International Political Economy Series

Series Editor
Timothy M. Shaw, University of Massachusetts Boston, Boston, USA;
Emeritus Professor, University of London, London, UK

The global political economy is in flux as a series of cumulative crises impacts its organization and governance. The IPE series has tracked its development in both analysis and structure over the last three decades. It has always had a concentration on the global South. Now the South increasingly challenges the North as the centre of development, also reflected in a growing number of submissions and publications on indebted Eurozone economies in Southern Europe. An indispensable resource for scholars and researchers, the series examines a variety of capitalisms and connections by focusing on emerging economies, companies and sectors, debates and policies. It informs diverse policy communities as the established trans-Atlantic North declines and 'the rest', especially the BRICS, rise.

NOW INDEXED ON SCOPUS!

Corrine Cash · Larry A. Swatuk
Editors

The Political Economy of Climate Finance: Lessons from International Development

palgrave
macmillan

Editors
Corrine Cash
Mount Allison University
Sackville, NB, Canada

Larry A. Swatuk
School of Environment, Enterprise and Development
University of Waterloo
Waterloo, ON, Canada

ISSN 2662-2483 ISSN 2662-2491 (electronic)
International Political Economy Series
ISBN 978-3-031-12618-5 ISBN 978-3-031-12619-2 (eBook)
https://doi.org/10.1007/978-3-031-12619-2

© The Editor(s) (if applicable) and The Author(s), under exclusive license to Springer Nature Switzerland AG 2022

This work is subject to copyright. All rights are solely and exclusively licensed by the Publisher, whether the whole or part of the material is concerned, specifically the rights of translation, reprinting, reuse of illustrations, recitation, broadcasting, reproduction on microfilms or in any other physical way, and transmission or information storage and retrieval, electronic adaptation, computer software, or by similar or dissimilar methodology now known or hereafter developed.

The use of general descriptive names, registered names, trademarks, service marks, etc. in this publication does not imply, even in the absence of a specific statement, that such names are exempt from the relevant protective laws and regulations and therefore free for general use.

The publisher, the authors, and the editors are safe to assume that the advice and information in this book are believed to be true and accurate at the date of publication. Neither the publisher nor the authors or the editors give a warranty, expressed or implied, with respect to the material contained herein or for any errors or omissions that may have been made. The publisher remains neutral with regard to jurisdictional claims in published maps and institutional affiliations.

Cover illustration: © RBFried/iStockphoto

This Palgrave Macmillan imprint is published by the registered company Springer Nature Switzerland AG
The registered company address is: Gewerbestrasse 11, 6330 Cham, Switzerland

Acknowledgements

This book is the product of a Social Sciences and Humanities Research Council (SSHRC) funded workshop that brought 11 specialists together from both development and climate finance. The goal of the workshop was to discuss "what can we learn from 60 years of development finance for climate finance?" The participants at the workshop represented academia, civil society organizations, think tanks and practice. The goal was to have a diversity of views and perspectives in the room. While not all authors from that workshop have contributed chapters to this book, we believe that the views expressed here represent the discussions that occurred over three days quite well.

We would like to thank the participants from that workshop, including: Dr. Blair Feltmate, Dr. Romeo Bertolini, Dr. Nick Mercer, Dr. Kate Ervine, Brian Tomlinson, Delaine Mccullough, Leslie Qammaniq, Simon Addison and Dr. Chijioke Oji. We would also like to thank the Coady International Institute for supporting that workshop. Tiffany MacLennan worked tirelessly to ensure the smooth running of the workshop. Laina Timberg contributed important last-minute editorial assistance. We thank them both.

Larry A. Swatuk would like to thank Corrine Cash for involving him from the start of this worthwhile project. Covid-19 presented many challenges but working together on this collection was not one of them. On behalf of all contributors, we would like to thank Anca Pusca and Ananda

Kumar Mariappan for their encouragement and support in the production of this volume.

We hope that the research and reflections within this collection provides insight into the considerable challenge of ensuring that climate finance reaches those who need it most.

Contents

1 **Climate Finance: Lessons from Development Finance**   1
Corrine Cash and Larry A. Swatuk

2 **How Lessons from Development Finance Can Strengthen Climate Finance**   21
Leia Achampong

3 **International Climate Finance and Development Effectiveness**   45
Brian Tomlinson

4 **Climate Finance and Principles for Effective Development Cooperation**   75
Brian Tomlinson

5 **What Can We Learn About the 'Country Ownership' of International Climate Finance by Employing a Relational Conception of Scale?**   99
Jonathan Barnes

6 **Towards Accountability in Climate Finance: Lessons from Nepal and Indonesia**   129
Cathy Shutt and Brendan Halloran

7	Delivering Adaptation Finance Through the Market? The Trouble with Using Carbon Offsets to Finance Climate Adaptation in the Global South Kate Ervine	153
8	Climate Finance and Neo-colonialism: Exposing Hidden Dynamics Rebecca Navarro	179
9	Climate Finance and the Peace Dividend, Articulating the Co-benefits Argument Catherine Wong	205
10	Toward Just and Effective Climate Action Larry A. Swatuk and Corrine Cash	233

Index 245

Notes on Contributors

Achampong Leia is a climate justice and women's rights activist and has a Masters's degree in Sustainability Science and Policy (MsC) from Maastricht University. With a background in research, policy analysis and advocacy on climate change issues, Achampong's current research focus is on the best ways to strengthen financial mechanisms to increase the quality and additionality of climate finance. Achampong presently works at Eurodad on climate finance and climate justice.

Dr. Barnes Jonathan is Researcher at the International Institute of Environment and Development where he focuses on climate governance and finance. He is a Visiting Fellow in the Department of Geography and Environment at the London School of Economics and Political Science. His Ph.D. explored questions of justice in climate finance, specifically looking at the Green Climate Fund in South Africa. He has a policy background in climate and development finance including roles at the Organisation of Economic Cooperation and Development and the Commonwealth Secretariat.

Cash Corrine holds a Ph.D. in Urban Planning from the School of Planning, University of Waterloo, Ontario, Canada. Dr. Cash is Assistant Professor in the Department of Geography and Environment at Mount Allison University in Sackville, New Brunswick, Canada. Prior to joining Mt. Allison, Dr. Cash was a member of the Programme Teaching Staff at the Coady International Institute as well as an Assistant Professor in the Climate and Environment Program at St. Francis Xavier University, Antigonish, Nova Scotia, Canada. Among her most recent publications are two co-edited collections: *Water, Energy, Food and People: The Nexus in an era of Climate Change* and *The Political Economy of Urban Water Security under Climate Change*.

Ervine Kate is Associate Professor in the Department of Global Development Studies at Saint Mary's University and a Faculty Associate of SMU's School of the Environment. Her research examines the global political economy of the environment, with a specific focus on climate change mitigation, carbon markets, carbon offsetting, climate finance to the Global South and climate justice. Among her recent publications is the book *Carbon* (Polity, 2018).

Halloran Brendan is International Budget Partnership's Head of Strategy and Learning. In this role, he facilitates strategy and learning processes at IBP—both the internal production of learning insights and drawing on evidence and ideas from broader research and practice in the governance space. Prior to joining IBP in 2016, Brendan lead the learning work of the Transparency and Accountability Initiative, where he played a role in shaping and interpreting evidence about what works, as well as supporting collective learning spaces. Before that, he spent five years living, researching and working in Guatemala. Brendan has a Ph.D. from Virginia Tech, and has published work in a variety of journals, think pieces and blogs, including his own—Politics, Governance, and Development.

Navarro Rebecca is a young Researcher at the Bonn International Centre for Conflict Studies (BICC) in Germany. As a geographer who recently graduated with a master's degree in Nature Conservation and Landscape Ecology at the University of Bonn, she has explored different areas related to climate change from an interdisciplinary perspective. Since 2018 she has been working in the field of sustainable technologies for agriculture in the Global South.

Shutt Cathy has over 28 years' experience of research, teaching and practice within the international development sector, which has included programme and evaluation work for a range of International NGOs, Foundations, commercial suppliers and complex multi-sectoral consortia. She holds a DPhil in International Development from the Institute of Development Studies where she is an Honorary Associate.

Cathy also teaches on Institutions of Aid and Policy Analysis in Energy and Sustainability at the University of Sussex.

Swatuk Larry A. is Professor in the School of Environment, Enterprise and Development at the University of Waterloo, Canada. He is also Extraordinary Professor in the Institute for Water Studies, University of the Western Cape, South Africa and External Researcher, Bonn International Centre for Conflict Studies (BICC), Bonn, Germany. His recent research focuses on the unintended negative consequences of state-led climate action leading to potential 'boomerang effects'. Among his most recent publications is the co-edited collection (with Corrine Cash) entitled *The Political Economy of Urban Water Security under Climate Change* (Palgrave).

Tomlinson Brian is Adjunct Professor in the Department of International Development Studies at Dalhousie University and Executive Director of AidWatch Canada. He has had a long career working with international civil society organizations in international development and is widely published on Canadian development cooperation, including editing and contributing to the biannual global Reality of Aid Reports. He follows closely trends and issues relating to Canadian international climate finance.

Wong Catherine is Team Leader for Climate and Security Risk and the technical lead on climate, peace and security in UNDP's Global Policy Network. She is matrixed to the Conflict Prevention, Peacebuilding and Responsive Institutions Team—Crisis Bureau and the Climate Strategies and Policy Team—Bureau of Policy and Programme Support. Catherine possesses more than 15 years' experience working on climate change and environment at headquarters and in-the-field. She serves as UNDP's focal point on the Climate Security Mechanism and the UN Water-led core group on Leveraging Water for Peace. Catherine was recognized as one of 25 Young Security Leaders by the Government of Germany, Körber-Stiftung and the Munich Security Conference (2021–2022) and is an observer of the International Military Council for Climate and Security.

Acronyms

3MR	Third Monitoring Round
AC	Adaptation Communications
ADEs	Anthropogenic Dark Earths
AF	Adaptation Fund
ANC	African National Congress
AWF	African Wildlife Foundation
BAU	Business-As-Usual
BMR	Biannual Monitoring Process
CBDR-RC	Common But Differentiated Responsibilities and Respective Capabilities
CCBC	Climate Change Budget Code
CDKN	Climate and Development Knowledge Network
CDM	Clean Development Mechanism
CER	Carbon Emission Reductions
CERs	Certified Emission Reductions
CFF	Climate Finance Facility
CIFs	Climate Investment Funds
CNA	Centre for Naval Analyses
CO_2	Carbon Dioxide
COP	Conference of the Parties
COP-PF4SD	Community of Practice on Private Finance for Sustainable Development
CPDE	CSP Partnership for Effective Communication
CPI	Climate Policy Initiative
CSA	Climate Smart Agriculture
CSOs	Civil Society Organisations

Acronym	Definition
CSP	Communication Service Provider
DAC	Development Assistance Committee
DAEs	Direct Access Entities
DBSA	Development Bank of South Africa
DECC	Department of Energy and Climate Change
DFIs	Development Finance Institutions
EFLG	Environment Friendly Local Government
EU	European Union
FIFs	Financial Intermediary Fund
FMIS	Financial Management Information System
FoE US	Friends of the Earth United States
GCF	Green Climate Fund
GEF	Global Environment Facility
GHGs	Greenhouse Gas
GNI	Gross National Income
GPEDC	Global Partnerships for Effective Development Cooperation
GWP	Global Warming Potential
HFC	Hydrofluorocarbons
HRD	Human Rights Defenders
IBP	International Budget Partnership
IDR	Indonesian Rupiah
IEA	International Energy Agency
IETA	International Emissions Trading Association
IEU	Independent Financial Unit
IFC	International Finance Corporation
IIED	International Institute for Environment and Development
IMF	International Monetary Fund
INCAF	International Network on Conflict and Fragility
INGOs	International NGOs
INISIATIF	National Center for Indonesia Leadership
IPCC	Intergovernmental Panel on Climate Change
IRENA	International Renewable Energy Agency
ITMOs	Internationally transferred mitigation outcomes
KTNI	Indonesian Traditional Union of Fisherfolk
LDCs	Least Developed Countries
LORTA	Learning-Oriented Real-Time Impact Assessment
LTSs	Long-term Low Greenhouse Gas Emissions Strategies
MDB	Multilateral Development Banks
MINUSMA	Multidimensional Integrated Stabilisation Mission in Mali
MoCA	Ministerial on Climate Action
MSF	Multi-Stakeholder Forum
NAPs	National Adaptation Plans
NCQG	New Collective Quantified Goal

NDA	National Designated Authority
NDCs	Nationally Determined Contributions
NGOs	Non-Governmental Organisations
ODA	Official Development Assistance
ODC	Official Development Cooperation
ODI	Overseas Development Institute
OECD	Organisation for Economic Cooperation and Development
OMGE	Overall Mitigation in Global Emissions
OI	Oxfam International
OPM	Oxford Policy Management
PAR	Participatory Action Research
PBF	Peacebuilding Fund
PCD	Petersberg Climate Dialogue
PDB	Public Development Banks
PITA	Participation, Inclusion, Transparency, and Accountability
PSA	Power Shift Africa
PSE	Private Sector Engagement
REDD+	Reducing Emissions from Deforestation and Forest Degradation
SACFA	South African Finance Assemblage
SANBI	South African National Biodiversity Institute
SCF	Standing Committee on Finance
SDGs	Sustainable Development Goals
SDSN	Sustainable Development Solutions Network
SIDS	Small Island Developing States
SOP	Share of Proceeds
SPARC	Supporting Pastoralism and Agriculture in Recurrent and Protracted Crises
SSDC	South-South Development Cooperation
TANAPA	Tanzania National Parks
TAP	Technology Action Plans
tCO2e	Tons of CO_2 equivalent
TFGB	Trees For Global Benefit
UN	United Nations
UNCTAD	United Nations Conference on Trade and Development
UNDESA	United Nations Department of Economic and Social Affairs
UNDP	United Nations Development Program
UNFCCC	United Nations Framework Convention on Climate Change
UNHCR	United Nations High Commissioner for Refugees
UNSD	United Nations Statistics Division
WBG	World Bank Group
WHO	World Health Organisation

List of Figures

Fig. 3.1	Trends in international climate finance (*Source* OECD, Climate Finance Provided and Mobilized by Developed Countries in 2013–2018, Bilateral Adjusted is OECD DAC Bilateral Provider Perspective, Significant Purpose [Rio Marker 1 adjusted to 30%, Loans adjusted at Grant Equivalency, Total Commitments])	54
Fig. 3.2	Modalities for MDB climate finance, percentage of total MDB climate finance (*Source* OECD DAC Climate Finance Recipient Perspective, Loans at gross face value)	55
Fig. 3.3	MDB adaptation finance (*Source* Joint Report on Multilateral Development Banks Climate Finance, Various Years)	61
Fig. 3.4	DAC providers bilateral adaptation finance (*Source* OECD DAC Provider Climate Finance, various years, significant purpose adjusted to 30% and loans at grant equivalency)	62
Fig. 3.5	Adaptation finance to vulnerable least developed and small island states: share of total bilateral and MDB adaptation climate finance	64
Fig. 3.6	Loans in bilateral climate finance as a share of total bilateral climate finance	66

List of Tables

Table 1.1	Group of 10 (G10) country climate finance performance	5
Table 3.1	Top 10 DAC providers, share of total (adjusted) bilateral climate finance, 2019	54
Table 3.2	Climate finance and DAC/EU gender marker	68
Table 3.3	Select providers, bilateral principal purpose climate finance as a share of real bilateral ODA commitments, 2019	70
Table 5.1	Analytical categories to operationalize relational scale vis a vis a hierarchical conception	105
Table 5.2	Accredited entity comparison	109

CHAPTER 1

Climate Finance: Lessons from Development Finance

Corrine Cash and Larry A. Swatuk

INTRODUCTION

We either choose to achieve rapid and large-scale reductions of emissions to keep the goal of limiting global warming to 1.5C—or we accept that humanity faces a bleak future on this planet. We either choose to boost adaptation efforts to deal with current extreme weather disasters and build resilience to address future impacts—or we accept that more people will die, more families will suffer, and more economic harm will follow. We

---

C. Cash (✉)
Department of Geography and Environment, Mount Allison University, Sackville, NB, Canada
e-mail: ccash@mta.ca

L. A. Swatuk
School of Environment, Enterprise and Development, University of Waterloo, Waterloo, ON, Canada
e-mail: lswatuk@uwaterloo.ca

© The Author(s), under exclusive license to Springer Nature Switzerland AG 2022
C. Cash and L. A. Swatuk (eds.), *The Political Economy of Climate Finance: Lessons from International Development*, International Political Economy Series, https://doi.org/10.1007/978-3-031-12619-2_1

either choose to recognize that business as usual isn't worth the devastating price we're paying and make the necessary transition to a more sustainable future—or we accept that we're investing in our own extinction. It is about much more than environment, it is about peace, stability and the institutions we have built to promote the wellbeing of all.
Patricia Espinosa (2021)

Anthropogenic climate change poses an existential threat to humanity. Abrupt changes to the climate at various scales are underway due primarily to the burning of fossil fuels in human industrial processes (see, e.g., https://climate.nasa.gov/evidence/). The planetary impact of these processes is commonly called 'global warming' and its cumulative impact is exacerbating humanity's lurch towards an unknown, largely unpredictable and, most certainly for large swaths of the planet, undesirable future. The most reliable scientific evidence suggests that action to limit warming to less than 2 °C can contribute meaningfully to minimizing negative long-term consequences for ecosystems and people. Poor and/or uncoordinated action, however, will lead to catastrophic outcomes at a variety of spatial and temporal scales. Recent extreme weather events—drought, flood, fire—offer but an inkling of our climate-changed future. While calls to action are persistent and increasingly alarmist in tone, the institutional and organizational systems that are in place seem ill-suited to the task at hand: sovereign states, inter-governmental organizations, development banks, private entrepreneurs, non-governmental organizations, global meetings which bring together actors with very different ideas about what is to be done how and when.

This collection focuses on climate finance as one of the emergent institutional mechanisms for dealing with the negative effects of anthropogenic climate change across the Global South. In terms of total global (public and private sector) finance deployed in support of climate action, it is a minor contributor. At the 2009 Conference of the Parties (COP) at Copenhagen, rich countries pledged to provide US $100 billion/per year in finance to developing countries to assist them in developing and implementing mitigation and adaptation measures. As shown in this collection, the avenues along which finance is to travel are many and varied, from the orthodox (e.g. bilateral and multilateral grants and loans) to the more creative (e.g. carbon markets, job-creating low-emission production processes). According to the UNFCCC (n.d.), 'Climate finance is needed for mitigation, because large-scale investments are required to significantly reduce emissions. Climate finance is equally important for adaptation, as significant financial resources are needed to adapt to the adverse effects and reduce the impacts of a changing climate'. Climate finance is meant to be 'new and additional' to already existing development finance. To put the $100 billion pledge into context, Dodd (2020) estimated the financial support needed for achieving Sustainable Development Goals 3 (Health) and 4 (Education). Dodd chose colleagues chose these two SDGs as they closely align with the central focus of Overseas Development Assistance (ODA). Whereas ODA in 2019 was estimated to be $147 billion, the costs of achieving SDG 3 varied from $227 to $406 billion per year up to 2030 (Dodd, 2020: 4). In comparison, for SDG 4 Dodd (2020) looked at two studies where the estimated costs varied dramatically from $222 billion per year between 2015 and 2030 (Wils, 2015) and $3 trillion per year by 2030 (Education commission, 2016).

Current debates regarding climate finance offer important insights into not only the facts and arguments regarding the ways and means to move away from fossil fuel dependence towards a clean energy near-term future, but a window into abiding problems of social organization broadly defined. Put differently, the political economy of climate finance mirrors closely the economic, political, social and ecological dynamics of a neoliberal, globalized world. Importantly, then, there are lessons to be learned from international development for climate finance, as shifts in development thinking and practice closely reflect changing dynamics of global political economy. We return to this point below. Suffice to say here, however, that current approaches to climate finance are already making many of the same mistakes that characterize experiences in international development: from funding 'white elephants' to anti-democratic practices, from being captured by political agendas to privileging 'expert' (Western, scientific) knowledge; from taking markets and private property as an uncontested baseline assumption to seeing techno-economic approaches as necessary and equally incontestable solutions to formidable and complex challenges.

Financing Climate Action

As human endeavour has dramatically altered the face of the Earth, undermining ecosystem resilience worldwide—from forests and grasslands to wetlands and coral reefs—the cumulative impact is being realized at planetary scale. The negative impact of human activities on particular types of ecosystems has long been recognized, with the demise of much of the world's wetlands being one example. At a slightly larger scale, the failure to act 'in time' or to recognize the folly of our ways, is a central feature of world history, with scholars regularly chronicling the rise and fall of civilizations, from Easter Island to the Inca, to Rome. Recognition of the human impact on the biosphere, however, is of more recent vintage. Whereas ecosystem impacts are local/regional (e.g. point source and diffuse pollution; deforestation; fish die-offs; eutrophication) and require comparative inquiry regarding problems and solutions, biosphere impacts (e.g. loss of biodiversity; global warming; sea level rise) are by definition a collective action problem.

Given that global climate change impacts at local/regional levels, existing socio-ecological challenges related to land degradation and deforestation, for example, may be exacerbated by permanent shifts to previously stable climate systems and predictable patterns of weather. Some scholars label this the move from the Holocene era to the Anthropocene. It is the abruptness of this shift, in addition to the human driver, that makes current era climate change significantly different from past climate change. Moreover, the interactions between biosphere and ecosystem phenomena require an integrated approach to climate action; piecemeal action will not suffice.

The UNFCCC Conference of the Parties 27 (COP 27) has adopted the tagline 'together for implementation', thereby acknowledging the need for a collective, integrated approach to addressing the sources and consequences of climate change. Yet, at the June 2022 Bonn climate talks, division, discord and acrimony were the order of the day. Developing countries pressed for a new finance mechanism to address 'loss and damages' due to developed country emissions effects. This was not only rejected but left out of the meeting's final agenda. At the same time, a recent ODI study reveals how far rich most countries are from meeting their climate action financial commitments (see Table 1.1 for a selection) (Colenbrander et al., 2022). At COP 15 in Paris, OECD countries agreed to contribute US$ 100 billion per year to assist developing countries to mitigate and adapt to changes in climate. This total was meant to be the minimum amount committed per year until 2025, after which the total would be revised upward. As shown in several chapters in this book, especially 2, 3 and 4, the funding was meant to come from a variety of public and private sources and to be disbursed in a number of ways.

In a June 2022 ODI working paper, Sarah Colenbrander and colleagues demonstrate that much of the rich world, especially the U.S.A., is failing to pay what they call their 'fair share'. 'The US is overwhelmingly responsible for the climate finance gap having provided just 5% of its fair share in 2020. Although its economy is 40% larger than the European Union's, it provided only one-twelfth as much climate finance' (Colenbrander et al., 2022: 10). The fair share is determined by three criteria: Gross National Income (GNI); cumulative CO_2 emissions (1990–2019); and population. While emissions totals reflect the polluter pays principle, GNI and population reflect both financial and human capabilities to act (so aligning with the UNFCCC principle of 'common but differentiated responsibility and respective capabilities').

As shown in Table 1.1, only five of the G10 countries are found to be paying their fair share.

The ODI report goes on to highlight how state performance in meeting climate finance commitments tends to vary directly with how well

Table 1.1 Group of 10 (G10) country climate finance performance

Country	Fair share (US$ billions)	Provided (US$ billions)	Progress towards meeting commitment based on fair share (%)
Sweden	0.91	1.47	161
France	5.39	8.66	161
Japan	11.89	16.09	135
Netherlands	1.76	2.14	122
Germany	8.33	9.91	119
Switzerland	0.94	0.68	72
United Kingdom	5.84	3.2	55
Belgium	1.13	0.59	52
Italy	4.73	1.43	30
Canada	4.13	0.74	18
United States	43.48	2.3	5

Source Adapted from Colenbrander et al. (2022)

states have performed in meeting their mutually agreed target of 0.7% of GNI in development finance. According to OECD calculations for 2018, only four countries—Denmark, Norway, Luxembourg and Sweden (in ascending order)—met this commitment.

Furthermore, the authors caution against reading too much into good performance. Most of France's resources 'were provided as loans rather than grants' (Colenbrander et al., 2022: 13). As shown in Chapter 3 (Ervine), of the $79 billion in climate finance generated for the Global South in 2018, 'only 20% was delivered as grants and 74% was delivered as loans' (see also OECD, 2020: 6). Ervine, citing OECD (2020), goes further to say that '20% of the loans from developed countries and 76% from multilateral development banks were in fact non-concessional.' Developing countries have spent more on debt service than they have received in climate finance from developed countries.

As highlighted in Chapter 2 (Achampong), climate finance is not meant to substitute for development finance but to constitute 'new and additional' support sourced from public and private, bilateral and multilateral institutions that complements ODA. Moreover, Tomlinson, in Chapter 4, states '[d]eveloping countries are not only seeking a commitment target that is additional to current levels of ODA, but also financing for "loss and damage" due to current and expected climate change events that is additional to finance for adaptation and mitigation'.

Yet, as climate finance increasingly turns towards adaptation it increasingly looks like development assistance. Donor states, eager to make good on their pledges, using the Rio Markers, are busy playing a game of 'tick box', claiming existing development actions as (partially or totally) climate focused (Chapter 4). Granted, there are a variety of legitimate challenges to accurately measuring climate finance, but claiming existing project/programme support as climate finance is primarily an exercise in climate action-washing.

Financing the Sustainable Development Goals (SDGs)

The SDGs constitute the focal point for orthodox thinking on international development. As such, they reflect not only the dominant discourse of development theory and practice, but a jumping-off point for debate regarding the forms, ways and means of 'development'. At the outset of the SDGs, a preliminary analysis from the SDSN (Schmidt-Traub, 2015:

1) estimated 'that incremental spending needs in low- and lower-middle-income countries may amount to at least $1.4 trillion per year ($340–360 billion for low-income countries and $900–944 billion for lower-middle-income countries)'. According to the UN SDG Report 2020 (UN, 2020), there were already several significant problems with implementation prior to the onset of the Covid-19 pandemic including funding shortfalls, data gaps, limited human resource capacity particularly in low-income developing states, restricted absorptive capacity of recipient states and weak uptake on several SDGs and targets, particularly mainstreaming protection and rehabilitation of biodiversity. According to a 2019 report from the Social Progress Imperative, performance was so poor that, other things being equal, the SDGs would be achieved only in 2073—almost five decades behind schedule (Green, 2019). In the intervening three years, however, the foundation under the global political economy has shifted dramatically.

The pandemic has turned most states inward. The socio-economic foundations of political stability have been badly shaken: clogged harbours; broken global supply chains; the (near) collapse of entire industries and sectors; social protest. Vaccine nationalism coupled with extensive rich state support for the pharmaceutical industry exposed the vast socio-economic inequalities within and across states today. The Russian invasion of Ukraine has exacerbated these and added new challenges for all states, rich and poor alike. Staple food shortages, the Western shift away from Russian petroleum and gas, combined with numerous socio-economic sanctions imposed on the Putin regime have driven worldwide inflation and economic stagnation. Irrespective of their capacity to meet their obligations, most rich countries point to these phenomena to help explain stagnation in development and climate finance. At the same time, these same states are pressing a market-oriented, private sector-led approach to development and climate action, citing constrained budgets and the 'benefits' of entrepreneurship as motivating factors.

Problems with 'Aid'

Obsession with amounts, methods and metrics serves to distract from more important questions regarding underlying assumptions, ideological positions and power relations. International development has long been a battleground of values, perspectives and ideas. Far from uniting behind the so-called 'global goals', sovereign state approaches to achieving the sustainable development goals are as diverse as are their sociopolitical/socio-economic agendas. Over recent decades there have been several attempts to clarify the global development agenda, in particular to put decision-making regarding action into the hands of recipient states. This is reflected in agreements such as the Paris Declaration, the Accra Agenda for Action and the Global Partnership for Effective Development Cooperation. Both the Millennium Development Goals (2000–2015) and SDGs (2015–2030) claim to be participatory and inclusive.

Despite the rhetoric of 'togetherness', irrespective of whether projects and programmes are developed and designed in the Global South, the ontological and methodological frameworks remain Western/colonialist, hierarchical and neoliberal capitalist in theory and practice. This is nothing new. The 'aid industry' has been critiqued extensively from all points on the political ideological spectrum. Commonly held critiques focus on the self-serving nature of 'aid', support for corrupt governments, and the forcing of geo-political agendas by powerful states into 'development' practice. From the ideological right there is an increasing chorus that aid should begin at home, with the Covid-19 pandemic augmenting these calls. From the left there is the abiding argument that neoliberal capitalist development impoverishes the many and 'liberates' the already empowered few. With the advent of the so-called 'debt crisis' of the early 1980s, Western states and banks began a coordinated assault on active and interventionist state behaviour across the Global South. Using debt financing as an entry point, donors and international financial institutions forced structural adjustment conditionalities into lending agreements. The literature is voluminous so there is no need to go into details here. The central point to be made is that structural adjustment programmes led to a multi-decadal debt crisis among the weakest states in Africa, south Asia, Latin America and the Caribbean. Having long paid back the principle, many states continue to pay on interest. Moreover, significant new debt has been taken on via public and private lending (domestic and international), with China playing a particularly prominent role. Much of this borrowing is against hypothesized future earnings, reflecting the long commodities boom on the African continent in support of China's dramatic economic rise. However, the pandemic stopped many economies dead in their tracks, leading to a renewed 'debt crisis'. In Sub-Saharan Africa, debt as percentage of GDP before the pandemic rose from 35.1% in 2014 to 55.4% in 2019. It is estimated that this has risen to more than 60% in 2021 (Heitzig et al., 2021: 4). The World Bank (2021) estimates the 2020 debt of low- and middle-income Sub-Saharan African countries to be $702 billion, approximately two and a half times greater than it was just ten years earlier. As a significant amount of this debt is taken on in support of infrastructure, both the (multilateral, bilateral) lender and the recipient are likely to claim that these loans are in support of climate action.

The global development architecture is entirely hierarchical and disciplinary in nature. Those countries most vulnerable to climate change are also the weakest in the global political economy; they are in no position to bargain to their advantage. History shows that financial institutions are more than willing to lend in support of dubious projects—rare is the country that defaults on its debts, as restructuring is the norm. One wonders, where is the oversight in such a relationship? Evidence also shows that when it comes time to restructure, it is the poor that pay—e.g. through the loss of state-supported services—not the politicians, bankers, entrepreneurs and global 'civil servants' who signed on to the agreement.

Social Organization

The problems with aid highlight the highly problematic character of social organization. The human world is beset by a complex array of challenges involving the built and natural environments. Organizations such as the United Nations characterize these as a collective management problem and seek to reduce this complexity into actionable pieces articulated as the SDGs, through specialized agencies, collaborative multi-stakeholder arrangements and so on. Generally known as 'global governance', this approach puts great faith in humanity's ability to rationally respond to empirically verifiable threats and vulnerabilities.

At the same time, and as shown above, effective collective action is hampered by numerous material, institutional and ideational factors. From a simple shortage of finance, to bureaucratic complexity, to differing world views, the number of factors getting in the way of positive collective social change is significant. At present, there is a resurgence of populist nationalism worldwide in reaction to the seeming failures of neoliberal globalization. With less than a decade remaining until the end of the SDGs in 2030, it seems highly unlikely that 'the world' will come anywhere close to achieving the 'global goals'.

Somewhat paradoxically, while the Russian invasion of Ukraine draws attention away from what many call the 'climate emergency', climate change-driven extreme events are increasing incidences, scales and impacts of natural disasters, driving millions out of the countryside into already massively overcrowded cities and adding climate-refugees to the already burgeoning number of people on the move, thereby heightening levels of intra-group conflict. In the absence of effective climate action, the need for humanitarian assistance will only grow. At the same time, it is increasingly apparent that all development planning needs to be 'climate ready', both in terms of mitigation—i.e. reducing the carbon footprint of all activities—and adaptation—i.e. preparing adequately for the 'new normal'.

While there is an increasing chorus of voices that varies from school children to artists, from city mayors to leaders of countries, all calling for rapid and effective climate action, those most empowered to act (and most responsible for the climate emergency in the first place) seem happy to plod along, dinosaur-like, making pronouncements, signing agreements, but largely choosing the time-honored path of delay, deny and blame others. The Covid-19 global pandemic provided an important window into this world. When faced with a global crisis, the willingness to work together for a global best result was absent. States pursued self-help, supported particular sections of (pharmaceutical) industry, hoarded personal protection equipment (PPEs) and vaccines and offered limited assistance to those most in need both within their own countries and in other parts of the world. Covid's uneven impacts varied directly with the neoliberal capitalist world's uneven socio-economic terrain. It is clear that this is only the latest in an ongoing series of global viral emergencies. Millions died and while the pandemic has abated in some parts of the world, it rages on largely out of the limelight of Western public consciousness. Climate change impacts also are being felt unevenly, helping to explain the divisions of opinion regarding the timing and scale of appropriate action. However, unlike coronavirus, in the absence of a sustained and coordinated response, the climate emergency will only worsen, ultimately engulfing us all.

The fact of the sovereign state functioning in a world of states; exercising a variety of forms of (ideational, institutional, material) power is a primary impediment to meaningful action. As suggested above, those most vulnerable to climate change are also those least able to influence the global agenda. Those most capable of facilitating 'transformative change' are least interested. In the context of neoliberal globalization, there has arisen a powerful constellation of social forces (companies, states, individuals, select non-governmental organizations) reluctant to let go of the ideational (market forces, sovereignty), institutional (financial markets, bond-rating agencies, World Economic Forum, World Trade Organization, World Bank, International Monetary Fund) and material (capital, military) bases of their power despite all of the evidence regarding the need for transformation (see Espinosa in the epigram at the start of this chapter).

It is this world out of which climate finance has emerged. Make no mistake, climate finance as currently articulated is a product of this neoliberal world order. We have highlighted a few of the ways in which international development mirrors this world. By aligning climate finance with development thinking and action, it seems to us that the capacity for meaningful action particularly where it is needed most is seriously hampered. It is no accident, then, that those most vocal in challenging the current development architecture, are the same who are now raising their voices in relation to climate finance (mis)steps, with Oxfam International's (2020) *Climate Finance Shadow Report 2020* serving as an appropriate example.

THE BOOK

As with this introductory chapter, the essays that follow constitute individual entry points into the complex and contentious topic of climate finance. Together, they constitute a critical voice whose primary message is to not repeat the errors of the past. Climate finance intersects with international development in two specific ways. First, where support for mitigation heavily focuses on infrastructure, it aligns with the historically primary development agents'—states, banks, engineering firms—long obsession with energy, transportation and services: multi-purpose dams (hydropower, irrigation, water supply), ports, railways, central-business districts (CBDs) and car-dependent suburbs. The aim being, of course, to mirror Western development by mimicking 'best practice'. Today, in the context of climate action, this means a focus on green design, green infrastructure, and the development of circular economies, otherwise known as ecological modernization. Second, with the recent turn towards climate finance for adaptation, this draws climate action directly in line with discourses of sustainable development and the 'triple bottom line':

social equity, economic efficiency, environmental sustainability. Irrespective of the entry point, and as highlighted above, development discourse remains dominated by techno-economic and techno-managerial thinking and practice. Put simply, the 'vicious cycle of poverty' model long discredited by critical development scholars and practitioners is alive and well in the offices of the world's most powerful states, inter-governmental organizations, private companies and financial institutions: if you put enough money behind it and create a particular set of incentives, 'development' will follow. But where is the evidence that such a process has ever worked? Especially a process driven by the global political and economic architecture devised to serve the most powerful interests in Western boardrooms and state houses?

Contrary to the dominant developmental discourse of neoliberal capitalist development through the market, the most successful 'developmental' states of the past fifty years are those in East and Southeast Asia, every one of which pursued a path to sustained economic growth through systematic state planning and careful control of finance and market forces. As climate finance draws closer to development finance, each of the chapters here offers cautionary tales regarding lessons from the past, present and future of international development.

In Chapter 2, Leah Acheampong states that tackling climate change and ensuring that there are liveable environments for people, biodiversity and ecosystems to flourish in is part of achieving the sustainable development agenda. Ensuring that communities address and adapt to climate impacts enables them to maintain and strengthen their livelihoods and helps future generations to thrive. It also supports the sustainable development of equitable societies within which citizens have access to education, justice, health and affordable energy. As such, climate finance is a vital and powerful sustainable development tool. Acheampong argues that in order for climate finance to adequately support vulnerable communities' efforts to tackle climate change and develop sustainably four elements deserve close consideration: (i) the climate finance agenda must be driven by the most vulnerable; (ii) the quality of climate finance must improve; (iii) greater access to new and additional climate finance is needed to minimize debt; and (iv) climate finance must be gender-responsive.

In Chapter 3, Brian Tomlinson highlights the ways in which successful climate actions are inextricably linked to improving the quality of life of the world's most vulnerable people. While the degree of decarbonization needed for a 1.5 °C target is politically ambitious for most developed countries, the consequences of missing this target for vulnerable populations in the Global South will be profound. Five decades of development, the ambition of *Agenda 2030* and the achievement of 17 Sustainable Development Goals (SDGs) agreed by the international community in 2015, are seriously undermined without a strong political consensus in developed countries, focusing on renewed commitments to deeply transformative action on the climate crisis at the highest level. As many countries stagger to rebuild from the still unpredictable implications of the pandemic, developed countries have responded with trillions of dollars for emergency finance to protect their citizens, demonstrating that "affordability" is less a technical constraint than a political one.

As with the Covid-19 pandemic, addressing the climate emergency is a global justice challenge of the first order, one which must include and prioritize the most vulnerable countries and peoples. With so little time to act effectively to avert the worst consequences, this chapter looks at the recent history of international public climate finance to situate how well the international community is prepared to meet this challenge in ways that bridge the implications of climate apartheid.

Considering these challenges for human rights and a just global order, this chapter examines (i) the current ambition in setting international climate finance goals against what is required; (ii) the degree to which existing goals have been met to date; (iii) the trends in the allocation of this climate finance against *Paris Agreement* commitments to give priority to vulnerable countries and peoples; and lastly, (iv) the implications of good practice approaches in effective development cooperation for realizing meaningful impacts through official climate finance.

In Chapter 4, Tomlinson then turns to an interrogation of development effectiveness, an idea that has been evolving over the past decade. At the same time, its implications for provider practices and development outcomes have been affected by a changing and more complex development finance landscape. Emerging cooperation modalities, such as South–South Development Cooperation (SSDC), global International NGOs (INGOs) or blended finance with the private sector, have become more prominent, deepening a debate on development effectiveness. Climate finance is now a growing and important dimension of this finance landscape. Developed country providers will be pressed to respond to the undeniable and urgent need for dramatically increased allocations of climate finance. But seemingly climate finance has yet to be analysed in relation to lessons from efforts to improve effective development cooperation. In putting forward a framework for assessing climate finance drawing on the principles for effective development cooperation, this chapter draws upon the third monitoring round (3MR) of the Global Partnerships for Effective Development Cooperation 2018/2019 biannual monitoring process. The GPEDC monitors the implementation of the four principles against ten indicators for effective development cooperation. The chapter argues that building trust will require major new commitments on the part of providers to set ambitious climate targets for themselves, to scale up their international climate finance based on real need, including for loss and damages, and to strengthen its overall effectiveness for developing country partners. Providers must pay much greater attention to the needs, interests and priorities of the many vulnerable countries and populations that will bear the major impacts of climate change so far largely unchecked. Lesson from 15 years of discourse and country attention to conditions for effective development cooperation can provide a useful framework for sharpening this finance as a tool for inclusive and transformative change for millions of affected people.

In Chapter 5, Jonathan Barnes asks the question 'What can we learn about the "country ownership" of international climate finance by employing a relational conception of scale?' In theory, country ownership re-frames development aid as development cooperation that empowers national governments to choose and implement policies. Barnes addresses a conceptual impasse where a lack of clarity about what it means and how to use it blunts country ownership. He argues that a relational conception of scale can un-pack development work and look beyond reified generalities that limit explanatory value in a hierarchical interpretation. The Green Climate Fund (GCF) exemplifies this muddled thinking, where country ownership is simultaneously presented as a principle, investment criteria and an outcome. South Africa has a varied and dynamic partnership with the GCF which the author frames as an assemblage to explore who and what steers climate finance in a relational ontology. Four analytical categories are distilled to operationalize and distinguish a relational approach from a hierarchical one. This permits an empirical analysis of how projects are assembled that acknowledges the wide range of contingency and possibility. These categories are as follows: (i) a material-human hybridity; (ii) how complex social actors imprint in proceedings indirectly; (iii) what shapes categories of actors that own proceedings in an emergent sense; and (iv) how raised expectations and misunderstandings help and hinder different project development processes. This re-affirms the value of relational scale in human geography and enlivens country ownership conceptually. It advances a heuristic generalization that highlights partial scalar effects and moves analysis beyond pre-figured labels and a version of ownership premised on multiplicity, immanence and emergence. This nuance is missed by a hierarchical conception of scale.

In Chapter 6, Cathy Shutt and Brendan Halloran draw on their experiences in Indonesia and Nepal to investigate accountability in climate finance. According to the authors, there is overwhelming evidence that those who are poor or marginalized will be disproportionately impacted by climate change. Poor people are more susceptible to climate hazards because they live in poorly constructed homes in high-risk areas; often rely heavily on natural resources for food, fuel and income; and have limited options. They also have little capacity to respond to climate hazards because of existing structural inequalities. How governments manage the funds needed to build the resilience of people and communities to climate change will determine whether climate change will further entrench or deepen existing poverty and force more of those who are "near poor" into poverty.

Hundreds of billions of dollars are being mobilized globally from donors and domestic sources to address the causes and impacts of climate change. Governments around the world are now establishing and operationalizing the budget systems, institutions and processes for managing these funds. At the same time, countries are facing increasing pressure to generate revenues domestically as donors scale back aid, heightening the need for effective and accountable climate finance management. Unfortunately, the budget systems in most of the countries that will generate and/or receive significant funds for addressing climate change are not transparent and accountable. Such systems are more likely to produce inadequate, poorly designed or poorly implemented investments in climate change mitigation and adaptation, placing those most effected by climate hazards at grave risk. And because of the interaction of climate change and poverty, failure to improve these systems would have serious implications on the International Budget Partnership's (IBP) mission to realize equitable, just and sustainable societies.

Kate Ervine, in Chapter 7, focuses her attention on the problematic idea of carbon offsets. According to Ervine, estimates reveal a consistent failure to fulfill climate finance targets, with adaptation finance receiving proportionately less than finance directed to mitigating climate breakdown. Financing for loss and damage is even more critically inadequate. Though likely an underestimate, official figures peg adaptation costs at approximately US $70 billion per year presently, growing to an estimated $140–300 billion by 2030 and $280–500 billion by 2050. Much of the scholarly literature and policy work is thus focused on determining how sufficient funds to finance adaptation will be raised and from where they will come. This challenge is perceived as especially acute given the absence of incentives for private sector investment in adaptation projects.

Ervine's chapter offers a critical intervention into discussions and debates on the related themes of adaptation finance and adaptation to climate breakdown with a particular focus on carbon markets. Abundant and well-documented evidence shows that carbon offsetting under the Kyoto Protocol allowed polluters in the Global North to avoid taking action, shifting the burden of responsibility for lowering emissions to distant nations and communities; that an overwhelming share of offset projects failed to fulfill their emission reduction commitments resulting in an overall increase in global emissions; and that carbon offsetting today represents a dangerous obstacle to achieving real and lasting emission reductions consistent with limiting heating to 1.5 °C above pre-industrial levels.

The chapter thus offers an intervention into critically oriented research on adaptation to climate breakdown in the Global South. Much of this literature has documented the problems with adaptation interventions—that they fail to problematize how pre-existing inequalities at the community level shape outcomes and heighten marginalization; that they fail to interrogate multi-scalar sources and structures of vulnerability and oppression, including relations of production and social reproduction, class, gender, race and more, thereby threatening to reproduce them; that they fail to offer spaces for democratic dialogue, mutual learning and participatory practice in adaptation projects; and that they conceptualize adaptation as a technical fix in response to external climate threats, thereby mystifying the imperative to understand climate breakdown and the need for adaptation as deeply enmeshed in, and constituted through, globalized socio-economic and political structures to which we must respond as part of adaptation interventions.

In Chapter 8, Rebecca Navarro exposes hidden, neocolonial dynamics within climate finance thinking and practice. Despite the manifold loopholes of carbon markets, the demand for climate offsets has never been higher than in recent years. Besides the questionable efficacy of such climate compensating measures, growing critique has also been voiced concerning their role in perpetuating global power dynamics and neocolonial patterns. The history of nature conservancy and its implementation in the global South under the veil of sustainable development prepared the ground for the deployment of carbon markets, which have also evolved, responding to criticism, presumably seeking ethical improvements. While many studies have addressed evident forms of physical land grabs as a consequence of environmental and climate action, Navarro's chapter highlights the subtler expressions of "carbon colonialism" found in recent research, showcasing them through different case studies. As climate finance diversifies to meet the needs of a growing awareness among both Western society and host communities, new challenges beyond land-use conflicts appear that need to be addressed. As opposed to land grabs, they take place in unseen dimensions of instrumentalization, where "contradictory knowledge translations" are used to ensure legitimacy. Exposing such hidden dynamics is essential to respond appropriately and seek solutions to decolonize climate finance.

In the final substantive contribution, Chapter 9, Catherine Wong focuses on climate finance and the peace dividend, articulating the co-benefits argument. The role and impacts of climate finance on peace and security in conflict-affected and fragile contexts—many of which are also vulnerable to climate change rank among the lowest recipients of climate finance—is an area still little investigated by either the climate finance, climate security or environmental peacebuilding fields. A recent UNDP report (2021) with the Climate Security Mechanism and the Nataij Group argues for the need to better understand peace co-benefits. Wong's chapter attempts to fill this void, highlighting that greater attention is needed to the allocation, access and thus distribution, quality and quantity of finance, and therein, the design of climate finance mechanisms and their inherent impacts on equity in conflict-affected and fragile contexts. Wong critically examines the literature and underlying arguments from the emerging fields of climate finance, climate security and environmental peacebuilding and the application of a co-benefits approach to strengthen policy coherence, before considering learnings from nascent practice, including the efforts of the UN system. The chapter identifies gaps for further investigation and key guiding principles on the measurement of peace and security co-benefits or dividends of climate finance and draws conclusions from a new meta-analysis by UNDP (2021) and advocates for a transdisciplinary approach. As one of the first attempts to systematically consider climate finance in climate-vulnerable conflict-affected and fragile contexts, it argues that better metrics accounting for peace co-benefits or dividends, reinventing Theories of Change, and establishing intersectoral Communities of Practices and special vehicles/calls for proposals could strengthen access and outcomes.

Conclusion

One of the great lies of international development is that the challenges of poverty and underdevelopment are largely related to having access to adequate capital and technology, human capacity, and appropriate forms of organization and management. Such a story serves to depoliticize the challenges before us. At best it provides some space for useful things to happen. At worst it supports business as usual. Is it not a telling fact that as we move towards the 70th anniversary of the Bandung Conference on development so few countries in Asia and Africa—indeed, in the world—can claim to have improved the lives of a majority of their peoples? How many trillions of dollars in 'aid' have flowed from the rich world to the poor? How many dams, railways and highways have been built in the name of 'modernization'? Today's world is more unequal than ever before. It is a world where a handful of men hold more wealth than the bottom half of humanity. And it is this world that stands at the precipice of climate chaos.

If there is one important lesson for climate finance to learn from international development, it is that progressive movement in support of those most in need of assistance is first and foremost a political struggle. As many activist academics can attest, shifting international development away from its basic framework of capital accumulation is a long-term project. Getting states, corporations and international financial institutions to recognize and meaningfully consider the gender, race, class, environmental and social justice aspects of their actions is an ongoing, and often frustrating, process. Transformation towards a socially equitable, environmentally sustainable, low-carbon future therefore requires a clear strategy and a type of social organization that seeks to build creative coalitions within and across the fragmented landscape within which we currently reside. We believe that the essays collected here provide insights and ideas in support of this worthy cause.

REFERENCES

Colenbrander, S., Cao, Y., Pettinotti, L., & Quevedo, A. (2022). *A fair share of climate finance? Apportioning responsibility for the $100 billion climate finance goal* (ODI Working Paper). ODI.

Dodd, A. (2020). *The cost of achieving SDG 3 and SDG 4. How complete are financing estimates for the health and education goals?* Development Initiatives.

Education commission. (2016). *The Learning Generation. Investing in education for a changing world*. The International Commission on Financing Global Education Opportunity.

Espinosa, P. (2021). *Remarks by UNFCCC Executive Secretary Patricia Espinosa to open COP26*. https://unfccc.int/news/remarks-by-unfccc-executive-secretary-patricia-espinosa-to-open-cop26. Accessed 29 June 2022.

Green, M. (2019). *We are 43 years behind schedule on achieving the SDGs and the US is going backwards*. Reuters Events: Sustainable Business. https://www.reutersevents.com/sustainability/we-are-43-years-behind-schedule-achieving-sdgs-and-us-going-backwards#:~:text=or%20e%2Dmail%20*-,'We%20are%2043%20years%20behind%20schedule%20on%20achieving%20the%20SDGs,the%20US%20is%20going%20backwards'&text=Business%20as%20usual%20is%20not,Sustainable%20Development%20Goals%20(SDGs). Accessed 4 July 2022.

Heitzig, C., Ordu, A. U., & Senbet, L. (2021). *Sub-Saharan Africa's debt problem: Mapping the pandemic's effect and the way forward*. The Brookings Institution.

OECD. (2020). *Climate Finance Provided and Mobilized by Developed Countries in 2013–18*. OECD.

Oxfam International. (2020). *Climate Finance Shadow Report 2020*. Oxfam Great Britain.

Schmidt-Traub, G. (2015). Investment needs to achieve the sustainable development goals: Understanding the billions and trillions. SDSN Working Paper (12 November). SDSN.

UNDP. 2021. *Climate finance for sustaining peace. Making climate finance work for conflict-affected and fragile contexts*. UNDP.

UNFCCC. (n.d.). Introduction to climate finance. Available at: https://unfccc.int/topics/introduction-to-climate-finance. Accessed September 25, 2022.

United Nations (UN). (2020). *The sustainable development goals report 2020*. United Nations.

Wils, A. (2015). Reaching education targets in low and lower-middle income countries: Costs and finance gaps to 2030. UNESCO. Available at: https://unesdoc.unesco.org/ark:/48223/pf0000232560. Accessed September 25, 2022.

World Bank. (2021). *International Debt Statistics 2022*. The World Bank.

CHAPTER 2

How Lessons from Development Finance Can Strengthen Climate Finance

Leia Achampong

INTRODUCTION

Covid-19 has exposed the precarity of the current economic and financial system. Aid budgets have been slashed (*The Guardian*, 2021), social security gaps have been exposed (KPMG, 2020) and the fragility of healthcare systems has been laid bare. The pandemic has further exacerbated the inequality and divide within and between societies—including gender inequalities, and has highlighted the impacts of historic disinvestment (Capital Impact Partners, 2020) in marginalized communities.

Tackling these crises will require a huge amount of resources. It is in the interest of all countries and international institutions to ensure that the world recovers from the pandemic together to engage in a pathway towards a peaceful, safe and dignified future. Without this, gains made

L. Achampong (✉)
Eurodad (European Network On Debt and Development), Climate Finance, Brussels, Belgium
e-mail: lachampong@eurodad.org

in poverty eradication and towards sustainable development risk being further undermined (UNDESA, 2020).

Tackling climate change and ensuring that there are liveable environments for people, biodiversity and ecosystems to flourish in is part of achieving the sustainable development agenda. Ensuring that communities address and adapt to climate impacts enables them to maintain and strengthen their livelihoods, and helps future generations to thrive. It also supports the sustainable development of equitable societies within which citizens have access to education, justice, health and affordable energy. As such, climate finance is a vital and powerful sustainable development tool.

The objective of this chapter is to help strengthen synergies between the agendas of the Paris Agreement and Sustainable Development Goals (SDGs). This chapter is comprised of three sections. The first section of this chapter outlines the key issues, and the second section highlights lessons learned from long-standing work on development finance that should be taken into account in climate finance discussions. The final section concludes with a set of policy options for the way forward.

This chapter argues that in order for climate finance to adequately support vulnerable communities' efforts to tackle climate change and develop sustainably:

i. The climate finance agenda must be driven by the most vulnerable
ii. The quality of climate finance must improve
iii. Greater access to new and additional climate finance is needed to minimize debt
iv. Climate finance must be gender-responsive.

CLIMATE FINANCE: THE KEY ISSUES

Country Ownership of Climate Finance

Many climate-vulnerable countries in the global south are attempting to respond to the impacts of the Covid-19 pandemic while experiencing ongoing climate impacts (*BBC News*, 2020; ReliefWeb, 2021). Although developing countries have contributed the least to climate change, they are experiencing the worst effects of climate change and have been for decades (Heinrich-Böll-Stiftung, 2020). The compounding nature of these impacts has made it difficult to put in place and implement domestic Covid-19 health measures (*The Daily Star*, 2020); thereby impacting the ability of developing countries to meet their own needs during these crises, which in turn is exacerbating vulnerable countries' risk of falling into a debt trap (Munevar, 2021a). Despite all of this, increasingly there is a lack of alignment between climate-vulnerable countries' strategies for climate resilient, sustainable development (UNDP, 2019) and developed countries' development cooperation commitments. Given the severity of climate change and its impacts on achieving sustainable development, countries must work to realign the two.

However, many climate-related meetings where discussions on aligning the two take place, are hosted by the large economic powers that are also the biggest contributors to the current climate crisis (UNFCCC, 2021a). Examples of such meetings include the Ministerial on Climate Action (MoCA) (European Commission, 2022) which is hosted by Canada, China, and the European Union (EU); the Petersburg Climate Dialogue (PCD) (UNFCCC, 2021b) hosted by Germany and the UNFCCC Climate negotiations (COP) Presidency in a given year. These two meetings only invite a select group of developed and developing countries to join, but hold political discussions on a range of technical issues that affect multiple stakeholders. The 'select' nature of these meetings excludes developing countries from important discussions and decisions, including discussions on access to climate finance. Thus the climate agenda is still largely controlled and driven by the largest emitters of greenhouse gases.

The multilateral nature of the UN climate negotiations makes it a useful forum for all relevant stakeholders to be a part of identifying the problems and solutions. Indeed, between 2021 and 2024 the UNFCCC climate negotiations will host the discussions for a New Collective Quantified Goal on climate finance (NCQG) (UNFCCC, 2021c) to be agreed and set, with the new goal expected to start in 2025. The last climate finance goal agreed under the UNFCCC was ultimately a political agreement among developed countries, that excluded developing countries and was not based on the needs of developing countries. As such, the current discussions to set a new global goal are an opportunity to ensure that all climate finance contributors learn from the experiences of efforts to achieve the existing global climate finance goal, and react to the feedback from developing countries on **pre**-2025 climate finance (Achampong, 2021a). This is to ensure that **post**-2025, solutions can be used to ensure that there is no global climate finance gap (Achampong, 2021b). It is crucial that the process to set this new goal includes all relevant countries and stakeholders, to ensure that these discussions—and the subsequent efforts agreed—are driven by equity and the needs of those most affected. All affected stakeholders, including members of civil society must be a part of policy development and implementation processes.

Quantity, Quality and Composition of Climate Finance

Implementing solutions and addressing climate impacts **will require a substantial amount of finance**. As evidenced by the UNFCCC *First Report on the Determination of the Needs of Developing Country Parties*, the costed needs of developing countries to implement Nationally Determined Contributions (NDC) amount to between $US 5.8 trillion and $US 5.9 trillion (Standing Committee on Finance, 2021). Out of this "USD 502 billion is identified as needs requiring international sources of finance" (Standing Committee on Finance, 2021), meaning that a country is not able to fund these measures through the use of domestic resources. These amounts do not include costed needs to implement other climate action plans from developing countries e.g. Technology Action Plans (TAP) or Adaptation Communications (AC), of which the needs are also substantial (Standing Committee on Finance, 2021). To add further context research published by the Climate Policy Initiative (CPI) states that total global climate finance flows have slowed in the last few years. Yet "[a]n increase of at least 590% in annual climate finance is required to meet internationally agreed climate objectives by 2030 and to avoid the most dangerous impacts of climate change" (Buchner, 2021). What is more, the 2021 NDC Synthesis report (UNFCCC, 2021d) shows there is a clear difference between developing countries' climate action needs and their financial capacities. Furthermore, 2022 estimates from the United Nations Conference on Trade and Development (UNCTAD) state that "[t]he gap in financing needed to achieve SDGs, such as ending poverty and halting climate change, now sits at $17.9 trillion for the 2020–2025 period [...] This puts the current annual gap at $3.6 trillion—more than $1 trillion wider than before the COVID-19" (UNCTAD, 2022). This is backed up by 2022 analysis from the Intergovernmental Panel on Climate Change (IPCC), which shows that "In a high-vulnerability development pathway, climate change in 2030 could push 35–132 million people into extreme poverty, in addition to the people already in poverty assuming climate is unchanged" (O'Neill et al., 2022).

These data sources all highlight that **the current quantity of climate finance is insufficient to meet current and future needs**. Yet the existing global climate finance goal of US$ 100 billion per year is not predicted to be met until 2023 and is not predicted to be surpassed until 2024 (COP26 Presidency, 2021).

Worryingly, there are three ongoing trends that are undermining the **quality of climate finance**:

i. non-concessional finance
ii. over-reporting on climate finance, and
iii. dichotomy between needs and granted finance.

The majority of climate finance is provided in the form of loans (OECD Library, 2021), which are often counted at their full face value (Oxfam International [OI], 2020), instead of only counting the grant equivalent of a loan.[1] When only the grant equivalent is factored in, then climate finance between 2017 and 2018 is estimated to be US$ 25 billion per year (OI, 2020), which is less than half of the estimated public climate finance for this same period (OECD Library, 2021). Moreover, according to the Organisation for Economic Cooperation and Development (OECD) public loans in 2019 (concessional and non-concessional) accounted for seventy-one per cent of climate finance amounting to $US 44.5 billion (OECD Library, 2021). Additionally, the IPCC highlights that "African countries expect grants rather than debt because loans add to already high debt levels that exacerbate fiscal challenges, especially given the debt crisis emerging out of COVID-19" (Trisos et al., 2022: 28). This comes when finance from international economic institutions (which is typically in the form of debt-generating instruments) is expected to grow significantly. As evidenced by the 2020 Joint Report of eight Multilateral Development Banks (MDB) on climate finance for developing countries, total loans, equity, lines of credit, and policy based financing (borrowed finance) from these institutions amounted to $US 58.8 billion out of $US 66 billion in total climate finance provided (World Bank Group et al., 2021). Thus, this excessive reliance on loans means that climate finance makes climate-vulnerable countries more vulnerable

---

[1] Grant equivalent: The final amount of money a developing country receives after repayments, interest rates, fees and other factors.

to debt, which in turn reduces the ability of these countries to adapt and to address loss and damage, or to invest in high-quality and universal public services and social protection.

Another worrying trend is that climate finance is being over-reported. Oxfam estimates that over-reporting of climate relevance means that bilateral climate finance could be around a third lower than reported (OI, 2020). This is further echoed by research from CARE Denmark and CARE Netherlands, which shows that the World Bank is over-reporting on climate finance provided for adaptation (CARE Climate Change, 2021). Usefully, both developed and developing countries agree there is a need for enhanced transparency on whether climate finance goals are being met or not. However, the extent to which progress should be tracked is a continuous matter for debate, including on the type of financial flows that should be tracked.

One of the reasons for over-reporting on climate-relevant finance is because the current methodologies used under the United Nations Framework Convention on Climate Change (UNFCCC) are not being applied consistently to the data reported by climate finance providers (Independent Expert Group on Climate Finance). All of this adds further complexity to determining whether climate finance providers are truly on track towards achieving existing, global climate finance goals. Vulnerable communities cannot afford to be 'short-changed' if they are to address the ongoing impacts of climate change, as well as develop sustainably.

In 2021, as part of a package agreeing the rules that guide the implementation of the Paris Agreement (UNFCCC, 2018a), countries agreed on a set of common tabular format reporting tables on financial support provided and received (UNFCCC, 2022). Significantly, these tables require developed countries to report on financial support pledged and disbursed via various channels, including bilateral and multilateral channels. Additionally, developed countries must also now report on the inflows and outflows of finance they provide to multilateral institutions separately, which makes it clearer to determine what disbursed multilateral climate finance is attributable to which reporting country. Previously, it was harder to determine how much finance provided to multilateral institutions by a country was actually disbursed as climate finance to a developing country.

However, these tables do not require developed countries to report on the grant equivalent of finance provided but developed countries can do so in a voluntary capacity. Knowing what the grant equivalent of finance is makes it more manageable to accurately track climate finance and its economic impact. Given the high-amount of finance that is provided using debt-generating instruments such as loans (OECD Library, 2021), the grant equivalent should always be reported. What is more, the funding source and financial instrument used are only required to be reported on to the 'extent possible'. If developed countries do not report the final instrument used to provide the finance it makes it harder to further the collective understanding of the impact of debt-generating instruments. Additionally, loss and damage finance cannot be reported as a type of support, but can be reported under 'additional information' when the information is available. While this is a significant development, considering that developing countries have repeatedly made it clear that they need finance to address loss and damage, it is crucial that this flow is actually tracked to ensure there is a collective understanding of the financing gap, on finance to address loss and damage.

Added to this, analysis by Oxfam shows that there is a **clear dichotomy between where climate finance is most needed and where it actually goes** (OI, 2020). 2019 climate finance figures from the OECD show that $US 50.8 billion out of $US 79.6 billion of provided and mobilized climate finance went to mitigation; amounting to 63.8% for mitigation measures (OECD, 2021). This shows that, while vulnerable communities have identified mitigation as an area where finance is needed (UNFCCC, 2021d), other areas of need are being severely under supported. As the UNFCCC *First Report on the Determination of the Needs of Developing Country Parties* shows, the most commonly identified areas where finance is needed are both **mitigation** (specifically on renewable energy, energy efficiency, transport and forestry) **and adaptation** (specifically on water, agriculture, coastal protection and resilience) (Standing Committee on Finance, 2021; UNFCCC, 2021d). Increasingly, these needs include access to finance to address severe losses and damages caused by ongoing climate impacts (Achampong, 2022; Chhetri et al., 2021; Standing Committee on Finance, 2021) **the severity of which cannot be overlooked**.

Despite these clear signals from developing countries about their needs, the Adaptation Fund (AF) remains severely underfunded. Total contributions to the AF up to September 2021 amounted to US$1103.26 million (World Bank Group, 2021), whereas finance for fossil fuels—from

G20 countries through their international public finance institutions—amounted to US$77 billion per year between 2015 and 2020 (OCI & FoE US, 2020). This is approximately 70 times more for fossil fuels via G20 countries' international public finance institutions in a one-year period than in the 20-year history of the Adaptation Fund. Such a disparity is highly worrying, particularly given the adaptation needs of climate-vulnerable communities.

Accessing High-Quality, New and Additional Climate Finance to Minimize Debt

Accessing finance is another component of quality finance. Between 1999 and 2018, seven out of the ten countries and territories most affected by climate change were developing countries, and losses between this period "amounted to around US$ 3.54 trillion (in purchasing power parities)" (Eckstein et al., 2019). Such severe impacts are disproportionately impacting developing countries, and they need access to additional financial support to tackle climate change impacts.

To date, access to climate finance is often via complicated access procedures that in some cases require the use of accredited entities as 'middle-persons'. All of which impedes developing countries and climate-vulnerable communities' ability to tackle climate change. The lack of access to climate finance, and the need for climate finance can sometimes result in developing countries agreeing bilateral climate finance between themselves and richer countries. Experiences from development finance agreements show that bilateral agreements often come with policy conditions that vastly favour the richer country, and severely impact the development of strong domestic economies in developing countries, as well as livelihoods (Maffei, 2019). This also limits the ability of developing countries to have democratic ownership over climate finance strategies.

Added to this is the complexity of climate finance flows. The Overseas Development Institute (ODI) states "[t]he climate finance architecture is too complex with insufficient resources spread thinly across many small funds with overlapping remits" (Nakhooda et al., 2014). In the midst of this complex landscape, development finance and climate finance streams are often drawn from the same well. Significantly, the OECD states that "Development finance and climate finance have distinct roles and aims. A complete conflation of these budgets and efforts would likely not succeed in achieving either of the critical climate or development agendas" (Ahmad & Carey, 2021).

One of the main issues with the quality of climate finance is whether or not it is additional to existing finance commitments, such as Official Development Assistance (ODA). Developing countries made it clear from the outset that climate finance must be 'new and additional' to existing aid budgets. However, when the current $US 100 billion goal was set in 2009 at the United Nations Framework Convention on Climate Change (UNFCCC) climate negotiations COP15 (it was formalized at COP16 in 2010), no baselines were set from which to count climate finance as additional to existing financial commitments (UNFCCC, 2009, 2011). Given the declining levels of humanitarian financial support (Global Citizen, 2019) and cuts to development finance (Devex, 2020), it is crucial to ensure that public climate finance providers do not divert finance away from existing finance commitments to fund climate efforts. However, it is estimated that, for 2017–2018, "reported climate-related development finance was 25.5 per cent of bilateral Official Development Assistance (ODA)", and the "majority of [this] climate finance was counted towards donor commitments to increase aid to 0.7% of gross national income" (OI, 2020). All of which highlights the difficulties in ensuring that climate finance is 'new and additional' to existing finance commitments.

Debt Implications

Low disbursement ratios coupled with a lack of access to climate finance are impacting developing countries' ability to carry out effective climate action. Particularly, as due to other financial commitments, developing countries often do not have the domestic financial flows to finance their own climate action measures. Lower-income countries are spending five times more on debt repayments than they are on tackling climate change (Jubilee Debt Campaign, 2021). In 2020, lower-income countries spent $372 billion on public external debt repayments (Munevar, 2021b). What is more, the IPCC reports that "[t]he total external debt servicing payments combined for 44 African countries in 2019 were USD 75 billion (World Bank, 2018), far exceeding discussed levels of near-term climate finance" (Trisos et al., 2022: 31).

Limited to no-capacity to tackle climate change in a fiscally responsible and sustainable manner creates a continuous cycle of (i) climate-impacts induced debt, which leads to (ii) debt-induced climate vulnerabilities, and repeats. Low resources and capacities to tackle climate change create the conditions for climate impacts to drain countries' financial resources, as countries are forced to redirect their budgets to address the immediate extreme climate impacts they face; this is climate-impacts induced debt.

The debt they accumulate then reduces their ability to invest in adaptation initiatives or to address the losses and damages that they are facing, which further exacerbates their climate vulnerabilities (Fresnillo, 2020), this is debt-induced climate vulnerabilities. Additionally, research from Imperial College London and SOAS University of London has shown that developing countries are paying extra interest due to their climate vulnerabilities—equivalent to an extra $1 for every $10 of interest paid (Buhr et al., 2018). 2016 projections estimated that an additional US$ 146 billion to US$ 168 billion could be paid in interest by developing countries over the next decade (Donavon, 2018; *Financial Times*, 2018).

This all highlights how finance tools and mechanisms, prudential assessments and risk management systems are contributing to this cycle of indebtedness—all of which is further impacting vulnerable communities' capacity to tackle the climate crisis that they have historically contributed to the least (ClimateWatch, n.d.). As such, it is imperative that when identifying financial instruments to use, climate finance providers must prioritize non-debt-generating instruments, and use methodologies that adequately account for climate impacts (physical manifestations of climate change), climate vulnerabilities (sensitivity to climate impacts) and climate risks (possible negative financial and non-financial impacts) as these all impact a country's fiscal space in different, mutually reinforcing ways.

Gender-Responsive Climate Finance

Gender policy is commonly seen as a way of mitigating the effect of the learned social differences between females and males. These social differences have deep cultural roots and are also changeable over time. Accordingly, research shows that women and men can have different solutions to addressing the same climate impact (UNFCCC, 2019; WHO, n.d.), and often outreach to engage women results in better outcomes for all parts of a community (WHO, n.d.). These alternative approaches to solutions are particularly relevant given that "[t]here is ample empirical evidence that the impacts of climate change are not of equal scope for men and women. Women, particularly the poorest, are more vulnerable and are impacted in greater proportion" (Castellanos et al., 2022: 84). Highlighting that pursuing gender-responsive finance investments is crucial and there is a real benefit for the whole community, particularly as it can help to transform power relations and structures within communities.

For example, a renewable energy project that powers a community fridge reduces the impact that heatwaves have on food stores and helps to ensure that food is available during heatwave-induced drought, as food preparation typically uses water. In turn, this reduces the time girls spend on food preparation and creates the opportunity for girls to have a similar level of access to education as boys. This highlights the benefit of gender-responsive climate finance for achieving both the Paris Agreement and several of the SDGs.

However, the rise in over-reporting of climate-relevant climate finance (OI, 2020) particularly from stakeholders that do not follow existing development effectiveness principles (GPEDC, 2019; OECD, n.d.) means there is also a lack of data on how gender-responsive finance is. This is because there's a lack of consistent, transparent and publicly available information on the various finance streams being reported as climate relevant (OI, 2020).

Significantly, research published by CPI shows that gender-tagging of climate-reported projects is still very low. Just zero point seven per cent of tracked mitigation projects used gender-tagging, eleven per cent of adaptation projects and twenty-seven per cent of projects with dual objectives incorporated used gender-tagging (Buchner, 2021). This is despite, the rules that guide the implementation of the Paris Agreement stating that developed countries should report (UNFCCC, 2018b) on whether finance provided is gender-sensitive or takes gender considerations into account. Similarly, "climate ODA that is dedicated to gender equality as the 'principal' objective stood at only USD 778 million in 2018–2019—a little over 0.04% of all climate-related ODA" (OECD, 2022), and principal[2] and significant[3] "climate ODA integrating gender equality (USD 18.9 billion)" (OECD, n.d.). While not perfect, it is fair to say that gender-tagging of climate-related ODA is implemented at a higher rate by development finance providers. However, it is also clear that transparency on gender-responsive climate finance flows is not comprehensive, and should be improved. Development finance providers should share best practices and lessons learned on gender-tagging of projects that climate finance providers could use to improve their own gender-tagging practices.

Moreover, understanding the intersectionality of gender inequality is also necessary to develop transformative policies that create deep-rooted, sustained and positive change. "Intersectionality refers to the way in which multiple forms of discrimination—based on gender, race, sexuality, disability and class, etc.—overlap and interact with one another to shape how different individuals and groups experience discrimination" (Gender & Development Network, n.d.). Indeed the 2022 IPCC report on *Impacts, Adaptation, and Vulnerability*, states that an "intersectional approach contributes to better capture the diversity of adaptive strategies that men and women adopt vis-à vis climate change" (Castellanos et al., 2022: 85). Thus understanding the intersectionality of gender inequality is necessary to further understand the impacts of climate change on various parts of society. Understanding the intersectionality of gender inequality can be adequately assessed through the use of gender analyses, which should also help reveal the interests, societal parity and power relations within a community. All of which can impact project development and implementation (CARE Climate Change, 2015).

---

[2] OECD DAC Rio Markers for Climate Handbook definition: "fundamental in the design of, or the motivation for, the activity". Available at: https://www.oecd.org/dac/environment-development/Revised%20climate%20marker%20handbook_FINAL.pdf.

[3] OECD DAC Rio Markers for Climate Handbook definition: "not the fundamental driver or motivation for undertaking [the activity]." Available at: https://www.oecd.org/dac/environment-development/Revised%20climate%20marker%20handbook_FINAL.pdf.

Learning from Development Finance to Ensure More Effective Climate Finance

Eurodad has identified six key lessons on development finance that are relevant for understanding how to strengthen climate finance as a tool for supporting sustainable development:

(1) **Instrumentalising policies for other interests does not allow for developing country ownership or enable democratic country-driven strategies** (Eurodad, 2020). Increasingly, developed country providers of public climate finance have been including their own interests within climate policies and agendas (Down to Earth, 2021; European Commission, 2021). Doing so reduces climate-vulnerable countries' ownership of climate finance, and also makes it easier for policy conditions to be attached to climate finance, which severely impacts the development of strong domestic economies, as well as livelihoods (Maffei, 2019).

(2) **Private sector involvement can be costlier than public service investments and can lead to additional, unplanned costs**. Research shows that policy conditions, such as those that encourage private sector access to the domestic markets of developing countries, or partly or fully privatize public services e.g. water services, among others things, severely impacts access to finance (International Trade Union Confederation, 2018), quality jobs (Maffei, 2019) and can lead to proposed forced displacement of communities (Bankwatch, n.d.; Romero, 2018).

(3) **Export-driven approaches to sustainable development have intensified an over-reliance on certain industries to support entire economies**. Export-driven strategies focus on using international trade as a growth strategy to achieve economic development. However, if these industries are fossil fuel based and reliant on fossil fuel subsidies to function, then the risk and reward aspect associated with export-driven approaches can actually lead to stranded assets, due to other countries' transition away from fossil fuels. What is more, export-driven approaches can lead to disastrous impacts on the local environment, impact livelihoods and have high financial risks for the public purse/taxpayers

(*Kaieteur News*, 2019), especially when they are not coupled with social programmes designed to support local communities and counter-cyclical benefits (ADB, 2008).
(4) **The economic prowess of certain (richer) economies influences countries' macroeconomic policies.** This can be seen in the results of studies on spatial inequality and justice (Israel et al., 2018; McKay & Perge, 2015; NRC, 2010). Some of these results highlight the effect of (higher) consumption rates of developed countries on what developing countries choose to produce and export, and the subsequent poor environmental and social conditions under which production is carried out (Felipe et al., 2014). This further highlights the need to ensure true country ownership of climate and development strategies.
(5) **The involvement of Public Development Banks (PDBs) does not automatically lead to positive development outcomes.** PDBs are state-owned financial institutions meant to serve the public good. Despite their overarching objective or mandate being to "deliver on public policy objectives to support the economic development of a country or region" (Romero, 2017), most of the practices and policies of these institutions have not adequately supported sustainable development outcomes, protected human rights and the environment or been accountable and democratic (McDonald et al., 2020).
(6) **Group dynamics play a significant role in project development and implementation.** The attitudes and behaviours of groups in society (e.g. policymakers, project implementers, change agents, etc.) affect project development and implementation. This depends as much on who is involved in the development of the project as it does on the capacity of local communities and local stakeholders to adequately engage with the project's implementation (Romero, 2018). Additionally, differences in power held by stakeholders, coupled with specific narratives, have an impact on the extent to which priorities and agendas are prioritized (Shawoo et al., 2020), which in turn can impact on project development and implementation.

Conclusion and Policy Recommendations

In the wake of the Covid-19 pandemic, there is an opportunity to ensure that a new norm in climate finance emerges that is structured to ensure that vulnerable communities have access to high-quality financial support, technological assistance and capacity building. To make sure this is the case, Eurodad makes the following recommendations:

Democratic country ownership of climate finance strategies is a necessity: It is imperative that climate-vulnerable countries have the agency to design policies to suit their own specific circumstances and domestic needs, as opposed to the priorities of other economies. Empowering domestic policy design will also help to build trust, contribute to empowering the domestic economies of climate-vulnerable countries and set a good precedent for continued, equitable, sustainable development.

Public climate finance in the form of grants should be prioritized: Particularly for projects related to strengthening the resilience of public services to climate impacts, as public climate finance can help reduce the risk of unnecessary higher public debt, which is typically incurred when private finance investments are used (Achampong & Geary, 2021; Romero, 2018). In addition to public finance, climate finance providers should also identify new finance instruments, or repurpose finance instruments, and use these innovative sources of climate finance[4] to provide a stream of scalable and predictable climate finance grants.

Mandatory debt cancellation and debt relief in the aftermath of climate disasters, coupled with direct access to new and additional climate finance: In the immediate aftermath of climate disasters, developed countries must agree on an automatic mechanism to suspend debt payments that is in addition to providing climate finance (Achampong, 2021a). Highly concessional loans should be used only under certain conditions. Furthermore, unconditional debt cancellation, covering both private and official creditors, should be granted to all countries in need of it, thereby allowing resources earmarked for debt repayment in national budgets to be used immediately for emergency relief and reconstruction.

Supporting greater access to finance for women and indigenous communities. Those most impacted by ongoing climate impacts and

---

[4] New or repurposed finance instruments being used by public climate finance providers to generate finance to fulfil their climate finance commitments.

inequality are also the core implementers of these pledges (UNFCCC, 2019). However, they often do not have the access to finance. A gender analysis must be conducted to determine the differing needs and interests, accessibility to finance mechanisms, and power dynamics. It will also help to understand what the gendered-intersectional impacts are (e.g. age, race, ethnicity, gender identity, etc.)—as well as help to determine what the social additionality of climate and development finance on local communities could be (e.g. creating equitable societies, social justice and economic empowerment within communities, notably for women and girls, including from indigenous communities). This will also support developing countries' objectives to have at least 70 per cent of climate finance going to support local-level climate action by 2030 (LDC-Climate Change, 2019).

PDBs must embed climate action and biodiversity objectives across all of their operations, investments and macroeconomic frameworks, and apply a 'do no harm' principle to all investments and approved projects. Additionally, PDB's asset purchases and refinancing operations must be aligned with the Paris Agreement's goals. High-quality climate risk and vulnerability data should be gathered and used to ensure risk management and to guide the direction of investments towards effective climate action measures. This is to ensure that their activities and operations do not undermine the goals of the Paris Agreement, and that they support sustainable development that enables climate-vulnerable countries to transition to net-zero emission economies. These institutions must implement global economic good governance, responsible finance standards, and design finance mechanisms that support the evolving needs of climate-vulnerable countries.

Creating a comprehensive monitoring and reporting framework that includes private finance and multilateral finance. Additionally, the grant equivalency of climate finance must always be reported. Reporting should also record how gender-responsive a climate finance intervention is and take place at the level of activity. Best practices and lessons learned on gender-tagging of projects should be shared between development aid and climate finance providers. This will help create clarity on the additionality of climate finance, and contribute to reducing double counting. It will also increase transparency, accountability and good governance, which in turn should allow the vested interests of those with significant levels of power to be exposed, instead of prioritized (Romero, 2018).

Policy coherence between the Paris Agreement and SDGs should be pursued by all climate finance providers. Climate and development finance decisions must be taken with a long-term view. While these two agendas have differing timelines and policy structures, they are mutually reinforcing and are an opportunity to develop coherent long-term domestic efforts to tackle climate change and achieve sustainable development. This recommendation fits with the trend of more and more countries seeking to create coherence between their climate efforts and the SDGs; with a particular focus on the opportunities of coherence for cost-effectiveness while under fiscal constraints brought on by the Covid-19 pandemic and subsequent unsustainable debt levels.

Countries should institutionalize engagement and participation processes to ensure that all relevant stakeholders are able to engage in policy and project development and implementation, listening to the views of all marginalized groups within society including women, indigenous and ethnic groups, rural communities, racialized communities, etc. These processes must also be gender-sensitive. In order to ensure that the voices of those in the communities carrying out the efforts are taken into account, more efforts should be made to decentralize decision-making, policy and project development processes, in order to support community-based policy development and implementation.

The link between climate change and stunted economic equity between countries and sustainable development is clear. The current global climate-financing gap is preventing developing countries from transitioning to net-zero economies, stopping vulnerable communities from being able to carry out adaptation activities, and is blocking efforts to address ongoing losses and damages. **If this global financing gap is not addressed, then climate change will likely continue to exacerbate inequalities within and between countries.**

Acknowledgements The author would like to express thanks for the feedback received from Isabelle Brachet (ActionAid International); Tess Woolfenden (Jubilee Debt Campaign, UK); and Eurodad's Julia Ravenscroft, Jean Saldanha, María José Romero, Nerea Craviotto and Iolanda Fresnillo.

REFERENCES

Achampong, L. (2021a). *Skilling up to scale up: A guide to COP26 for development finance organisations.* Eurodad. https://www.eurodad.org/skilling_up_to_scale_up_a_guide_to_cop26_for_development_finance_organisations. Accessed 9 March 2022.

Achampong, L. (2021b). *How lessons from development finance can strengthen climate finance.* Eurodad. https://www.eurodad.org/lessons_climate_finance. Accessed 9 March 2022.

Achampong, L. (2022). *Making loss and damage finance the third pillar of the new collective quantified goal on climate finance.* Loss and Damage Collaboration. https://www.lossanddamagecollaboration.org/publication/making-loss-and-damage-finance-the-third-pillar-of-the-new-collective-quantified-goal-on-climate-finance. Accessed 22 March 2022.

Achampong, L., & Geary, K. (2021). *Myanmar's Myingyan public-private partnership gas power plant Pitfalls of private sector involvement.* Infrastructure Case Study. Eurodad & Recourse. https://d3n8a8pro7vhmx.cloudfront.net/eurodad/pages/2581/attachments/original/1633597776/case-study-myanmar-FINAL.pdf?1633597776. Accessed 29 March 2022.

ADB. (2008, February 3). *Liquid gold: The oil palm and disregard of social and environmental norms (Papua New Guinea).* NGO Forum. https://www.forum-adb.org/post/liquid-gold-the-oil-palm-and-disregard-of-social-and-environmental-norms-papua-new-guinea-1. Accessed 6 July 2022.

Ahmad, Y., & Carey, E. (2021). *Development co-operation during the COVID-19 pandemic: An analysis of 2020 figures and 2021 trends to watch.* OECD. https://www.oecd-ilibrary.org/sites/e4b3142a-en/index.html?itemId=/content/component/e4b3142a-en&_ga=2.84877713.984016436.1623763095-2059374352.1573486326#section-d1e1003. Accessed 9 March 2022.

Bankwatch. (n.d.). *Mombasa-Mariakani Road Project, Kenya.* https://bankwatch.org/project/mombasa-mariakani-road-project-kenya. Accessed 28 March 2021.

BBC News. (2020, May 21). *Amphan: Kolkata devastated as cyclone kills scores in India and Bangladesh.* https://www.bbc.com/news/world-asia-india-52749935

Buchner, B. (2021). *Global landscape of climate finance 2021.* Climate Policy Initiative. https://www.climatepolicyinitiative.org/publication/global-landscape-of-climate-finance-2021/. Accessed 9 March 2022.

Buhr, B., Volz, U., et al. (2018). *Climate change and the cost of capital in developing countries assessing the impact of climate risks on sovereign borrowing costs.* Imperial College London and SOAS University of London. https://imperialcollegelondon.app.box.com/s/e8x6t16y9bajb85inazbk5mdrqtvxfzd. Accessed 28 March 2021.

Capital Impact Partners. (2020, May 21). *Racial inequity: As cause and effect—In the Time of COVID-19.* https://www.capitalimpact.org/racial-inequity-as-cause-and-effect-covid-19/

CARE Climate Change. (2015). *Making it count: Integrating gender into climate change and disaster risk reduction.* https://careclimatechange.org/making-it-count-integrating-gender/. Accessed 29 March 2022.

CARE Climate Change. (2021, January 21). *Climate adaptation finance: Fact or fiction?* https://careclimatechange.org/climate-adaptation-finance-fact-or-fiction/

Castellanos, J. E. et al. (2022). Chapter 12: Central and South America. In *Climate Change 2022: Impacts, adaptation and vulnerability—Full report in IPCC Sixth Assessment Report.* IPCC. https://www.ipcc.ch/report/ar6/wg2/. Accessed 30 March 2022.

Chhetri, P. R. et al. (2021). *Loss and damage finance: A long time in the making but not without its challenges.* ClimateWorks Foundation. https://www.climateworks.org/report/loss-and-damage-igst/. Accessed 28 March 2021.

Climate Watch. (n.d.). *Greenhouse gas (GHG) emissions | Climate watch.* https://www.climatewatchdata.org/ghg-emissions?end_year=2018&start_year=1990. Accessed 28 March 2021.

COP26 Presidency. (2021). *Climate finance delivery plan: Meeting the US $100 billion goal.* https://ukcop26.org/wp-content/uploads/2021/10/Climate-Finance-Delivery-Plan-1.pdf. Accessed 9 March 2022.

Devex. (2020, November 25). *Breaking: UK cuts aid budget to 0.5% of GNI.* Devex. https://www.devex.com/news/sponsored/breaking-uk-cuts-aid-budget-to-0-5-of-gni-98640

Donovan, C. (2018). *Developing countries are paying twice for climate change.* Imperial College Business School. https://www.imperial.ac.uk/business-school/ib-knowledge/finance/developing-countries-are-paying-twice-climate-change. Accessed 28 March 2021.

Down to Earth. (2021). *EU and France hijacking Africa's renewable energy initiative, allege civil society groups.* https://www.downtoearth.org.in/news/energy/eu-and-france-hijacking-africa-s-renewable-energy-initiative-alleges-arei-57742. Accessed 28 March 2021.

Eckstein, D., Künzel, V., Schäfer, L., & Winges, M. (2019). *Global Climate Risk Index 2020.* Germanwatch. https://germanwatch.org/en/17307. Accessed 27 September 2021.

Eurodad. (2020, January 29). *European parliament hearing on aid effectiveness.* https://www.eurodad.org/hearing_on_aid_effectiveness. Accessed 28 March 2021.

European Commission. (2021). *Council adopts conclusions on climate and energy diplomacy.* https://www.consilium.europa.eu/en/press/press-releases/2021/01/25/council-adopts-conclusions-on-climate-and-energy-diplomacy/. Accessed 28 March 2021.

European Commission. (2022). *Ministerial on climate action.* https://ec.europa.eu/clima/news-your-voice/events/ministerial-climate-action_en. Accessed 9 March 2022.

Felipe, J., Mehta, A., and Rhee, C. (2014). Manufacturing matters ... but it's the jobs that count. ADB economics working paper series No. 420. Asian Development Bank.

Financial Times. (2018, July 2). Countries face higher debt bills due to climate risks. https://www.ft.com/content/18103b92-7ae6-11e8-bc55-50daf11b720d

Fresnillo, I. (2020). *A tale of two emergencies: The interplay of sovereign debt and climate crises in the global south.* Eurodad. https://www.eurodad.org/a_tale_of_two_emergencies_the_interplay_of_sovereign_debt_and_climate_crises_in_the_global_south. Accessed 28 March 2021.

Gender and Development Network. (n.d.). *Intersectionality, race and decolonisation.* https://gadnetwork.org/issues/intersectionality. Accessed 29 March 2021.

Global Citizen. (2019, July 18). *Foreign aid is falling 'alarmingly' short, humanitarian organization warns.* Global Citizen. https://www.globalcitizen.org/en/content/foreign-aid-funding-falling-short/. Accessed 6 July 2022.

Global Partnership for Effective Development Co-Operation. (2019). *Kampala principles on effective private sector engagement through development co-operation.* https://www.effectivecooperation.org/content/kampala-principles-effective-private-sector-engagement-through-development-co-operation. Accessed 28 March 2021.

Heinrich-Böll-Stiftung. (2020). *Lessons from COVID-19 for addressing loss and damage in vulnerable developing countries.* Heinrich Böll Stiftung. https://us.boell.org/en/2020/12/11/lessons-covid-19-addressing-loss-and-damage-vulnerable-developing-countries. Accessed 28 March 2021.

Independent Expert Group on Climate Finance. (2020, December). *Delivering on the $100 billion climate finance commitment and transforming climate finance.* https://www.un.org/sites/un2.un.org/files/100_billion_climate_finance_report.pdf

International Trade Union Confederation. (2018). *Aligning blended finance to development effectiveness: Where we are at.* https://www.ituc-csi.org/aligning-blended-finance. Accessed 28 March 2021.

Israel, E., et al. (2018). Social justice and spatial inequality: Toward a conceptual framework. *Progress in Human Geography, 42*(5), 647–665. https://doi.org/10.1177/0309132517702969

Jesus, F., Utsav, K., & Arnelyn, A. (2014). How rich countries became rich and why poor countries remain poor: It's the economic structure...duh! *Japan and the World Economy, 29*, 46–58. https://doi.org/10.1016/j.japwor.2013.11.004

Jubilee Debt Campaign. (2021). *Lower income countries spend five times more on debt than dealing with climate change*. https://jubileedebt.org.uk/press-release/lower-income-countries-spend-five-times-more-on-debt-than-dealing-with-climate-change. Accessed 9 March 2022.

Kaieteur News. (2019, July 21). Extensive review of 130 oil contracts exposes inferiority of Guyana & ExxonMobil's PSA. https://www.kaieteurnewsonline.com/2019/07/21/extensive-review-of-130-oil-contracts-exposes-inferiority-of-guyana-exxonmobil-psa/

KPMG. (2020, December 8). *Canada: KPMG Global*. https://home.kpmg/xx/en/home/insights/2020/04/canada-government-and-institution-measures-in-response-to-covid.html. Accessed 6 July 2022.

LDC-Climate Change. (2019). *LDC long term initiatives*. http://www.ldc-climate.org/about-us/long-term-initiatives/. Accessed 28 March 2021.

Maffei, L. (2019). *Blended finance in development—Chile: A shift from people's needs to business demands in country cases: Blended finance in development*. International Trade Union Confederation. https://www.ituc-csi.org/country-cases-blended-finance-in-development. Accessed 28 March 2021.

McDonald, D. A., Marois, T., & Barrowclough, D. (2020). *Public banks and COVID-19: Combatting the pandemic with public finance*. Municipal Services Project, UNCTAD; Eurodad.

McKay, A., & Perge, E. (2015). 'Spatial inequality and its implications for growth: Poverty reduction relations. In: A. McKay, & E. Thorbecke (Eds.), *Economic growth and poverty reduction in sub-Saharan Africa: Current and emerging issues*. Oxford University Press. https://doi.org/10.1093/acprof:oso/9780198728450.003.0007. Accessed 6 July 2022.

Munevar, D. (2021a). *A debt pandemic: Dynamics and implications of the debt crisis of 2020*. Eurodad. https://www.eurodad.org/2020_debt_crisis. Accessed 28 March 2021.

Munevar, D. (2021b). *Eurodad submission to the call for contributions on international debt architecture reform and human rights*. https://www.ohchr.org/Documents/Issues/IEDebt/Int-debt-architecture-reform/Eurodad-input-IDAreform-EN.pdf. Accessed 9 March 2022.

Nakhooda, S. et al. (2014). *Climate finance: Is it making a difference? A review of the effectiveness of multilateral climate funds'*. Overseas Development Institute. https://odi.org/en/publications/climate-finance-is-it-making-a-difference-a-review-of-the-effectiveness-of-multilateral-climate-funds/. Accessed 28 March 2021.

National Research Council (NRC). (2010). *Understanding the changing planet: Strategic Directions for the Geographical Sciences*. The National Academies Press. https://doi.org/10.17226/12860. Accessed 28 March 2021.

OECD. (2022). *Development finance for gender responsive climate action*. Gender Equality Perspectives Series. https://www.oecd.org/dac/development-finance-gender-climate-action.pdf. Accessed 30 March 2022.

OECD. (n.d.). The Busan partnership for effective development co-operation. https://www.oecd.org/development/effectiveness/busanpartnership.htm. Accessed 28 March 2021.

OECD DAC (Development Assistance Committee). (n.d.). *OECD DAC Rio markers for climate handbook*. https://www.oecd.org/dac/environment-development/Revised%20climate%20marker%20handbook_FINAL.pdf. Accessed 6 July 2022.

OECD Library. (2021). *Climate finance provided and mobilised by developed countries: Aggregate trends updated with 2019 data*. https://www.oecd-ilibrary.org/finance-and-investment/climate-finance-provided-and-mobilised-by-developed-countries-aggregate-trends-updated-with-2019-data_03590fb7-en. Accessed 1 October 2021.

OECD & World Health Organisation. (2020). Chapter 2. The impact of the COVID-19 outbreak on Asia-Pacific health systems. In *Health at a glance: Asia/Pacific 2020: measuring progress towards universal health coverage*. https://www.oecd-ilibrary.org/sites/aaa5448f-en/index.html?itemId=/content/component/aaa5448f-en#chapter-d1e7323. Accessed 28 March 2021.

Oil Change International (OCI) & Friends of the Earth U.S. (FoE US) (2020). *Still digging: G20 governments continue to finance the climate crisis*. http://priceofoil.org/2020/05/27/g20-still-digging/. Accessed 27 September 2021.

O'Neill, B. et al. (2022). Chapter 16: Key risks across sectors and regions. In *IPCC, Climate Change 2022: Impacts, adaptation and vulnerability—Full report in IPCC Sixth Assessment Report*. https://www.ipcc.ch/report/ar6/wg2/. Accessed 30 March 2022.

Oxfam International. (2020). *Climate Finance Shadow Report 2020*. https://www.oxfam.org/en/research/climate-finance-shadow-report-2020. Accessed 20 October 2020.

ReliefWeb. (2021, March 1). *Regional dialogue calls for scaled up climate finance for hard-hit Caribbean region*. https://reliefweb.int/report/antigua-and-barbuda/regional-dialogue-calls-scaled-climate-finance-hard-hit-caribbean-region

Romero, M. J. (2017). *Public development banks: Towards a better model*. Eurodad. https://www.eurodad.org/public_development_banks_towards_a_better_model. Accessed 28 March 2021.

Romero, M. J. (2018). *History RePPPeated—How public-private partnerships are failing*. Eurodad. https://www.eurodad.org/historyrepppeated. Accessed 28 March 2021.

Shawoo, Z., Dzebo, A., Hägele, R., Iacobuta, G., Chan, S., Muhoza, C., Osano, P., Francisco, M., Persson, Å., Linner, B-O., & Vijge, M. J. (2020). *Increasing policy coherence between NDCs and SDGs: A national perspective*. SEI Policy Brief. Stockholm Environment Institute.

Standing Committee on Finance. (2021). *First report on the determination of the needs of developing country parties*. UNFCCC. https://unfccc.int/topics/climate-finance/workstreams/needs-report. Accessed 9 March 2022.

The Daily Star. (2020, April 16). *Will covid-19 change how we hold climate change talks?* https://www.thedailystar.net/opinion/politics-climate-change/news/will-covid-19-change-how-we-hold-climate-change-talks-1893190

The Guardian. (2021, January 27). *UK aid cuts of up to 70% a "gut punch" to world's poorest, experts say*. http://www.theguardian.com/global-development/2021/jan/27/uk-aid-cuts-of-up-to-70-a-gut-punch-to-worlds-poorest-experts-say

Trisos, H. C. et al. (2022). Chapter 9: Africa. In *IPCC, Climate Change 2022: Impacts, adaptation and vulnerability—Full report in IPCC Sixth Assessment Report*. https://www.ipcc.ch/report/ar6/wg2/. Accessed 30 March 2022.

UNCTAD. (2022), *Ukraine war risks further cuts to development finance*. https://unctad.org/news/ukraine-war-risks-further-cuts-development-finance. Accessed 23 March 2022.

United Nations Department of Economic and Social Affairs (UNDESA). (2020, July 7). *UN report finds COVID-19 is reversing decades of progress on poverty, healthcare and education*. https://www.un.org/development/desa/en/news/sustainable/sustainable-development-goals-report-2020.html. Accessed 6 July 2022.

UNDP. (2019). *Making development co-operation more effective: How partner countries are promoting effective partnerships*. https://www.undp.org/content/undp/en/home/librarypage/development-impact/Making-development-co-operation-more-effective.html. Accessed 28 March 2021.

UNFCCC. (2009). *Report of the conference of the parties on its fifteenth session, held in Copenhagen from 7 to 19 December 2009 Addendum part two: Action taken by the conference of the parties at its fifteenth session*. https://unfccc.int/resource/docs/2009/cop15/eng/11a01.pdf#page=4. Accessed 28 September 2021.

UNFCCC. (2011). *Report of the conference of the parties on its sixteenth session addendum part two: Action taken by the conference of the parties at its sixteenth session*. https://unfccc.int/resource/docs/2010/cop16/eng/07a01.pdf. Accessed 28 September 2021.

UNFCCC. (2018a). *The Katowice climate package: Making the Paris Agreement work for all*. https://unfccc.int/process-and-meetings/the-paris-agreement/katowice-climate-package. Accessed 9 March 2022.

UNFCCC. (2018b). *Report of the conference of the parties serving as the meeting of the parties to the Paris Agreement on the third part of its first session, held in Katowice from 2 to 15 December 2018b Addendum part two: Action taken by the conference of the parties serving as the meeting of the parties to the Paris Agreement*. https://unfccc.int/sites/default/files/resource/cma 2018b_3_add1_advance.pdf#page=35. Accessed 30 March 2022.

UNFCCC. (2019). *5 reasons why climate action needs women*. https://unfccc.int/news/5-reasons-why-climate-action-needs-women. Accessed 28 March 2021.

UNFCCC. (2021a). *GHG data from UNFCCC*. https://unfccc.int/process-and-meetings/transparency-and-reporting/greenhouse-gas-data/ghg-data-unfccc/ghg-data-from-unfccc. Accessed 28 March 2021.

UNFCCC. (2021b). *Petersburg climate dialogue charts path to net-zero emissions*. https://unfccc.int/news/petersberg-climate-dialogue-charts-path-to-net-zero-emissions. Accessed 9 March 2022.

UNFCCC. (2021c). *New collective quantified goal on climate finance*. https://unfccc.int/documents/310505. Accessed 9 March 2022.

UNFCCC. (2021d). *NDC synthesis report*. https://unfccc.int/process-and-meetings/the-paris-agreement/nationally-determined-contributions-ndcs/nationally-determined-contributions-ndcs/ndc-synthesis-report. Accessed 9 March 2022.

UNFCCC. (2022). *Report of the conference of the parties serving as the meeting of the parties to the Paris Agreement on its third session, held in Glasgow from 31 October to 13 November 2021. Addendum part two: Action taken by the conference of the parties serving as the meeting of the parties to the Paris Agreement at its third session*. https://unfccc.int/documents/460951. Accessed 9 March 2022.

World Bank Group. (2021). *'Adaptation fund' in financial intermediary funds (FIFs)*. https://fiftrustee.worldbank.org/en/about/unit/dfi/fiftrustee/fund-detail/adapt. Accessed 27 September 2021.

World Bank Group (WBG) et al. (2021). *MDBs' climate finance for developing countries rose to US$ 38 billion, joint report shows*. https://www.worldbank.org/en/news/press-release/2021/07/02/mdbs-climate-finance-for-developing-countries-rose-to-us-38-billion-joint-report-shows. Accessed 9 March 2022.

World Health Organization. (n.d.). *Gender, climate change and health*. https://www.who.int/globalchange/publications/reports/gender_climate_change/en/. Accessed 28 March 2021.

CHAPTER 3

International Climate Finance and Development Effectiveness

Brian Tomlinson

A Deepening Climate Crisis, Particularly for Poor and Vulnerable People

The global climate crisis is accelerating rapidly with deepening and irreversible impacts on people, nature and ecosystems. In 2020 this crisis was compounded as the world's population confronted an unprecedented global pandemic, with unrelenting infections and death, with severe economic and political impacts in many countries, North and South, from the spread of the COVID-19 virus. The pandemic has revealed the deeply disturbing limits in global solidarity, particularly on the part of the international donor community, in the face of profound vulnerabilities for hundreds of millions of people throughout the Global South.

B. Tomlinson (✉)
Department of International Development Studies, Dalhousie University, Halifax, NS, Canada
e-mail: brian.t.tomlinson@gmail.com

AidWatch Canada, Waterville, NS, Canada

© The Author(s), under exclusive license to Springer Nature Switzerland AG 2022
C. Cash and L. A. Swatuk (eds.), *The Political Economy of Climate Finance: Lessons from International Development*, International Political Economy Series, https://doi.org/10.1007/978-3-031-12619-2_3

A recently published United Nations Report, *2021 Financing for Sustainable Development*, warns that the pandemic could lead to a lost decade for development, noting that there is a sharply diverging and unequal world emerging from the lack of access to resources by poor countries and people to combat the crisis (United Nations [UN], 2021). In the words of the WHO Director General, we are witnessing a "catastrophic moral failure" in the wake of "vaccine apartheid" and the "me-first" northern allocation of vaccines ("WHO Director-Genera's Opening Remarks", 2021). The UN report cites growing global systemic risks arising from interlinkages between economic, social (e.g. health, inequality) and environmental (e.g. climate) conditions.

In late 2020, the World Bank predicted that as many as 150 million people may be pushed into extreme poverty (i.e. destitution) by 2021 as a result of the pandemic. With 1.9 billion people, or 30% of the population of developing countries, living below the $3.20 social poverty line (and close to 50% of people in Sub-Saharan Africa), vulnerability to the economic and social shocks of the pandemic remains very high. Many people were already living on the margin of extreme poverty (Civicus, 2020; ILO et al., 2020; UN Women, 2020; World Bank, 2020).

As the pandemic unfolds, time is also running out in tackling the climate emergency. In October 2018, the UN Intergovernmental Panel on Climate Change (IPCC) issued a landmark report with a clarion call for transformative and unprecedented shifts in energy systems and use. Without deep cuts in greenhouse gas emissions in the next decade (45% by 2030 over 2010 levels) the planet is likely to fail to achieve the 2015 *Paris Agreement* pledge to keep temperature increases between 1.5 and 2 °C. The report concludes "with very high confidence" that severe climate change and instability "will worsen existing poverty and exacerbate inequalities, especially for those disadvantaged by gender, age, race, class, caste, indigeneity and (dis)ability" (IPCC, 2018: 451). Yet with the accumulated effect of each year of inaction, scientists are predicting that the 1.5 °C could be breached in less than a decade, and a catastrophic 3 °C heating by the end of the century (Hausfather, 2020).

Already parts of the world have experienced severe climate impacts on food and water security, health conditions, livelihood loss, migration, and loss of species and habitat. At a 1.5 °C increase, the IPCC Report estimates that 122 million additional people could experience extreme poverty, with substantial income losses for the poorest 20% in 92 countries, and with significant impacts on poor countries, regions and places where poor people live and work (IPCC, 2018: 452).

By 2050, up to 140 million people could be forced to move within their own countries due to climate-induced disruptions to their livelihoods. In 2019 over 70% of the internally displaced persons population was the result of extreme weather events and natural disasters, more than three times the displacements caused by conflict and violence in that year (Bronkhorst & Bousquet, 2021). In 2018 more than 100 million people required humanitarian assistance as a result of storms, floods, droughts and wildfires. This number is expected to grow to over 200 million each year by 2050 (as cited in European Commission, 2021). The International Federation of the Red Cross estimates that the costs for climate-related humanitarian needs will be approximately $20 billion by 2030, which is almost the current level for the entire humanitarian sector (as cited in Konyndyk & Aly, 2021).

Philip Alston, the UN Special Rapporteur on Poverty and Human Rights, has pointed to the multiple implications of the climate crisis for the rights of poor and vulnerable people. "We risk a 'climate apartheid' scenario where the wealthy pay to escape overheating, hunger and conflict, while the rest of the world is left to suffer" (Alston, 2019: 14).

The exclusive monopoly of developed countries over first access to COVID-19 vaccines may portend a world fractured by even deeper inequalities, marginalizing the health and economic welfare of billions of people. In relation to the climate emergency, Alston noted that developing countries would bear an estimated 75% of the costs of global impacts, despite the fact that the poorest half of the world's population, mainly residing in these countries, are responsible for just 10% of historical carbon emissions. He issued a worrying prognosis for the future of human rights:

> Democracy and the rule of law, as well as a wide range of civil and political rights are every bit at risk. ... The risk of community discontent, of growing inequality, and even greater levels of deprivation among some groups, will likely stimulate nationalist, xenophobic, racist and other responses. Maintaining a balanced approach to civil and political rights will be extremely complex. (Alston, 2019: 14)

What will be the implications of large-scale climate migration, which will be inevitable as the equatorial belt warms towards uninhabitability? How will this migration affect or strengthen already rising "authoritarian nationalist" forces? The climate crisis "is a justice challenge of the first order" (Athanasiou, 2019).

With the degree of decarbonization needed for a 1.5 °C target being politically ambitious for most developed countries, the consequences of missing this target for vulnerable populations in the Global South will be profound. Five decades of development, the ambition of *Agenda 2030* and the achievement of 17 Sustainable Development Goals (SDGs) agreed by the international community in 2015, are seriously undermined without a strong political consensus in developed countries, focusing on renewed commitments to deeply transformative action on the climate crisis at the highest level. As many countries stagger to rebuild from the still unpredictable implications of the pandemic, developed countries have responded with trillions of dollars for emergency finance to protect their citizens, demonstrating that "affordability" is less a technical constraint than a political one.

As with the pandemic, addressing the climate emergency is a global justice challenge of the first order, one which must include and prioritize the most vulnerable countries and peoples. With so little time to act effectively to avert the worst consequences, this chapter looks at the recent history of international public climate finance to situate how well the international community is prepared to meet this challenge in ways that bridge the implications of climate apartheid.

Considering these challenges for human rights and a just global order, this chapter examines (1) the current ambition in setting international climate finance goals against what is required; (2) the degree to which existing goals have been met to date; (3) the trends in the allocation of this climate finance against *Paris Agreement* commitments to give priority to vulnerable countries and peoples; and lastly, (4) the implications of good practice approaches in effective development cooperation for realizing meaningful impacts through official climate finance.

Setting International Climate Finance Goals

All developed countries have an urgent obligation to heighten their ambition for climate commitments for the coming decade, at both the domestic and international levels. Increasing numbers of governments at all levels have stated that they are aligning public policies and actions towards transformed energy systems that reflect a commitment to the Paris 1.5 °C target and establish a pathway to carbon neutrality by 2050.

In Copenhagen in 2009, at the UNFCCC Conference of the Parties (COP15), the international community committed to $100 billion in total annual international climate finance by 2020.[1] This annual commitment was extended to 2025 at the 2015 Paris CSO21, which also adopted the *Paris Agreement* on climate change.[2] Negotiations for a more ambitious target for the period 2025–2030, one that is better aligned to country needs for mitigation and adaptation, will be initiated at the Glasgow COP26 in November 2021 (Dagnet et al., 2021).

The loose structure for delivering existing international climate finance commitments creates significant challenges for the international community in responding with new ambitious international finance initiatives, particularly those that can give priority to those countries and people most vulnerable to the evolving climate crisis.

Aside from the overall target of $100 billion agreed more than 10 years ago in Copenhagen, there are no individual or collective provider (donor) targets for their share of this target.[3] In 2016, the Organisation for Economic Cooperation and Development (OECD) and a number of Development Assistance Committee (DAC) providers created a *Roadmap* (as mandated by the Paris COP21) for achieving this $100 billion target by 2020. Accordingly, developed country providers are expected by 2020 to contribute annually a minimum of $66.8 billion in public resources, of which $37.3 billion is bilateral funds and $29.5 billion is multilateral funds attributed to developed country providers.[4] The remaining

---

[1] All figures are in current US dollars.

[2] See the UNFCCC *Paris Agreement* at https://unfccc.int/process-and-meetings/the-paris-agreement/the-paris-agreement.

[3] This paper uses the lexicon of "provider" for a donor in development cooperation, and "partner country" for a recipient at the country level in development cooperation, common to the Global Partnership for Effective Development Cooperation.

[4] Multilateral banks (MDBs) also allocate climate finance from their own internal resources generated by investments and loan portfolios. The $100 billion Roadmap tracks only allocations by the MDBs that can be traced to a developed country provider core contribution to that MDB. The MDBs produce an annual Joint Report on all climate finance provided by the MDBs. The latest version of this Joint Report is accessed at https://publications.iadb.org/publications/english/document/2019-Joint-Report-on-Multilateral-Development-Banks-Climate-Finance.pdf.

$33.2 billion (33%) is expected to be mobilized from the private sector ("Roadmap to US$100 Billion," 2016: 8). But these "targets" were only best guess-projections in 2016 of the components of the $100 billion climate finance in 2020 and the latter was itself a negotiated amount unrelated to the scale of need.

Determining the Levels of International Climate Finance Commitments

In November 2020, the OECD reported that $64.3 billion in public international climate finance was committed by developed countries in 2018, with an additional $14.6 billion mobilized by these providers from the private sector. Overall, the OECD concludes that $78.9 billion has been directed to the climate crisis in 2018 by developed countries against the goal of $100 million in annual commitments by 2020 (OECD, 2020).

An analysis of this climate finance, however, is fraught with methodological issues, different practices in counting climate finance by different providers, and by the proliferation of different bilateral and multilateral channels for allocation of this finance. Of the $64.3 billion identified above, $32.7 billion was "bilateral public climate finance" derived from provider biennial reports to the United Nations Framework Convention on Climate Change (UNFCCC) and direct reporting to the OECD. This finance was allocated directly through providers' institutions to partners in the Global South. Most developed country providers use the OECD DAC Rio Marker for climate to determine the levels of bilateral climate finance reported to the UNFCCC. But unfortunately, the rules for determining bilateral climate finance are not agreed among all providers. In particular, providers report a bilateral project, where climate mitigation or adaptation is only one among several objectives of the project, to the UNFCCC.[5]

---

[5] The Rio Markers for climate mitigation and adaptation is implemented in the OECD DAC CRS. Project marked 0 have no climate objectives; projects marked 1 have one climate objective among several other project objectives; projects marked 2 have climate as their principal objective. Providers report the full budget for projects with Rio Marker 2 to the UNFCCC, but the value reported for Marker 1 range from 100 to 20%. See *OECD DAC Rio Markers for Climate Handbook* at https://www.oecd.org/dac/enviro nment-development/Revised%20climate%20marker%20handbook_FINAL.pdf. For a list of the share of significant purpose budgets reported see OECD DAC, "Results of the Survey on the Coefficients Applied to Rio Marker Data When Reporting to the UN Conventions on Climate Change and Biodiversity," DCD/DAC/STAT(2020)41/REV1,

These shares range from 100% (Japan) to 30% (Canada), with several reporting 40% of significant purpose budgets. To fairly compare DAC climate finance providers, all provider budgets and disbursements for significant purpose of climate finance have been adjusted to a share of 30% dedicated to climate finance on average.

In 2018 $29.6 billion was reported as "multilateral public climate finance attributable to developed countries." This finance is a calculation of outflows from Multilateral Development Banks (MDBs) coming from core provider contributions to the MDB and the MDB retained earnings (from previous loans) dedicated for climate adaptation or mitigation, which can be attributed to developed countries (based on their relative share of core contributions). But these amounts are also affected by technical differences between the methodology used by the OECD and the MDB's own determination of climate finance from their core resources.[6] Provider allocations to climate-specialized multilateral organizations or funds dedicated to climate mitigation and/or adaptation, such as the Adaptation Fund or the Green Climate Fund, are considered bilateral flows by the OECD DAC.

The lack of consistent rules creates significant credibility issues for developed countries in meeting their climate finance commitments. It undermines trust in the UNFCCC political process on the part of developing countries, as they are increasingly called upon to implement the *Paris Agreement*.[7] The focus of Conference of the Parties (COP)24 in December 2018 was to achieve consensus on a "Paris Rulebook" for guiding its implementation. Among these rules were those intended to resolve and bring order and transparency to both the measurement and to the reporting to the UNFCCC of international climate finance.[8]

27 April, 2021, accessed July 2021 at https://www.oecd.org/officialdocuments/publicdisplaydocumentpdf/?cote=DCD/DAC/STAT(2020)41/REV2&docLanguage=En.

[6] See OECD, "2020 Projections of Climate Finance Towards the USD 100 billion Goal: Technical Note," 2016, accessed at https://www.oecd.org/environment/cc/Projecting%20Climate%20Change%202020%20WEB.pdf.

[7] See for example, "Antonio Guterres on the climate crisis, 'We Are Coming to a Point of No Return,'" Guardian, June 11, 2021, accessed July 2021 at https://www.theguardian.com/environment/2021/jun/11/antonio-guterres-interview-climate-crisis-pandemic-g7.

[8] For an explanation and overview of the "Paris Rulebook", see World Resources Institute, "Explaining the Paris Rulebook," June 2019, accessed October 2019 at https://wriorg.s3.amazonaws.com/s3fs-public/unpacking-paris-agreement-rulebook.pdf.

The negotiated compromise reached at COP24 revolved around greater transparency, specificity and detail on climate finance, with reporting mandatory for developed countries (and encouraged and voluntary for other countries). However, much is still left to the discretion of the reporting party, with a high degree of flexibility in determining what is climate finance (e.g. support for fossil fuel-related activities that reduce carbon intensity) and how to report it.

What will be different after 2020 when the rules come into force is greater transparency in developed country UNFCCC reports. They are required to provide information on what they are reporting (what they consider to be international climate finance) and how they are calculating their contributions.[9] But there is still no agreed consistency in a common approach to these questions between reporting parties. When implemented in their 2020 reports to the UNFCCC, close scrutiny will still be required for assurance that all providers are reporting climate finance fairly and consistently. Developing country trust is likely to continue to be a significant issue in climate finance negotiations.

As mentioned above, for bilateral developed country providers, the OECD DAC Rio Marker is the main option for determining their climate finance based on their own assessment of the main objectives of each project. Since providers have different practices regarding Marker 1 (climate one objective among several), the credibility of the OECD's total bilateral climate finance can be questioned, and it is difficult to compare providers' relative efforts. Therefore, to compare providers fairly, budgets for Marker 1 projects must be adjusted with a common approach across all providers. As noted above, the approach taken in this paper is to include

---

[9] For example, there are no rules around reporting fossil fuel energy as part of climate finance (e.g. "clean coal"). At this point the OECD does not include clean coal in their reporting, but some providers such as Japan consider such support climate mitigation. Many of the reporting rules are qualified "to the extent possible" leaving broad room for differences. Climate finance under the agreement can include not only concessional loans and grants to developing country partners, but also non-concessional loans, equity, guarantees, insurance and other forms of finance. With loans a major part of climate finance (see below) there is no compulsory reporting of net finance accounting for loan repayments. Loan and investment guarantees require no budgetary allocation on the part of developed country providers. See Tomlinson, *The Reality of Canada's International Climate Finance* op. cit. 2019 for more detail on the results of COP24 and the Paris Rulebook.

Marker 1 climate-related projects at 30% of their budget or disbursements.[10] While the level of this adjustment is arbitrary, it acknowledges the importance of mainstreaming climate concerns in projects, but also takes into account the fact that these projects have different overall objectives and sectoral priorities.

The implications for trends in reported OECD DAC climate finance with an adjusted bilateral climate finance are presented in Fig. 3.1. There is a noticeable difference in trends. The OECD data shows a significant increase in bilateral climate finance from an average of two-year $24.5 billion in 2014 and 2015 to $32.7 billion in 2018 (by 33%). Adjusted provider data, on the other hand, indicates a slight decrease in bilateral climate finance from a two-year average of $14.4 billion in 2014 and 2015 to $14.2 billion in 2018, which is just over a third of the $37.3 billion *Roadmap* target for 2020. In 2019, the bilateral adjusted total declined again to $13.6 billion. Bilateral climate finance (adjusted) has been essentially flat lined for three years since 2014.

Bilateral climate finance has also been highly concentrated among a few providers. In 2018, just five providers, including the European Union, made up 71% of bilateral climate finance (adjusted) commitments. The top 10 accounted for 89% (Table 3.1).

As is apparent in Fig. 3.1, much of the growth in climate finance since 2014 has been through multilateral channels (which is even more pronounced if bilateral finance channelled through MDBs would also be considered). According to the OECD, multilateral financing has increased from a two-year average of $18.3 billion in 2014–2015 to $29.6 billion in 2018 (by more than 60%). However, non-concessional loans make the largest share of climate financing by the MDBs (79% of finance in 2019) (Fig. 3.2).

Non-concessional loans have zero value from the perspective of grant equivalency. In a recent report on international climate finance, Oxfam International argued that these loans should be discounted in an assessment of the public finance component of the $100 billion commitment as they ultimately represent a cost to recipient partner countries. Under

---

[10] The paper adjusts bilateral climate finance by including all principal purpose climate finance (Marker 2) at 100% of budget, dividing equally between the two purposes the budget of projects where the purpose is both mitigation and adaptation, including Marker 1 at 30% of budget, and excluding projects as Marker 1, when Marker 2 is indicated for one or other of mitigation or adaptation (in which case the budget is included at 100%).

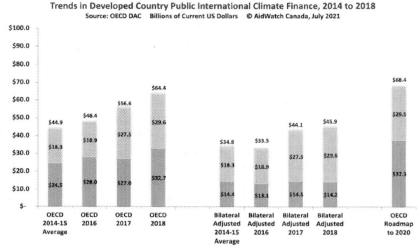

Fig. 3.1 Trends in international climate finance (*Source* OECD, Climate Finance Provided and Mobilized by Developed Countries in 2013–2018, Bilateral Adjusted is OECD DAC Bilateral Provider Perspective, Significant Purpose [Rio Marker 1 adjusted to 30%, Loans adjusted at Grant Equivalency, Total Commitments])

Table 3.1 Top 10 DAC providers, share of total (adjusted) bilateral climate finance, 2019

Donor	Share of climate finance (%)	Donor	Share of climate finance (%)
(1) Germany	23.2	(6) United States	4.7
(2) European Union	17.3	(7) Netherlands	4.4
(3) France	13.4	(8) Norway	3.3
(4) Japan	10.9	(9) Sweden	3.1
(5) United Kingdom	6.5	(10) Denmark	2.1

3 INTERNATIONAL CLIMATE FINANCE AND DEVELOPMENT ... 55

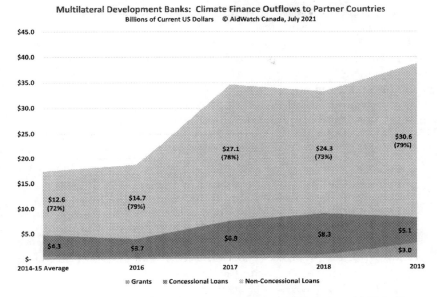

Fig. 3.2 Modalities for MDB climate finance, percentage of total MDB climate finance (*Source* OECD DAC Climate Finance Recipient Perspective, Loans at gross face value)

the reporting rules established through the Paris Agreement, however, non-concessional loans can be reported in a provider's biannual reports to the UNFCCC. Oxfam's estimate of total public net climate finance in 2017/2018 (two-year average) is between $18 billion and $22.5 billion, in contrast to the $60 billion reported by the OECD DAC for these years (Oxfam International, 2020).[11] These wide disparities in determining progress in reaching the $100 billion target affect future negotiations on

---

[11] Similar to the adjustments on bilateral climate finance in Chart One, the Oxfam authors have also adjusted bilateral climate finance, significant purpose, to 30–40%, and grant equivalency for loans, with results consistent with Chart One adjusted bilateral climate finance.

climate finance, post-2025. Without improved standards and accounting rules, trust is significantly eroded.[12]

The $100 billion target also includes private finance for climate mitigation or adaptation if it was mobilized through public finance (e.g. through a Development Finance Institution). In 2018, the OECD determined that $14.6 billion in private sector finance was mobilized through public finance instruments. The methodology deployed by the OECD for determining mobilized private sector climate finance has evolved but remains unclear, with differences in methodology with the MDBs (OECD, 2020).

Determining a causal attribution of the mobilized private finance for climate purposes to a public finance instrument can be problematic. Would the investment take place in the absence of public finance? The latter can include public finance guarantees for loan and investments (accounting for more than 40% of blended financing overall). It is important to note that guarantees are not actual expenditures, which only take place if the loan or investment defaults. Unfortunately, there is no transparency at the level of project detail to verify the amounts and allocations of this finance (and in the case of the World Bank's International Finance Corporation (IFC), OECD officials themselves were only allowed to view data in an IFC secured room).

Weak Accountability for International Climate Finance

Systematic accountability in addressing the climate crisis has been very problematic over the past decade. As demonstrated in the previous section, after a decade, even the allocations of international climate finance against the 2020 $100 billion commitment are highly contested. There are also limited official assessments of this finance in relation to its potential effectiveness as a development resource. The remaining sections of the chapter look at the development effectiveness of climate finance in two dimensions—(a) allocation of this finance for direct impact on vulnerable populations and countries; and (b) consistency with the

---

[12] See Anca Gurzu, "Unmet climate finance promises are damaging global trust: UN climate chief," Devex, April 22, 2021, accessed at https://www.devex.com/news/unmet-climate-finance-promises-are-damaging-global-trust-un-climate-chief-99730.

long-standing principles that define effective development cooperation (democratic country ownership, a focus on country-determined results, inclusive partnerships, and transparency and mutual accountability).

First, in terms of finance allocated in relation to the Paris Agreement, developed countries prepare a biannual report to the UNFCCC on their greenhouse gas emissions and on international climate finance. As noted above, while transparency has improved, the rules for inclusion of a project or flow are determined solely by the respective provider and not the UNFCCC.[13] There are therefore significant challenges in assessing provider performance in relation to reported climate finance flows (Independent Experts Group on Climate Finance, 2020).

Much of these climate resources, both bilateral and multilateral, have also been reported by providers to the OECD DAC as Official Development Cooperation. The OECD DAC publishes an annual report on climate finance, which is widely cited in climate finance negotiations at the annual UNFCCC Conference of the Parties.[14] While the DAC is careful in avoiding double counting, particularly in relation to multilateral finance, they too rely on provider reports to the UNFCCC in constructing their annual reports.

Compounding accountability challenges, climate finance has been allocated through many different channels, some of which are bilateral projects, others dedicated to multilateral funds in existing institutions, and still others newly created multilateral vehicles, such as the Green Climate Fund (GCF). Developing countries face an uncoordinated, project-based

---

[13] See https://unfccc.int/process-and-meetings/transparency-and-reporting/reporting-and-review-under-the-convention/national-communications-and-biennial-reports-annex-i-parties/third-biennial-reports-annex-i for the latest biannual reports submitted to the UNFCCC in 2018.

[14] The latest OECD DAC report on climate finance, *Climate Finance Provided and Mobilized by Developed Countries, 2013 to 2017*, accessed at http://www.oecd.org/env ironment/climate-finance-provided-and-mobilised-by-developed-countries-in-2013-17-39f af4a7-en.htm. DAC data for climate finance can be found in its CRS tables under the Rio Marker for climate adaptation and/or mitigation as well as on this dedicated OECD page: http://www.oecd.org/dac/financing-sustainable-development/development-fin ance-topics/climate-change.htm.

and often opaque international climate finance architecture, which is difficult to navigate and certainly a barrier to clear accountability in coherent international financing strategies for financing their climate priorities.[15]

The GCF has been launched and mandated by the UNFCCC to be its primary channel for climate finance. The Global Environment Facility (GEF) has a North / South governance structure for decision-making, giving it legitimacy as a financing instrument. It is seen to be transparent in its operations. But resourcing the GEF has been fraught with early difficulty, with both the United States and Australia withdrawing their pledges in 2016. Less than $8 billion in pledges were honoured in its first iteration and a first replenishment launched in 2018 achieved a modest target of $10.3 billion (as of September 2020). In April 2021, the United States special climate envoy, John Kerry, recommitted the US administration to finance the GEF, as an "indispensable player" in climate finance, with no indication of a multi-year pledge. An initial request to Congress for $1.25 billion was made in the current budgetary cycle, representing part of the $2 billion that was revoked by the Trump Administration (Green Climate Fund, 2021). While a crucial resource for partner countries, the GCF is not yet seen to be the pre-eminent climate-financing channel as intended with its launch in the Paris Agreement.

Much more is required of the international community, particularly in relation to accountability to the most vulnerable people and countries. They are the ones to bear a high cost from the climate crisis in the coming decades, with limited capacities and resources to respond. A focus on their priorities is crucial for an approach to climate finance that is consistent with Agenda 2030 (and its commitment to leave no one behind), international human rights norms and international climate justice (those responsible for the climate crisis should bear the burden). According to Philip Alston, the UN Special Rapporteur on Poverty and Human Rights,

> It is crucial that climate action is pursued in a way that respects human rights, protects people in poverty from negative impacts, and prevents more

---

[15] See Watson, Charlene (ODI), and Schalatek, Liane (HBS), "The Global Climate Finance Architecture," ODI and Heinrich Boll Stiftung, February 2020, accessed at https://climatefundsupdate.org/wp-content/uploads/2020/03/CFF2-2019-ENG-DIGITAL.pdf. See the diagrammatic representation of this architecture on page 2.

people from falling into poverty. This would include ensuring that vulnerable populations have access to protective infrastructure, technical and financial support, relocation options, training and employment support, land tenure, and access to food, water and sanitation, and healthcare. Women face particular challenges in the face of climate change. (Alston, 2019)

It is then important to ask whether current allocations in climate finance are meeting these needs. As will be developed in the last section, this accountability may be more possible at the country level than globally through the UNFCCC.

Climate Finance Allocations that Address the Needs of the Most Vulnerable

With existing challenges in data, transparency and consistency in rules on what constitutes climate finance for providers, there are limited options for analysing the degree to which climate finance focuses on the needs of the most vulnerable countries and populations. However, several proxies can serve to indicate some trends in climate finance up to 2019.

These indicators include:

1. The balance between adaptation and mitigation;
2. A focus on Least Developed Countries (LDCs) and Small Island Developing States (SIDSs);
3. The role of loans and grants in climate finance;
4. Gender equality objectives in climate finance commitments; and
5. The impact of principal purpose mitigation finance on providers' Official Development Assistance (ODA).

Vulnerable countries and peoples require substantial allocations of finance to adapt to climate impacts already build into current levels of atmospheric greenhouse gases. The LDCs and SIDSs have the least capacity and resources to meet their climate change objectives and many developing countries are challenged by increasing debt burdens. Strengthening women's equality and empowering women as development actors will be an essential dimension of responses that are inclusive and just. Finally, the impact of climate finance taken from aid budgets is an important factor affecting the allocation of aid for other poverty reduction purposes.

The Balance Between Adaptation and Mitigation

The *Paris Agreement* calls for "the provision of scaled-up financial resources [which] should aim to achieve a balance between adaptation and mitigation, taking into account country-driven strategies, and the priorities and needs of developing country Parties, ... considering the need for public and grant-based resources for adaptation" [Article 9, 4].

The Global Commission on Adaptation, led by former Secretary-General Ban Ki-moon, Bill Gates and Kristalina Georgieva, CEO, World Bank, launched *Adapt Now: A Global Call for Leadership on Climate Resilience* in September 2019, with an urgent call to ramp up adaptation finance (The Global Commission on Adaptation, 2019). The Commission notes the critical importance of addressing plausible and highly damaging and catastrophic scenarios (for example, increased drought and storms, deteriorating ocean environments affecting livelihoods, increase in the spread of diseases for which health systems are ill prepared). These impacts threaten the existence and livelihoods of many communities and societies. They draw attention to World Bank evidence that climate change could push 100 million more people below the extreme poverty line by 2030, with disproportionate impacts on women and girls.

The Commission calls on providers to invest $1.8 trillion in five key areas for adaptation by 2030.[16] The UNEP's *Adaptation Gap Report 2020* puts the annual adaptation costs in developing countries currently at $70 billion, which is expected to reach $140 to $300 billion by 2030 and $280 to $500 billion by 2050. While there have been some modest improvements in recent years, the adaptation gap is far from narrowing to reach these targets (UNEP, 2021).

What have been the trends in climate adaptation finance? According to the OECD, mitigation financing has consistently represented over two-thirds of total climate finance provided and mobilized in recent years. In relative terms, the share for adaptation finance grew modestly from 17% of climate finance in 2016 to 21% in 2018 (OECD, 2020: 15). Oxfam, in its shadow report, notes a large increase in volume for adaptation finance between 2016 and 2018, but they still put adaptation finance

---

[16] The five areas that the Commission considered for this estimate are early warning systems, climate-resilient infrastructure, improved dryland agriculture crop production, global mangrove protection, and investments in making water resources more resilient. They acknowledge that these areas are not intended to exclude other aspects of adaptation such as health systems or small-scale agriculture.

at 25% of climate finance in the two-year period, 2017 and 2018 (Oxfam International, 2020: 17).

Some of the growth in adaptation finance has been from the MDBs, albeit starting from a low level. MDB adaptation finance has more than doubled since 2016 to $14 billion in 2019, but is still only 24% of total MDB climate finance (Fig. 3.3).

At the multilateral level, even the UNFCCC-mandated GCF struggles to achieve an adaptation/mitigation balance. A review of 128 projects financed up to March 2020 ($6.1 billion) reveals that only 38% of committed funds have been directed to adaptation (Tomlinson, 2020).

DAC providers had been improving their performance in adaptation finance as a share of total climate finance up to 2017, but this share has declined since 2017 to 38% of their adjusted total climate finance by 2019 (Fig. 3.4). The dollar value of adaptation also declined by 12% from $6.7 billion to $5.2 billion. More than half of bilateral adaptation finance is

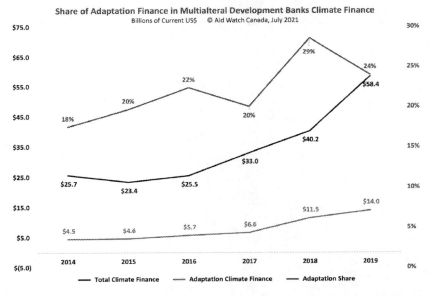

Fig. 3.3 MDB adaptation finance (*Source* Joint Report on Multilateral Development Banks Climate Finance, Various Years)

through projects where adaptation is only one of several objectives. Examining the performance of principal purpose adaptation finance (adaptation is the main objective of the project), the share of adaptation in principal purpose climate finance declined from 42% in 2017 to 26% in 2019, and from $4.1 billion to $2.1 billion.

A recent report by CARE offers a unique review of 112 multilateral and bilateral adaptation projects, with the conclusion that "donors routinely exaggerate the adaptation finance component of their projects." Figures for adaptation finance "are severely overstated and far too high," equivalent to 42% of the reported totals for these 112 projects, which represented a broad spectrum of adaptation finance. Some of the projects that were examined, for example, included large infrastructure projects that had little to do with adaptation (Hattle, 2021). Researchers have also questioned the impacts of adaptation finance, pointing to negative results, what the authors term 'maladaptation'. This work reveals that

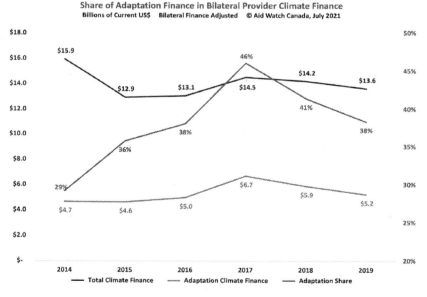

Fig. 3.4 DAC providers bilateral adaptation finance (*Source* OECD DAC Provider Climate Finance, various years, significant purpose adjusted to 30% and loans at grant equivalency)

some adaptation projects have made people more, not less, vulnerable to climate change. These analysts highlight a lack of sensitivity to sociopolitical dynamics that made people vulnerable in the first place, including the livelihoods of poor people in adjacent areas of a project, and the critical importance of considering systemic inequalities (Eriksen et al., 2021; Schipper et al., 2021).

The authors of these studies concluded that maladaptation often occurs when there is little or no participation by marginalized groups in the design and implementation of projects. For example, despite women's critical roles in key sectors, such as agriculture and food security which are highly affected by climate change, women-led climate change responses tend to be largely excluded from global climate finance flows.[17]

Clearly, much greater efforts are also needed in mitigation international finance to achieve the 1.5 °C Paris Agreement target (as well as making mitigation an urgent priority in provider countries themselves). But given the likely future impacts on climate already built into existing and expected greenhouse gas levels, current allocations for adaptation are woefully inadequate to create greater resilience in development approaches and to adapt infrastructure that is needed to protect vulnerable populations. Providers not only fall short of their commitment to achieving a balance for adaptation finance, but also in closing the widening adaptation financing gap.

A Focus on Least Developed Countries (LDCs) and Small Island Developing States (SIDS)

The *Paris Agreement* calls for developed countries to pay particular attention to "those that are particularly vulnerable to the adverse effects of climate change and have significant capacity constraints, such as the LDCs and SIDS, considering the need for public and grant-based resources for adaptation" (Article 9, [4]). The degree to which current climate finance for adaptation addresses the needs of these countries is an indicator of provider coherence with this Paris commitment.

---

[17] See The Equity Fund and the Nobel Women's Initiative, "Supporting Women's Organizations and Movements: A Strategic Approach to Climate Action," February 2020, accessed at https://nobelwomensinitiative.org/wp-content/uploads/2007/02/Climate-Brief_Feb2020_Final.pdf.

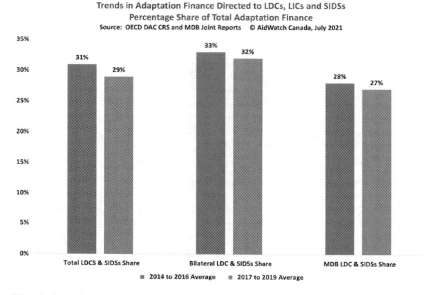

Fig. 3.5 Adaptation finance to vulnerable least developed and small island states: share of total bilateral and MDB adaptation climate finance

A review of bilateral and MDB climate finance estimates that only 29% of adaptation finance was directed to Least Developed, Low Income and Small Island Developing States (SIDS) on average between 2017 and 2019. This share has declined in recent years from an average of 31% between 2014 and 2016. Bilateral providers perform somewhat better than the MDBs, with an average of 32% of climate finance in the years 2017–2019 devoted to adaptation, compared to 27% for MDBs (Fig. 3.5). The GCF performed much better with LDCs and SIDSs receiving 53% of total GCF funds explicitly devoted to adaptation (Tomlinson, 2020).[18]

---

[18] This estimate includes half of commitments where adaptation and mitigation are cross purposes in the same projects.

The Role of Loans and Grants in International Climate Finance

While the *Paris Agreement* stresses the importance of "grant-based resources for adaptation" (Article 9, para. 4), the level of loans in the overall profile of climate finance is an ongoing concern. The International Monetary Fund (IMF) is paying increasing attention to the financial sustainability of debt in low-income countries and some middle-income countries. The widespread use of loans to governments and the private sector in developing countries for climate projects will seriously exacerbate debt distress for many of these countries, now compounded by the pandemic (UNCTAD, 2019).[19]

The economic and fiscal fallout of the pandemic for developing countries critically exacerbated their debt crisis. There are currently 36 low-income countries at or near serious debt distress (List of LIC DSAs for PRGT-Eligible Countries, 2022). EURODAD, a European NGO that monitors debt and development issues, recently calculated that at least 62 developing countries spent more on debt service than on health care in 2020, despite a moratorium on debt servicing for the poorest countries. Much of the World Bank and IMF special pandemic assistance for the poorest countries has been provided as concessional loans. Already in 2020, developing countries were spending $194 billion more on servicing their external public debt than they received in new loans, more than the total value of ODA in that period (Ellmers, 2021; Munevar, 2021). The deployment of loans in official international climate finance can only intensify this debt crisis and limit the fiscal capacities of many developing countries to implement their Nationally Determined Commitments (NDCs) under the Paris Agreement.

As a basic principle of climate justice, developing countries should not be responsible for paying developed countries (principal and interest on loans) for measures to adapt or mitigate the impacts of climate change, for which developed countries alone are largely responsible.

The overall use of loans on the part of bilateral providers has been declining modestly from 45% of climate finance in 2014 to 35% in 2019

---

[19] "Nonfinancial corporate debt in Emerging Market Economies has tripled since the global financial crisis, reaching roughly [US] $25 trillion, or 112 percent of GDP, in mid-2016" (Beltran et al., 2017: 1). Such dependence exposes developing countries to international financial markets with strong speculative features.

(Fig. 3.6). Reflecting the commitment in the *Paris Declaration*, the use of loans for adaptation has declined significantly since 2017, but still makes up 20% of adaptation finance. Three providers—France, Germany and Japan—account for almost all loans in climate finance, and these three are among the largest climate finance providers. Together they make up 95% of loans in 2019. Almost two-third (64%) of the climate finance for these providers together was delivered through loans. France provided 64% of their finance to adaptation as loans, while Japan's share was 50%, and Germany's share was 29% of its adaptation finance.

See "Determining the Levels of International Climate Finance Commitments" above (Fig. 3.2) noted the very high proportion of loans in climate finance provided by the MDBs, the vast majority with non-concessional terms. Oxfam's Shadow Report concluded that 20% of reported public climate finance was delivered as grants, compared to 80% as loans and other non-grant instruments, of which 40% was non-concessional. Non-concessional finance was seen to have increased by

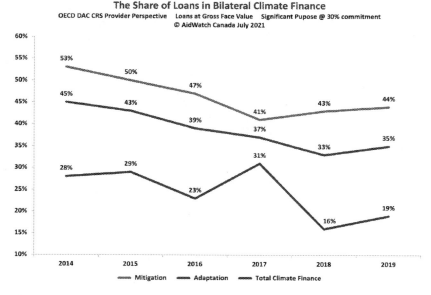

Fig. 3.6 Loans in bilateral climate finance as a share of total bilateral climate finance

10% between the 2015–2016 average and the 2017–2018 average. They also note that grant-based climate finance has flatlined as a share of total climate finance (Oxfam International, 2020: 14–15).

Gender Equality Objectives in Climate Finance Commitments

Mainstreaming gender equality in climate finance is a critical dimension that will ensure inclusive and potentially transformative impacts for both adaptation and mitigation. For example, women play crucial roles in the adoption of resilient agricultural practices. In relation to mitigation, current initiatives tend to ignore small-scale projects supporting clean development mechanisms of greater benefit to women's roles in the household, and women are often disproportionately affected by unintended consequences of large-scale energy infrastructure development, all crucial areas for mitigation efforts.

Currently, the only measure of gender equality objectives in development or climate projects is the OECD DAC's Gender Equality Marker. This Marker identifies projects in which gender equality is the principal objective (Marker 2) and projects in which gender equality is "mainstreamed" as one among several project objectives (Marker 1).

Projects where gender equality is the principal objective are a good indicator of the degree to which providers are serious about their policies relating to gender equality and women's empowerment. Gender Equality Marker 1 has serious limitations in measurement and quality assurance.[20] Merely placing an objective for relating to gender equality within a project's many objectives will not accomplish the mainstreaming of issues for vulnerable women and girls in responding to the climate crisis.

A recent CARE analysis of gender-transformative adaptation, based on case studies, concluded that such projects must carry out climate vulnerability analysis that addresses the power dynamics, priorities and preferences of women (Deering, 2019). They must devote specific budget

---

[20] Marker 1 projects are counted for gender equality by the DAC at 100% of their budget/disbursements even though gender equality is only one of several objectives. Unlike climate finance where activities tend to be distinct, gender mainstreaming is more complex and not easily reducible to a percentage share of the budget/disbursements for marker 1 projects.

to activities that will drive gender transformation on the ground. In many cases they must be accompanied by actions that also address structural barriers to gender equality, such as land ownership, division of labour and roles of women in decision-making. Unfortunately, there are no provider measures in place to assess such approaches or even verify the gender-mainstreaming Marker in climate finance projects.

There is insufficient data to assess gender equality and empowerment in total climate finance. But the OECD data on DAC bilateral and European Union climate finance gross annual disbursements for climate-related projects provides a proxy for the degree to which these issues likely inform climate finance as a whole. In 2019, just under half (46%) of climate disbursements had no gender equality objective, which has improved from 66% in 2017 (Table 3.2). A mere $300 million in project climate finance or 2% of total DAC/EU climate finance for that year had a focus on gender equality as a principal purpose of the project (irrespective of the mitigation or adaptation objectives). The remaining 52% of disbursements were for projects where there was at least one gender equality objective, and a disproportionate amount (67%) was concentrated among adaptation projects.

A commitment to develop gender equality policies in relation to climate finance is improving. But applying these policies to understand success factors and respond with gender-transformative climate adaptation and mitigation is an essential condition for climate finance addressing major vulnerabilities for women and girls in climate change impacts.

Table 3.2 Climate finance and DAC/EU gender marker

DAC gender marker Billions of US$	Mitigation	Adaptation	Total climate disbursements
0 (No gender objectives)	$6.1 (54% of mitigation)	$1.5 (29% of adaptation)	$7.6 (46% of total climate)
1 (One gender objective among others)	$5.1 (45% of mitigation)	$3.4 (67% of adaptation)	$8.5 (52% of total climate)
2 (Gender is principal purpose)	$0.1 (1% of mitigation)	$0.2 (4% of adaptation)	$0.3 (2% of total climate)

DAC CRS Gross Commitments, Provider Perspective, 2019, Significant purpose climate finance at 30% of Project Disbursements

Impact of Climate Finance on Providers' ODA

At the Bali COP13 in 2007, developed countries assured developing countries that ramping up international climate finance would not affect ODA dedicated to other urgent purposes such as health, education or improved governance. In 2009, developed countries reaffirmed in the COP15 *Copenhagen Accord* to, "scaled-up, new and additional, predictable and adequate funding … to developing countries [emphasis added, §9]" (UNFCCC, 2010).

But what constitutes "new and additional" climate finance? Almost all providers' climate finance has been included in their ODA. They are allowed to do so under OECD DAC ODA criteria for ODA if these resources are concessional and focus on the development and welfare of people in developing countries. The 2015 *Paris Agreement* further confused the notion of new and additional by defining it as "a progression beyond previous efforts" [Annex, Article 9]. This approach allows providers to establish their own benchmarks for what constitutes "new and additional" (Calleja, 2021: 21, 66). In practice almost all climate finance has been included and reported as ODA.

The original commitment that climate finance be new and additional to existing ODA has been a crucial concern for developing country parties, further eroding trust. From a climate justice point of view, developing countries should not be paying for the impacts of climate change they had little part in creating; from a development finance perspective, increased development cooperation for all development goals (meeting the ODA target of 0.7% of Gross National Income (GNI)) will be crucial if developing countries are to achieve the SDGs. The impact on providers' ODA is therefore an important measure of the degree to which climate finance is responding to the needs of poor and vulnerable countries and populations.

Table 3.3 provides an overview of the share of bilateral climate finance commitments in total bilateral commitments for select climate finance providers. The focus is on principal purpose climate finance in providers' ODA, with the assumption that mainstreaming climate challenges in all development programming is increasingly essential in a climate-challenged world. The actual impact of climate finance on ODA by this measure has changed over time and is different for each provider. Table 3.3 examines the current shares in 2019 for the top 10 providers for principal purpose climate finance (representing 92% of this financing).

Table 3.3 Select providers, bilateral principal purpose climate finance as a share of real bilateral ODA commitments, 2019[21]

Provider (three-year average, 2015–2017)	Principal purpose, total climate finance, as share of bilateral commitments (%)	Principal purpose, mitigation only, share of bilateral commitments (%)
Austria	55	53
France	26	20
Germany	18	14
Sweden	13	8
Norway	11	10
Netherlands	8	5
EU	5	3
United Kingdom	4	3
United States	2	2
Japan	2	2
DAC providers	9	7

Source OECD DAC Climate Finance, Provider Perspective, and OECD DAC1 ODA data
Real Bilateral ODA is bilateral ODA net of in-donor refugee and student costs, debt cancellation and interest received

For five providers (Austria, France, Germany, Sweden and Norway) principal purpose climate makes up more than 10% of their current bilateral commitments. In the case of France and Germany, 26% and 18%, respectively, of their bilateral aid commitments are directed to climate

[21] This analysis looks only at principal purpose climate finance where the objectives of the project are exclusively devoted to climate mitigation or adaptation. It is assumed that significant purpose climate finance is rightly a part of the approach of a given project where one objective might relate to climate purposes. It is therefore the former projects that should be considered as "new and additional" to existing ODA.

Given the limitations of data sources, it is not possible to consider the impact of total climate finance on ODA. It is important to keep in mind that the majority of climate finance is allocated through multilateral channels including the MDBs own resources (much of which can be attributed to bilateral providers). Table Three examines only bilateral climate finance included in bilateral ODA multi-year commitments based on available data. Total real bilateral aid is net of in-donor refugee costs, imputed student costs and debt cancelation. Including attributable multilateral finance would likely accentuate the trends for most individual providers, depending on their share in multilateral organizations' finance. Since multi-year commitments fluctuate from year to year for many small and medium size providers, the average of the three most recent years has been calculated. Table Three is therefore only indicative of the current impact of climate finance on ODA as a whole. But bilateral development finance is a crucial indicator of providers' priorities since it is allocated directly by the provider.

mitigation or adaptation purposes, leaving significantly reduced amounts for other urgent areas of development.

For all DAC providers an average of 9% of $115 billion in total bilateral aid is devoted to climate finance in 2019. This share is certain to grow as climate finance increases and ODA is flatlined by illiberal politics in many provider countries, which is marginalizing ODA.[22] Without a change in policy and approach by providers and the OECD DAC, as international climate finance increases in response to the urgency of the climate crisis, ODA and its availability for realizing the SDGs (addressing widespread poverty and leaving no one behind) will be seriously compromised.

Conclusion

While mitigation finance is a crucial ingredient to achieving the goals of the *Paris Agreement*, concern should be focused particularly on the widespread use of existing ODA resources for mitigation, which is the largest share of climate finance. Adaptation may be more consistent with good development practice, strengthening resilience in many areas. The failure to substantially increase ODA to address SDGs in relation to widespread conditions of poverty, exclusion and vulnerability, particularly in states with fragile governance, will only exacerbate the impacts of climate change. The latter may affect the capacity of the international community itself to govern in a worsening climate crisis and will lead to substantial demands from developing countries for finance for "loss and damage" as additional climate finance.

References

Alston, P. (2019). *Climate change and poverty: Report of the Special Rapporteur on extreme poverty and human rights.* Retrieved August 2019, from https://www.ohchr.org/sites/default/files/Documents/Issues/Poverty/A_HRC_41_39.pdf

Athanasiou, T. (2019). *Globalizing the movement.* Great Transition Initiative. Retrieved October 2019 from https://greattransition.org/gti-forum/climate-movement-athanasiou

---

[22] DAC ODA grew in 2020, but increases were largely the result of increased allocations relating to the COVID-19 pandemic.

Beltran, D., Garud, K., & Rosenblum, A. (June 2017). *Emerging market nonfinancial corporate debt: How concerned should we be? IFDP notes*. Board of Governors of the Federal Reserve System.

Bronhhorst, B. V., & Bousquet, F. (2021). *Tackling the intersecting challenges of climate change, fragility and conflict*. World Bank Blogs. Retrieved from https://blogs.worldbank.org/dev4peace/tackling-intersecting-challenges-climate-change-fragility-and-conflict

Calleja, R. (2021). *How do development agencies support climate action?* Centre for Global Development. Retrieved from https://www.cgdev.org/publication/how-do-development-agencies-support-climate-action

Civicus. (2020). *People power under attack, 2020*. Civicus Monitor. Retrieved January 2021, from https://findings2020.monitor.civicus.org/

Dagnet, Y., Cogswell, N., Gonzalez, L., Holt, M., Warszawski, N., & Chakrabarty, S. (2021). *Challenging climate negotiations deliver limited progress toward COP26*. World Resources Institute. Retrieved July 2021, from https://www.wri.org/insights/challenging-climate-negotiations-deliver-limited-progress-toward-cop26

Deering, K. (2019). *Gender-transformative adaptation: From good practice to better policy*. Care Insights. Retrieved August 2019, from https://insights.careinternational.org.uk/publications/gender-transformative-adaptation-from-good-practice-to-better-policy

Ellmers, B. (2021). *The new debt crisis and what to do about it policy proposals and political opportunities*. Retrieved from https://www.globalpolicy.org/sites/default/files/download/Briefing_0621_Debt_Crisis.pdf

Eriksen, S., Schipper, E. L. F., Scoville-Simonds, M., Vincent, K., Adam, H. N., Brooks, N., Harding, B., Khatri, D., Lenaerts, L., Liverman, D., Mills-Novoa, M., Mosberg, M., Movik, S., Muok, B., Nightingale, A., Ojha, H., Sygna, L., Taylor, M., & West, J. J. (2021). Adaptation interventions and their effect on vulnerability in developing countries: Help, hindrance or Irrelevance? *Science Direct, 141*(105383). Retrieved from https://www.sciencedirect.com/science/article/pii/S0305750X20305118

European Commission. (2021). *COMMUNICATION FROM THE COMMISSION TO THE EUROPEAN PARLIAMENT AND THE COUNCIL on the EU's humanitarian action: New challenges, same principles*. Retrieved from https://ec.europa.eu/echo/files/aid/hacommunication2021.pdf

Green Climate Fund. (2021). *US climate envoy supports "indispensable" GCF role during climate forum*. Green Climate Fund. Retrieved from https://www.greenclimate.fund/news/us-climate-envoy-supports-indispensable-gcf-role-during-climate-forum

Hattle, A. (2021). *Climate adaptation finance: Fact or Fiction?* CARE Denmark and CARE Netherlands. Retrieved from https://careclimatechange.org/wp-content/uploads/2021/01/CARE_Synthesis-report_Final_April-2021.pdf

Hausfather, Z. (2020). *UNEP: Net-zero pledges provide an 'opening' to close growing emissions 'gap'.* Carbon Brief. Retrieved July 2021, from https://www.carbonbrief.org/unep-net-zero-pledges-provide-an-opening-to-close-growing-emissions-gap/

ILO, FAO, IFAD, & WHO. (2020). *Impact of COVID-19 on people's livelihoods, their health and our food systems.* FAO. Retrieved November 2020, from https://www.fao.org/news/story/en/item/1313598/icode/

Independent Experts Group on Climate Finance. (2020). *Delivering on the $100 billion climate commitment and transforming climate finance.* United Nations. Retrieved from https://www.un.org/sites/un2.un.org/files/100_billion_climate_finance_report.pdf

IPCC. (2018). *Global Warming of 1.5°C. An IPCC special report on the impacts of global warming of 1.5°C above pre-industrial levels and related global greenhouse gas emission pathways, in the context of strengthening the global response to the threat of climate change, sustainable development, and efforts to eradicate poverty.* IPCC. Retrieved August 2019, from https://www.ipcc.ch/sr15/

Konyndyk, J., & Aly, H. (2021). *Aid's climate challenge: Rethinking humanitarianism episode 8.* Centre for Global Development. Retrieved from https://www.cgdev.org/blog/aids-climate-challenge-rethinking-humanitarianism-episode-8

List of LIC DSAs for PRGT-Eligible Countries. (2022). IMF. Retrieved from https://www.imf.org/external/Pubs/ft/dsa/DSAlist.pdf

Munevar, D. (2021). *A debt pandemic dynamics and implications of the debt crisis of 2020.* Eurodad. Retrieved from https://d3n8a8pro7vhmx.cloudfront.net/eurodad/pages/2112/attachments/original/1622627378/debt-pandemic-FINAL.pdf?1622627378

OECD. (2020). *Climate finance provided and mobilised by developed countries in 2013–18.* OECDiLibrary. Retrieved July 2021, from https://www.oecd-ilibrary.org/finance-and-investment/climate-finance-provided-and-mobilised-by-developed-countries-in-2013-18_f0773d55-en;jsessionid=l54WAeVYLf_0sz6hLIAe79pMSIGlSEH34JzMjl7m.ip-10-240-5-71

Oxfam International. (2020). *Climate finance shadow report 2020.* Oxfam International. Retrieved from https://www.oxfam.org/en/research/climate-finance-shadow-report-2020

Roadmap to US$100 Billion. (2016). Department of Foreign Affairs and Trade. Retrieved from https://dfat.gov.au/international-relations/themes/climate-change/Documents/climate-finance-roadmap-to-us100-billion.pdf

Schipper, L., Scoville-Simonds, M., Vincent, K., & Eriksen, S. (2021). *Why avoiding climate change 'maladaptation' is vital.* Carbon Brief. Retrieved from https://www.carbonbrief.org/guest-post-why-avoiding-climate-change-maladaptation-is-vital/

The Global Commission on Adaptation. (2019). *Adapt now: A global call for leadership on climate resilience.* https://cdn.gca.org/assets/2019-09/Global Commission_Report_FINAL.pdf

Tomlinson, B. (2020). *The reality of Canada's international climate finance, 2021.* AidWatch Canada. Retrieved October 2019, from http://climatechangeanddev.ca/wp-content/uploads/2021/10/2021-Final-Canada-Climate-Paper.pdf

UNCTAD (United Nations Conference on Trade and Development). (2019). *The least developed countries report 2019.* United Nations.

UN Women. (2020). *Spotlight on gender, COVID-19 and the SDGs: Will the pandemic derail hard-won progress on gender equality?* Retrieved July 2021, from https://www.unwomen.org/-/media/headquarters/attachments/sections/library/publications/2020/spotlight-on-gender-covid-19-and-the-sdgs-en.pdf?la=en&vs=5013

UNFCCC. (2010). *Report of the conference of the parties on its fifteenth session, held in Copenhagen from 7 to 19 December 2009.* United Nations. Retrieved from https://unfccc.int/resource/docs/2009/cop15/eng/11a01.pdf

United Nations. (2021). *Financing for sustainable development report 2021.* United Nations. Retrieved from https://developmentfinance.un.org/fsdr2021

United Nations Environment Programme. (2021). *Adaptation gap report 2020.* UNEP. Retrieved July 2021, from https://www.unep.org/resources/adaptation-gap-report-2020

WHO Director-General's Opening Remarks at 148th Session of the Executive Board. (2021). World Health Organization. Retrieved from https://www.who.int/director-general/speeches/detail/who-director-general-s-opening-remarks-at-148th-session-of-the-executive-board

World Bank. (2020). *Poverty and shared prosperity 2020: Reversals of fortune.* World Bank. Retrieved July 2021, from https://openknowledge.worldbank.org/bitstream/handle/10986/34496/9781464816024.pdf

CHAPTER 4

Climate Finance and Principles for Effective Development Cooperation

Brian Tomlinson

INTRODUCTION

The notion of development effectiveness has been evolving over the past decade (GPEDC, 2022; Kindornay, 2011; Rahman & Farin, 2019). At the same time, its implications for provider practices and development outcomes have been affected by a changing and more complex development finance landscape. Emerging cooperation modalities, such as South–South Development Cooperation (SSDC), global International NGOs (INGOs) or blended finance with the private sector, have become more prominent, deepening a debate on development effectiveness. Climate finance is now a growing and important dimension of this finance

B. Tomlinson (✉)
Department of International Development Studies, Dalhousie University, Halifax, NS, Canada
e-mail: brian.t.tomlinson@gmail.com

AidWatch Canada, Waterville, NS, Canada

© The Author(s), under exclusive license to Springer Nature Switzerland AG 2022
C. Cash and L. A. Swatuk (eds.), *The Political Economy of Climate Finance: Lessons from International Development*, International Political Economy Series, https://doi.org/10.1007/978-3-031-12619-2_4

landscape. Developed country providers will be pressed to respond to the undeniable and urgent need for dramatically increased allocations of climate finance. But seemingly climate finance has yet to be analysed in relation to lessons from efforts to improve effective development cooperation.[1]

Since 2001, providers and developing country partners have engaged in High Level Fora, which have established benchmarks for assessing the effectiveness of Official Development Assistance (ODA) in the context of development cooperation. All stakeholders made commitments to improve the effectiveness of aid and its development impact (2005 Paris Declaration on Aid Effectiveness and the 2011 Busan Partnership for Effective Development Cooperation).[2]

Since 2011, the Global Partnership for Effective Development Cooperation (GPEDC) has brought together providers, multilateral institutions, partner countries, Civil Society Organisations (CSOs), the private sector, parliamentarians, and foundations as a unique platform to advance the effectiveness of development efforts by all actors. It aims to support country-level implementation of its internationally agreed development effectiveness principles, which also inform the United Nations' framework for ODA in development finance (see the 2015 UN Financing for Development Conference Outcome Document). The principles that were agreed in Busan for effective development cooperation expand upon the earlier 2005 Paris Declaration concept of aid effectiveness.

---

[1] The responses of SSDC and INGO actors will also be increasingly driven by the climate crisis, but the application of development effectiveness principles to these modalities in development cooperation is distinct and beyond the scope of this analysis. See for example, Neissan Besharati, "Measuring the Effectiveness of South South Cooperation," Southern Voice, Occasional Paper # 52, April 2019, accessed October 2019 at http://southernvoice.org/wp-content/uploads/2019/10/191010-Ocassional-Paper-Series-No.-52_final-1.pdf. See also Open Forum, "The Siem Reap CSO Consensus on the International Framework for CSO Development Effectiveness," 2011, accessed October 2019 at https://www.csopartnership.org/single-post/2018/02/15/The-Siem-Reap-CSO-Consensus-on-the-International-Framework-for-CSO-Development-Effectiveness and Costanza De Toma, Accelerating the Implementation of the Istanbul Principles by INGOs in a Changing Development Landscape. CPDE, April 2019, accessed at https://csopartnership.org/resource/cpde-icso-guidelines-paper/

[2] See the 2005 Paris Agreement, the 2008 Accra Agenda for Action and the 2011 Busan Declaration at https://www.oecd.org/dac/effectiveness/parisdeclarationandaccraagendaforaction.htm, https://www.oecd.org/dac/effectiveness/49650173.pdf and https://www.oecd.org/dac/effectiveness/.

The four Busan principles that were agreed should guide effective development cooperation are the result of decades of learning and reflection on the experience of aid and development:

a. Ownership of development priorities by developing countries;
b. Focus on results that have a lasting impact on eradicating poverty and reducing inequality, on sustainable development, aligned with the priorities of developing countries;
c. Inclusive development partnerships, recognizing the different and complementary roles of all actors; and
d. Transparency and accountability to each other.

It was agreed that these principles must be implemented in ways that deepen, extend and operationalize the democratic ownership of development policies and processes, consistent with agreed international commitments on human rights [*Busan Outcome Document*, §11 and §12(a)].

The Busan principles provide a robust framework for assessing development stakeholders' development cooperation. There is a substantial literature on the degree to which these principles have in fact been implemented or even taken into account by development actors in their aid practices: What are the major challenges and influences on provider practices, and how can development practice on the part of all stakeholders be strengthened accordingly? (Blampled, 2016; Development Cooperation Directorate, 2021). But to date public debates on climate finance seem to have largely focused on expanding the amounts of finance committed and delivered, with little attention to the determinants of its effectiveness for transformative change that protects the interests of vulnerable populations.

In putting forward a framework for assessing climate finance drawing on the principles for effective development cooperation, this paper draws upon the third GPEDC's 2018/2019 biannual monitoring process (3MR). The GPEDC monitors the implementation of the four principles against ten indicators for effective development cooperation. It is an exercise that was led by developing country partners in more than 80 countries.[3]

Since significant portions of climate finance are allocated as ODA, the results of this monitoring should apply extensively to climate finance. Without a more explicit analysis of climate finance practices, which will require dedicated research, the analysis below can only be indicative of potential issues for effective climate finance, highlighted in the outcomes of the GPEDC monitoring.

COUNTRY OWNERSHIP OF CLIMATE FINANCE PRIORITIES

Country ownership is a key principle for *Agenda 2030*, which affirms that each government "will set its own national targets guided by the global level of ambition" and that the "global targets should be incorporated into national planning, policies and strategies" [*Transforming our world*, §55].

The *Paris Agreement* [Article 4, para. 2] is consistent with a national planning framework, requiring each Party to prepare, communicate and maintain successive Nationally Determined Contributions (NDCs) that it intends to achieve in reducing greenhouse gases. Developed countries' support "for developing country Parties (NDCs) will allow for higher ambition in their actions" [Article 4, para. 5].

Similarly, Article 7 of the *Agreement* calls for international cooperation to support adaptation plans in developing countries that are "country-driven, gender-responsive, participatory and a fully transparent approach, taking into consideration vulnerable groups, communities and ecosystems, and should be based on and guided by the best available science and, as appropriate, traditional knowledge, knowledge of

---

[3] The results of the GPEDC's 2018 third monitoring round is available at http://effectivecooperation.org/monitoring-country-progress/making-development-co-operation-more-effective/. This paper draws on a detailed parallel 2018-2019 analysis by CSOs of progress in development effectiveness practices prepared by the author, Brian Tomlinson, *Civil Society Reflections on Progress in Achieving Development Effectiveness: Inclusion, accountability and transparency*, a 2019 report prepared for the CSP Partnership for Effective Development (CPDE), June 2019, accessible at www.aidwatchcanada.ca or https://docs.wixstatic.com/ugd/9f29ee_44f4e59a973f47fb920f6ce8d66cba08.pdf.

indigenous peoples and local knowledge systems, with a view to integrating adaptation into relevant socioeconomic and environmental policies and actions, where appropriate [emphasis added]" (Article 7, para. 5).

Democratic country ownership is an essential basis for inclusive country ownership of development plans and strategies, which must include full participation by all country stakeholders in the development of priorities for NDCs. The GPEDC monitoring framework looks not only at the degree to which providers align their aid to country development plans and strategies, but also at country-level processes for stakeholder inclusion in the determination, and therefore the legitimacy of country strategies, priorities and results frameworks to which providers are aligning. What can be learned from the results in GPEDC's Third Monitoring Round (3MR) in 2018?

To what degree are developing country development priorities the result of inclusive and structured processes? CSOs consulted in the 3MR process observed that various forms of multi-stakeholder processes exist for dialogue on development priorities. But many of these processes are highly compromised by a lack of institutionalized regularity and can be perfunctory mechanisms to endorse existing government priorities with limited CSO engagement. CSOs continue to rate broad government consultation practices, in terms of timeliness, transparent documentation, openness and iterative processes, either as very poor or needing significant improvement.

The case of Kenya seems indicative: "Whereas some CSOs are sometimes meaningfully consulted, there is no unified process of consultative input, and thereafter implementation, monitoring and validation of the results of development efforts are similarly limited" (as quoted in Tomlinson, 2019: 25). Years of development experience suggests that transformative and sustainable development strategies "owned" across sectors, so essential for climate mitigation and adaptation focusing on transformation, but also for poverty reduction, will likely fail to galvanize support in the absence of meaningful inclusive processes of governance.

Of the hundreds of projects examined in partner countries by the 3MR developing country focal points, only 57% of bilateral projects were seen to be aligned with country results frameworks (derived from country plans and strategies), down from 64% in 2016 (Part 2, pages. 28–29)

(OECD & UNDP, 2019).[4] The 2019 *Progress Report* notes an improvement in country-level planning, which in some cases is more inclusive. But it also concludes, "more systematic and meaningful engagement of diverse stakeholders throughout the development processes is needed" {Part I, page. 36). While almost all Governments in the 3MR (77%) report consulting with CSOs in designing national development strategies, only a small number (17%) confirmed that they allowed CSOs to engage in a participatory process to shape the national development strategy.

How aligned are providers' climate finance allocations with developing country NDCs and stated needs for adaptation? There is little direct evidence, although it can be assumed that monitoring conclusions above on country alignment for bilateral aid broadly applies to bilateral climate finance. In a follow-up study by the EU, they observed that "climate change is another evolving priority that can be programmed through partner country systems but often is not" (DEVCO, 2020: 63). They note that many of these projects are implemented internationally or regionally, often avoiding partner country systems, which has not been a priority.

Within the climate finance architecture, the Green Climate Fund (GCF), with direct participation of developing countries in GCF governance, and its reliance on proposals from developing country governments and other stakeholders, may validate a new approach that ensures greater country ownership of climate initiatives. The GCF establishes ownership through National Designated Authority or Focal Point, which governments identify as the interface between the country and the Fund.[5] A strong reliance on UN-related multilateral channels for climate finance in general can also allow for greater trends in these directions, but with the very notable exceptions of provider-dominated MDBs.

The OECD DAC has set out systematic reflections and guidelines for the alignment of development cooperation with the *Paris Agreement* (OECD DAC, 2019, 2021). These reflections and guidelines point to

---

[4] All references are to OECD and UNDP, "Making development cooperation more effective: How partner countries are promoting effective partnerships," Part I and Part II, Global Partnership 2019 Progress Report, Global Partnership for Effective Development Cooperation, June 2019, accessed October 2019 at http://effectivecooperation.org/monitoring-country-progress/making-development-co-operation-more-effective/.

[5] See https://www.greenclimate.fund/document/nomination-national-designated-authority-nda-or-focal-point.

the centrality of ownership for global climate objectives that are delivered at both the national and subnational level that are guided by NDCs and long-term low greenhouse gas emissions strategies (LTSs). The Guidelines highlight that climate risks are in many cases country and sector specific, and that connecting climate-centric processes with other development and sectoral plans are essential (OECD DAC, 2019: 21–22).

The OECD DAC also points to several challenges in fully aligning development cooperation with climate commitments. A summary of their review of provider policies and practices concludes,

> most providers have not defined what Paris alignment looks like. Climate strategies and mainstreaming approaches have yet to effectively enhance the consistency of development cooperation. Many providers also lack capacity to support transformative climate action in developing countries. (OECD, 2019: 10)

On the other hand, developing countries face major capacity and institutional challenges in integrating their climate change objectives and commitments into their development planning processes, with inclusion of relevant subnational and non-state actors. Developing and updating NDCs and National Adaptation Plans (NAPs) is also challenging. For example, at least 120 developing countries have started to formulate NAPs, but only 20 have been submitted to the UNFCCC as of January 2021 (OECD DAC, 2021: 21).

The DAC recognizes the critical role of non-state actors in addressing climate vulnerabilities at the country and local levels, but in practice "non-state actors often have limited access to decision-making processes, including those related to domestic finance allocation and access to international climate finance (OECD DAC, 2021: 34. ff). Despite global commitments, only a minority of governments seem to be engaging civil society in determining Sustainable Development Goal (SDG) priorities and their implementation, including Goal 13 on addressing climate change.[6] These limitations will carry forward to the essential task of

---

[6] See evidence in Forus, *Prioritizing the Capacity Building of Civil Society for Effective SDG Implementation: An analysis of the 2020 VNRs to assess government action on SDG 17*, July 2021, accessed July 2021 at https://www.forus-international.org/en/extra/hub/resources-publications?modal_page=pdf-detail&modal_detail_id=77140-prioritizing-the-capacity-building-of-civil-society-for-effective-sdg-implementation&tab=list and Forus, *Progressing National SDG Implementation,* Cooperation Canada and BOND, March

building country consensus on societal priorities for climate mitigation and adaptation policies and plans.

The DAC reflections on climate action also point to the critical dimension of policy coherence in provider alignment with the *Paris Agreement*. The OECD observes that "the volumes of export credits reported for non-renewable energy production plants nearly quadrupled between 2010 and 2016, from $12 billion to $46 billion," an amount that dwarfs provider bilateral support for climate finance during this period (OECD, 2019: 10). ODA from several DAC donors (e.g. Japan) continue large investments in concessional finance of fossil fuels. The DAC recently identified $4 billion in support for electricity generation and fossil fuel infrastructure through ODA in 2019. DAC donors contribute 34% of energy sector financing, of which 13% is for fossil fuel electricity generation. Negotiations are underway at the DAC to set rules for the carbon intensity of supported ODA activities in the energy sector, which may reduce but not eliminate the continued deployment of ODA investments in the use of fossil fuels ("Alignment of ODA," 2021).

Enabling CSOs for Inclusive Development Partnerships

Given the scale of challenges arising from the climate crisis, sustained citizen engagement is a critical path towards decarbonization and resilience, with ambitious goals for mitigation and adaptation across the globe. Recent mass mobilizations have taken the form of student strikes and massive citizen demonstrations uniting diverse constituencies in a deepening concern for the future of the planet, its people and biodiversity. Targeted resistance by indigenous nations and peoples alongside community-level environmental activists, organizing to call attention to particularly destructive projects, have had a long history.

Together, they are a vital force to increase political pressure for credible responses to the climate crisis—ones that begin to set genuine targets and take systemic actions to reduce greenhouse gases, while addressing

2021, accessed July 2021 at https://www.forus-international.org/en/extra/hub/resources-publications?modal_page=pdf-detail&modal_detail_id=75964-progressing-national-sdgs-implementation-report&tab=list.

massive needs for adaptation affecting the most vulnerable. They are demanding real accountability from politicians and corporations to these ends.

Open civic space, where people can freely organize and express their concerns and alternatives, is a crucial political foundation for inclusive development outcomes; it is a recognized condition for inclusive partnerships for SDGs through development cooperation. This space is particularly critical for civil society organizations (CSOs) that are seen to be politically challenging by existing power structures, whether in government or extractive corporations in minerals, oil and gas. These CSOs often represent poor communities, marginalized and repressed populations, bring together indigenous peoples' voices and interests or work to empower women and girls. Open civic space is a vital condition for innovative partnerships that can press for just solutions in the climate crisis, often contesting powerful interests rooted in a fossil fuel economy.

In recent years, attacks on civil society across the globe by governments and other powerful interests are growing and have taken many legal and extra-legal forms.[7] Frontline Defenders, a human rights organization based in Ireland, confirms that 1268 human rights defenders (HRDs) were killed in the most recent four-year period (2017 to 2020), mainly in developing countries. Of those killed, nearly two-thirds (63%) were "defenders working on land, indigenous peoples' and environmental rights." Since 2017, 327 Indigenous Peoples' rights defenders were among those killed (Frontline Defenders, 2021).

Beyond killing HRDs, hundreds more environmental activists are designated "criminals" or "foreign agents" in both the Global North and South. They and their organizations continually face many forms of harassment and aggressive measures brought by government and corporations seeking to silence them. Women human rights defenders in general, but including those who are active on environmental rights and climate issues, face constant sexual harassment and abuse as well as continuous denigration of women's voices and issues (UN Human Rights, 2019).

---

[7] Among those documented by human rights organizations include: restrictive laws and regulations to harass and marginalize CSOs, limited policy dialogue and access to information, systematic violence against human rights advocates, increasing public intolerance (religious fundamentalisms and political intolerance), Stigmatization narratives (self-serving, foreign agents, threats to social stability), cyber harassment and surveillance, limitations on access to funding and advocacy roles under charity laws, and restrictions at the multilateral level (denial of access, severe limitations on speaking in meetings.

Many of these conditions were compounded by the pandemic whereby "murderers took advantage of lockdowns to target defenders whose security strategies would have previously involved frequent changes in location" (Frontline Defenders, 2021: 12).

Effective and inclusive partnerships are seen to be a core principle and approach in development cooperation, which aims to move from "whole-of-government" (i.e. exclusively inter-governmental partnerships) to a whole-of-society approach. Increasingly the latter is seen to be essential for effective climate adaptation:

> Underlying factors that were found influential for improving climate resilience and livelihoods included: a focus on community empowerment, capacities, institutions and participation in decision-making; ... engagement with key actors at the subnational level, including community-based organisations, civil society organisations and local governments; ... facilitation of dialogue and cooperation among different stakeholders in the public and private sector ... (Bird, 2020: 55–56)

But conditions for inclusive partnerships that are effective in reaching poor and vulnerable populations are not nearly a given for many civil society organizations. For CSOs, working through inclusive partnerships that are equitable and respect different societal interests, require all development actors to create an enabling policy and legal environment for CSOs. Civil society can reach vulnerable people and communities, bring context-specific development knowledge to the table, hold governments to account, defend the rights of vulnerable and marginalized populations and support transformative change, all of which are crucial in raising government ambition in the climate crisis.

But evidence collected by the GPEDC's 2018/2019 country monitoring exercise largely confirms the experience of human rights organizations. The GPEDC's 2019 *Progress Report*, summarizing observations by government, providers and CSOs, concluded, "constraints on civil society have increased, negatively affecting its ability to participate in and contribute to national development processes" (Part I, page. 40). GPEDC reports from 82 countries are consistent with "the widely reported view that space for civil society is shrinking" (Part I, page. 40).

This evidence suggests that opportunities for policy dialogue with government have increased in many of the GPEDC participating countries, yet most CSOs said that these are episodic and often perfunctory engagement on policies and priorities established by government. Unreasonable legal and regulatory measures affecting CSOs have become widespread across many countries, with restrictions on receiving external funding or regulatory harassment becoming more common practice.[8] As noted above, environmental activists and organizations have been increasingly targeted. Further research is needed to disaggregate and synthesize impacts of this civic environment for inclusion in adaptation climate initiatives or respect for affected communities' free, prior and informed consent in new mitigation infrastructure supported by providers through private sector partnerships.

Development cooperation providers can be playing a constructive role to strengthen enabling conditions for civil society actors, including through climate finance partnerships. But the GPEDC's 3MR found major barriers for progress: (1) providers were not raising issues of CSO enabling conditions systematically in provider/government policy dialogue and projects; (2) providers consulted CSOs at the country level episodically, if at all; and (3) good practice in providing financial support for CSOs was weak, with very limited direct support to local CSOs in developing countries, and a move away from flexible programmatic CSO funding by some providers (Tomlinson, 2019: 40–41).[9]

More specific research is needed to understand better whether climate finance partnerships are strengthening capacities and roles for local actors, including civil society, to implement country NDC priorities, and hold their governments to account at all levels.[10] The evidence suggests worrying trends, but also a lack of recognition of these challenges for civil society among climate actors and institutions.

---

[8] See a detailed summary of the evidence in Annex Three in Tomlinson, 2019, Civil Society Reflections, *op. cit.*

[9] In July 2021, the members of the DAC adopted a strong Recommendation on Enabling Civil Society, which will improve their accountability to measures that reverse these donor practices in their relationships with civil society. See https://legalinstruments.oecd.org/en/instruments/OECD-LEGAL-5021#backgroundInformation and https://crosol.hr/en/dac-recommendation-on-enabling-civil-society-in-development-co-operation-and-humanitarian-assistance/.

[10] The International Institute for Environment and Development (IIED) is an exception with its substantial work on local responses to poverty, climate and nature. See various reports and blogs at https://www.iied.org/climate-change. See also IIED, "Principles for Locally-led Adaptation," January 2021, accessed at https://www.iied.org/principles-for-locally-led-adaptation.

Development Partnerships and the Private Sector

Many bilateral and multilateral mitigation projects are carried out through public sector loans and guarantees, with private sector finance in blended finance managed by Development Finance Institutions (DFIs). Providers argue that the use of public resources to catalyze this private sector finance is essential to make up the massive shortfall in capital (hundreds of billions of dollars annually) required to finance the transition to a non-carbon economy throughout the Global South. Recent research highlights issues in scale and purpose, but also transparency and accountability for blended finance, which are basic principles for effective development cooperation.

The OECD has attempted to measure private sector finance mobilized by the public sector through blended finance (OECD, n.d.c; OECD, 2017). According to this research, $258.1 billion was mobilized from the private sector for sustainable development purposes, in the eight years between 2012 and 2019. In 2019, $45.0 billion in mobilized finance was reported by various DFIs to the OECD DAC. Three quarters of mobilized finance was reported by multilateral providers with the World Bank's International Finance Corporation (IFC) being the largest at $12.1 billion on average between 2018 and 2019. The largest bilateral providers for mobilized private sector finance were the United States at $5.4 billion, France at $2.8 billion and the United Kingdom at $1.2 billion. Almost all of this finance for 2018/2019 targeted middle-income countries—lower-middle-income 39% and upper middle-income at 49%, leaving only 11% for least developed and low-income countries (OECD, 2021: various slides).

A very significant share of this mobilized finance focused on the climate crisis—33% or approximately $15 billion in 2018/2019 (OECD, 2021: various slides). There was no breakdown between adaptation and mitigation in this most recent data. But an earlier OECD study on mobilized finance for the period 2012 to 2015 reported that 87% of this finance was directed to mitigation and 13% to adaptation (OECD, 2017).

There are several critical issues in the expanding role of DFIs in development cooperation in general, which also apply to blended finance for climate mitigation and adaptation. Among these challenges are

   a. The question of whether private finance is truly additional because of the public contribution, or a public subsidy of an existing private sector initiative, which would take place without the public input;

b. The need for much improved transparency at the transaction level;
c. The lack of impact analysis of development outcomes;
d. An exacerbation of a debt crisis through increased loans in development cooperation (as noted above); and
e. Demonstrated consistency with development effectiveness principles.

In responding to some of these challenges as they relate to development effectiveness and impact, in October 2017, members of the OECD DAC have agreed to a broad set of principles to guide the practices of DFIs, *Blended Finance Principles for Unlocking Commercial Finance for the Sustainable Development Goals*.[11] While the DAC has developed detailed guidance for these principles, this guidance ignores key aspects of local democratic ownership, including the human rights principle of free, informed and prior consent by those most affected by development investments, particularly in energy and infrastructure, where blended finance is most common.

Creating a framework for assessing actual contributions of blended finance to development and the SDGs, including climate adaptation and mitigation, will be essential to their credibility. In this regard, at its July 2019 Senior Level Meeting, the GPEDC endorsed the *Kampala Principles on Effective Private Sector Engagement in Development Cooperation* (GPEDC, n.d.). These principles were developed through an in-depth multi-stakeholder process, which included the full participation of CSOs. Bringing in key elements for effective development cooperation, the *Kampala Principles* can serve as a framework for monitoring private sector engagement, including blended finance, through the GPEDC biannual country-led monitoring process.

The *Kampala Principles* acknowledge "a number of challenges with private sector engagement [PSE] important for development effectiveness … [including] lack of safeguards on the use of public resources;

---

[11] See the OECD DAC web landing page on blended finance at https://www.oecd.org/dac/financing-sustainable-development/blended-finance-principles/. The OECD DAC have expanded on these principles with detailed guidelines for the implementation of the five principles—(1) Anchoring blended finance use to a development rationale, (2) Designing blended finance to increase mobilization of commercial finance, (3) Tailoring blended finance to local contexts, (4) Focusing on effective partnering for blended finance, and (5) Monitoring blended finance for transparency and results.

insufficient attention to concrete results and outcomes (particularly for the benefit of those furthest behind); and limited transparency, accountability and evaluation of PSE projects [page. 4]." Five principles are fully elaborated and provide normative guidance for assessing private sector engagement in effective development cooperation.

a. Inclusive country ownership—Define provider/government national private sector engagement (PSE) strategies through inclusive processes, which should be aligned with national priorities and strategies;
b. Results and targeted impact—Focus on maximizing sustainable development results while engaging in partnerships according to agreed international standards, including the International Labour Organisation labour standards, the United Nations Principles on Business and Human Rights and the OECD guidelines for multinational enterprises.
c. Inclusive partnerships—Support institutional inclusive dialogue on PSE and promote bottom-up innovative partnerships "in the spirit of leaving no one behind" [page. 5].
d. Transparency and accountability—Measure and disseminate results, remaining "accountable to the partners involved, beneficiary communities and citizens at large" [page. 5].
e. Leave no one behind—Targeting those furthest behind means recognizing, sharing and mitigating risks for all partners. Ensure that a private sector solution is the most appropriate way to reach those furthest behind. Carry out a joint assessment of the potential risks for the beneficiaries of the partnership as part of due diligence.

Implementation of the *Kampala Principles* by providers, DFIs and partner governments would bring a significant development effectiveness lens to blended finance projects, including those relating to mitigation and adaptation. But the overall weak track record of providers over the past decade in carrying through reforms in their development practice based regular monitoring of implementation of the four GPEDC development effectiveness principles, unfortunately, does not give strong assurance that they will be seriously taken on board. Domestic political pressures in provider countries to tie blended finance to their domestic private sector partners, and the expanding role of the MDBs to mobilize the corporate private sector in filling financing gaps, may accentuate a marginalization of these important *Principles*.

TRANSPARENCY AND ACCOUNTABILITY IN DEVELOPMENT COOPERATION FOR CLIMATE COMMITMENTS

Accountability to Nationally Determined Commitments (NDCs) at the level of the *Paris Agreement* is both voluntary and weak. Mechanisms for reviewing compliance are non-binding and largely consultative (Karlsson-Vinkhuyzen et al., 2018). The mechanism established in Article 15 of the *Paris Agreement* is intended to be expert-based, non-adversarial and non-punitive, "taking account the national capabilities of Parties." The word "accountability" does not appear in the text of the *Paris Agreement*. On the other hand, the December 2018 negotiated Paris Rulebook for implementing the *Agreement* added substantial improvements in transparency (see previous chapter), while largely avoiding issues of accountability. Developed countries are now obliged to send more rigorous biennial reports, but there are no political forums in the context of the UNFCCC for discussing individual reports.

The UNFCCC Standing Committee on Finance prepares an overarching and synthesizing biennial report.[12] These reports are based on national reports submitted by developed country Parties and bring attention to overall trends in patterns in finance (subject to the limitations of national reports and inconsistencies between them).

Given the overall weaknesses of the multilateral system for holding governments to account, including the UN and its bodies, the path to stronger accountability may lie at the country level (Karlsson-Vinkhuyzen et al., 2018). The GPEDC stresses the critical importance of partner country country-led mutual accountability mechanisms in its framework for effective development cooperation.

Country-level accountability mechanisms are an opportunity to hold providers (and partner country governments) to account for their financing commitments. They can also build incentives for behaviour change for all development actors, which is crucial to effective measures

---

[12] See https://unfccc.int/SCF.

that respect country ownership in development cooperation. But meaningful country accountability requires country mechanisms that go beyond provider/government dialogues, with processes that are both transparent and inclusive of all development actors such as civil society, parliamentarians, and the private sector.

The GPEDC's Third Monitoring Round (3MR) in 2018/2019 was an opportunity to review the realities of mutual accountability in development cooperation at the country level. To what degree are there regular, institutionalized and inclusive mutual accountability dialogue on development cooperation priorities and finance? Are there country frameworks in place to guide these dialogues? Are there specific targets for the different development partners? To what extent are the results of accountability assessments transparent and accessible in a timely way to the public? These were the questions country-level facilitators for the monitoring exercise asked in relation to current practices in their country.

The *Progress Report* found that quality mutual accountability mechanisms were seen by providers and government to be strong and improving in the poorest countries that rely heavily on ODA. But among the full set of 86 countries reviewed (many of which are middle-income countries), fewer than half were found to have quality mechanisms. Most partner countries (86%) reported that they had targets for effective development cooperation with traditional bilateral and multilateral partners. But do various country stakeholders share them? How inclusive are these mechanisms?

Parallel data from the UN Development Cooperation Forum reported that a third of countries surveyed reported that CSOs were not involved and another 20% reported minimal involvement. CSOs from 42 of the 86 countries involved in the GPEDC 3MR concluded that mutual accountability mechanisms for most partner countries require significant attention to improving institutionalization, deeper and meaningful inclusion across a diversity of stakeholders, greater predictability and full transparency in their documentation, deliberations and decisions for follow-up (ECOSOC Development Cooperation Forum, 2018; OECD & UNDP, 2019: 54–62; Tomlinson, 2019).

Where mutual accountability mechanisms exist and function with reasonable effectiveness, they present an opportunity for dedicated discussion of international climate finance in support of NDCs and adaptation needs. Climate finance is substantially integrated into concessional ODA flows, which should be included in aid targets and assessments at the country level. Unfortunately, climate finance allocations are biased towards middle-income countries, where the GPEDC evidence suggests that few mutual accountability mechanisms exist at the country level. This gap in accountability is more complicated in these countries with a diversity and multiplicity of international financial relationships for climate mitigation and adaptation. But as this financing expands, partner governments and country stakeholders may benefit from strengthening dialogue at the country (and local) level with all development partners involved.

Conclusion

Is the international community effectively addressing the profound implications of climate apartheid in its current commitments and allocations of international climate finance? Based on the evidence provided here and in Chapter 3, several summary observations can be made:

a. Ten years on from COP21 in Copenhagen, it is still very difficult to assess even the basics of international climate finance against the 2020 $100 billion target, which is the foundation for trust in moving forward the climate agenda with developing country parties in the UNFCCC. Clear provider accountability for this finance still lacks both a common institutional space for a critical examination of reported finance as well as an agreed framework for assessing performance. Greater transparency in developed country reporting agreed at COP24 in December 2018 is undermined by a continued lack of agreement on what constitutes legitimate climate finance and on how different modalities of climate finance should be counted.

b. What can be discerned about provider performance since the *Paris Agreement* is under-whelming. Bilateral climate finance in 2019 seems to be closer to $14 billion than the OECD reported $33 billion; $30 billion in multilateral climate finance has been accelerating for mainly mitigation initiatives, particularly through the MDBs, but a reality check on MDB reporting is largely non-concessional loans and is hampered by little accessible transparency at the project level; and mobilized private sector finance (said to approximate $15 billion) is largely self-reported by DFIs and is even less transparent. Germany and Canada, supported by research at the OECD DAC, confirmed on behalf of the UNFCCC that donors would not realize their commitment to $100 billion in climate finance by 2020 and would be unlikely to do so until 2023 (UNFCCC, 2021). This finance remains highly concentrated in six major providers (France, Germany, Japan, Norway, the United Kingdom and the United States).

c. Climate justice requires attention and priority to the rights and interests of the most vulnerable people and countries. These six providers, along with the European Union and the MDBs, have shaped climate finance allocations in ways that largely fail to protect and promote their interests.

- About a third of bilateral climate finance (38%) and less than a quarter (24%) of MDB climate finance is being allocated to adaptation for countries and people most exposed to the impacts of the climate crisis. Similarly, the share of adaptation finance to Least Developed Countries and Small Island Developing States seems to be declining (from 31% in 2014 to 2016 average to 29% in the 2017 to 2019 average) and is affected by low levels of adaptation finance overall.
- With Germany, France and Japan being among the largest providers, loans to developing countries are a significant modality for delivering climate finance (35% for all bilateral providers). Including MDBs, approximately 80% of climate finance is delivered as loans, of which 40% was non-concessional. Countries and people, who have contributed the least to the crisis, are being asked to pay back developed country lenders for developing country efforts to mitigate further greenhouse gases and adapt to its major impacts on their livelihoods.
- Women and girls, particularly those living in vulnerable countries and conditions, receive no priority in climate finance—almost half (46%) of bilateral climate finance project disbursements in 2019 had no gender equality objectives.
- Climate finance is more than 10% of ODA allocations for several strong climate finance providers—Austria, France, Germany, Sweden and Norway. Overall, in 2019, 9% of DAC bilateral ODA commitments were devoted to principal purpose climate finance initiatives. Increased climate finance is urgently required, but mitigation finance in particular should not be

budgeted at the expense of ODA intended for poverty eradication. Efforts to reduce poverty and inequalities, increase access to social services and support good governance are essential to success in tackling the climate crisis.

d. Further research is needed to more fully elaborate the implications of good practice approaches in effective development cooperation for implementing climate finance through aid relationships. Democratic country ownership, enabling environments for inclusive partnerships, accountable private sector initiatives, and robust transparency and accountability at the country level are seen to be essential pillars for effective development cooperation, including climate finance.

e. Preliminary evidence suggests that major challenges may limit the effective delivery of climate aid and its sustainable impact at the country level.

- The *Paris Agreement* calls for country-driven, participatory and fully transparent approaches at the country level. The UNFCCC encourages countries to develop Nationally Determined Contributions (NDCs) and adaptation plans; some providers have facilitated NDCs at the request of developing countries; and the Green Climate Fund responds to country proposals and includes developing countries in its core governance. Yet evidence from the GPEDC's Third Monitoring Round (3MR) in 85 countries said that only just over half of major bilateral projects, which would include major climate finance projects, were aligned with country results frameworks in 2018. Non-governmental stakeholders reported restricted and ineffective opportunities for engagement with government for the development and assessment of country development strategies.
- Political space for sustained citizen involvement in public life is an essential foundation for social inclusion in effective country climate action strategies. But the ability of citizens to hold governments to account and press for planet and people-friendly policies and initiatives is under serious attack in increasing numbers of countries. Governments harass and undermine the credibility of environmental and human rights organizations through unreasonable prosecution under CSO

laws and regulations, with 60% of the world's population estimated to be living in countries where civic space is closed, repressed or obstructed. Between 2017 and 2020, at least 1268 human rights defenders were murdered, with almost two-thirds (63%) from indigenous, land rights and environmental rights backgrounds.
- The involvement of Development Finance Institutions in climate finance through blended initiatives, combining government public resources with private sector finance, has escalated in recent years. Blended finance is an important modality for climate mitigation projects. Yet there has been little attention to whether public finance in these initiatives is little more than a subsidy to the private sector, whether projects can demonstrate consistency with development effectiveness principles and whether increased loans in blended finance are exacerbating a growing debt sustainability problem in poor and middle-income countries. The development of robust principles and guidance for providers' blended finance at the OECD DAC and through the GPEDC to assure the development effectiveness of these initiatives has yet to be tested in practice.
- Accountability in the climate finance architecture at the global level is very weak. Inclusive country-level accountability mechanisms for development cooperation may be an opportunity for various stakeholders to hold climate finance providers to account. It is a key modality to incentivize behaviour change among development actors to be more consistent with development effectiveness principles. According to the results of the 3MR, these accountability mechanisms have been improving in some countries that are highly dependent on aid, but unfortunately were weak in other middle-income countries with more complex financing flows (which are also the largest recipients of climate finance). In more than half of the country mechanisms examined, inclusivity is absent, with CSOs reporting no involvement or just minimal token participation.

As the global crisis accelerates with the COVID pandemic largely unfolding unchecked in most developing countries, urgent measures to address the climate emergency is an essential framework for recovery and a sustainable future. In light of gross inequalities in securing and allocating vaccines, developing countries' trust in international climate negotiations is deeply compromised. The latter will depend upon developed countries demonstrating that they have met their international commitments to the $100 billion annual flows in 2020 and will make up any unfulfilled amounts by 2025.

Building trust will also require major new commitments on the part of providers to set ambitious climate targets for themselves, to scale up their international climate finance based on real need, including for loss and damages, and to strengthen its overall effectiveness for developing country partners. Providers must pay much greater attention to the needs, interests and priorities of the many vulnerable countries and populations that will bear the major impacts of climate change so far largely unchecked. Lesson from 15 years of discourse and country attention to conditions for effective development cooperation can provide a useful framework for sharpening this finance as a tool for inclusive and transformative change for millions of affected people.

REFERENCES

Alignment of ODA with international climate agreements: The case of fossil fuels. (2021). Unpublished manuscript.

Bird, N. (2020). *Evaluation of Danish support for climate adaptation in developing Countries.* ODI. Retrieved from https://um.dk/en/danida-en/results/eval/eval_reports/publicationdisplaypage/?publicationID=A9CC034B-9F7B-4F61-B733-6F8370EC442B

Blampled, C. (2016). *Where next for development effectiveness?* Overseas Development Institute. Retrieved October 2019 from https://www.odi.org/sites/odi.org.uk/files/resource-documents/11089.pdf

DEVCO. (2020). *Effective development cooperation, Does the EU deliver? Detailed analysis of EU performance.* Retrieved from https://ec.europa.eu/international-partnerships/system/files/eu-development-effectiveness-monitoring-report-2020_en.pdf

Development Cooperation Directorate. (2021). *DAC effectiveness compendium 2020, Takeaways of the DAC information reference group on effective development cooperation.* Retrieved July 2021, from https://www.oecd.org/officialdocuments/publicdisplaydocumentpdf/?cote=DCD/DAC(2021)14&docLanguage=En

ECOSOC Development Cooperation Forum. (2018). *National mutual accountability and transparency in development cooperation: Study on the findings of the Fifty DCF Survey*. United Nations. Retrieved July 2021, from https://www.un.org/ecosoc/sites/www.un.org.ecosoc/files/files/en/dcf/UNDESA_2018%20DCF%20Study%20on%20mutual%20accountability.pdf

Frontline Defenders. (2021). *Global analysis 2020*. Retrieved July 2021, from https://www.frontlinedefenders.org/en/global-analysis

GPEDC. (n.d.). *Kampala principles on effective private sector engagement in development cooperation*. GPEDC. Retrieved August 2019, from https://effectivecooperation.org/wp-content/uploads/2019/06/Kampala-Principles-final.pdf

GPEDC. (2022). *Knowledge platform for effective development cooperation*. GPEDC. Retrieved from https://knowledge.effectivecooperation.org/

Karlsson-Vinkhuyzen, S., Groff, P., Tamás, P., Dahl, A., Harder, M., & Hassall, G. (2018). Entry into force and then? The Paris agreement and state accountability. *Climate Policy, 18*(5). Retrieved July 2021, from https://sciencepolicy.colorado.edu/students/envs-geog_3022/karlsson-vinkhuyzen_2018.pdf

Kindornay, S. (2011). *From aid to development effectiveness: A Working Paper*. The North-South Institute. Retrieved October 2019, from http://www.nsi-ins.ca/wp-content/uploads/2012/10/2011-From-aid-to-development-effectiveness.pdf

OECD. (2017). *Private finance for climate action: Estimating the effects of public interventions*. Retrieved July 2021, from http://www.oecd.org/env/researchcollaborative/WEB%20private-finance-for-climate-action-policy-perspectives.pdf

OECD. (2019). *Aligning development and climate action*. Retrieved July 2021, from http://www.oecd.org/dac/environment-development/aligning-development-co-operation-with-the-objectives-of-the-paris-agreement.htm

OECD. (2021). *Community of practice on private finance for sustainable development (COP-PF4SD), Meeting on blended finance data* [Powerpoint Presentation of Data]. Unpublished manuscript.

OECD DAC. (2019). *The only way forward: Aligning development cooperation and climate action*. Retrieved July 2021, from https://www.oecd.org/dac/aligning-development-co-operation-and-climate-action-5099ad91-en.htm

OECD DAC. (2021). *Strengthening climate resilience: Guidance for governments and development cooperation*. Retrieved July 2021, from https://doi.org/10.1787/4b08b7be-en

OECD, & UNDP. (2019). *Making development cooperation more effective: How partner countries are promoting effective partnerships*. Global Partnership for Effective Development Cooperation. Retrieved October 2019, from http://effectivecooperation.org/monitoring-country-progress/making-development-co-operation-more-effective/

Rahman, M., & Farin, S. M. (2019). Rethinking development Effectiveness: Lessons from a literature review. *Southern Voices*, (Occasional Issue 53). Retrieved October 2019, from http://southernvoice.org/wp-content/uploads/2019/10/Ocassional-Paper-Series-No.53-new.pdf

Tomlinson, B. (2019). *Civil society reflections on progress in achieving development effectiveness: Inclusion, accountability and transparency*. CSO Partnership for Development Effectiveness. https://www.effectivecooperation.org/system/files/2019-07/Inclusion%2C%20Accountability%20and%20Transparency.pdf

UN Human Rights. *Women human rights defenders*. United Nations. Retrieved October 2019, from https://www.ohchr.org/en/issues/women/wrgs/pages/hrdefenders.aspx

UNFCCC. (2021). *Climate finance delivery plan: Meeting the $100 billion goal*. https://www.canada.ca/content/dam/eccc/documents/pdf/climate-change/cop26/Climate%20Finance%20Delivery%20Plan_EN.pdf

CHAPTER 5

What Can We Learn About the 'Country Ownership' of International Climate Finance by Employing a Relational Conception of Scale?

Jonathan Barnes

INTRODUCTION

Country ownership is a central tenet of modern development cooperation, where aid used to be 'done in' or 'given to' beneficiary countries, today it is nominally done in partnership (Savedoff, 2019). The aid effectiveness agenda reflects donor-awareness of the inefficiencies of their work and, in some cases, harms. This prompted a renewed emphasis on partnership (OECD, 2005) and today, development assistance seeks to build

---

J. Barnes (✉)
International Institute for Environment and Development, London, England
e-mail: J.M.Barnes@lse.ac.uk

© The Author(s), under exclusive license to Springer Nature Switzerland AG 2022
C. Cash and L. A. Swatuk (eds.), *The Political Economy of Climate Finance: Lessons from International Development*, International Political Economy Series, https://doi.org/10.1007/978-3-031-12619-2_5

capacity and empower decision makers in recipient countries (OECD, 2011). It is intended to reinforce and advance national policy and planning with the overarching goal of supporting sustainable, lasting, positive change. This approach comes together under the rubric of country ownership with broad support from donors, recipients, critics, NGOs, private actors alike. Most agree that it is a good idea, and it is readily incorporated into many aid relationships today.[1] The issue is that it is hard to define or operationalize this central term, rendering it meaningless (Buiter, 2007; Winkler & Dubash, 2016). I argue that this reflects the hierarchical conception of scale that country ownership is based on. Development cooperation involves the transfer of resources, technology and ideas between different territorial actors and remains oriented around nation states. This is still conceived as a transfer from North to South and often a downwards channel. Scale is a foundational concept in human geography (Herod, 2010), yet the diverse deployment and malleability of the concept have exasperated geographers to the point that there have been calls to do away with it (Marston et al., 2005). Marston et al. (2005) claim that scale reinforces the binary opposition leading to problems in distinguishing between concrete and abstract forms so resort to a flat ontology instead.

This chapter contributes to academic and policy literatures by reframing country ownership with a relational conception of scale. I employ assemblage theory to analyse the desires (Buchanan, 2020) that shape and steer country ownership. I conceive and deploy the South African Climate Finance Assemblage (SACFA), which is an ordering of desire to produce Green Climate Fund (GCF) projects in South Africa. This centres on two contrasting national organizations that are accredited to access the GCF and the surrounding stakeholders and material context. The GCF is the primary financial instrument of the United Nations Framework Convention on Climate Change (UNFCCC) and has since its inception in 2010 made country ownership a guiding principle.[2] There remains plenty of doubt about how to operationalize this, however. Subsequent GCF policy (GCF, 2017) and research (GCF, 2019a) have explored the issue yet there remains only a very broad definition and little consensus on how the

---

[1] Country ownership is less applicable in some aid dynamics, for example in some fragile state contexts.

[2] https://www.greenclimate.fund/about.

concept should be operationalized. Assemblage theory employs a diffuse and disbursed conception of agency and resists reified generalities (Savage, 2020) which problematizes country ownership in this contribution. This facilitates novel insights that complicate the picture about who and what determines the use of GCF resources.

Background

Country Ownership

Country ownership is a central principle of the aid effectiveness agenda (OECD, 2005). The OECD asked the provocative question if country ownership was 'Political correctness or a practical key to better aid?' (2011), before concluding that it is in fact a 'challenge to both partner countries and donors to actually carry out their respective responsibilities and get better development results from aid spending' (ibid.). Country ownership is ever-present in GCF policy. All parties—donors, developing countries and civil society—were unequivocal in calling for its inclusion (Zamarioli et al., 2020) and it was readily incorporated (GCF, 2018). The problem is that there remains conceptual plurality around what country ownership means. There are calls to do away with country ownership altogether (Buiter, 2007), but as the term remains in constant use I take it seriously and problematize it in order to add to critical literatures. Country ownership can reproduce injustices and create structures that perpetuate the exclusion of subnational actors (Omukuti, 2020), but stops short of theorizing why. Others question if the concept is any different to the conditionality that shaped development previously (Dornan, 2017) and that some beneficiary countries are able to 'own' development cooperation more than others (De Renzio et al., 2008). Neither of these contributions distil what ownership should, or could, look like instead, however.

Country Ownership and the GCF

Country ownership remains central to the GCF's operations, policy and results. The GCF released advanced guidelines for country ownership in 2017 where it was defined as a 'measure through which countries, through meaningful engagement, including consultation with relevant national, local, community-level, and private sector stakeholders, can demonstrate ownership of, and commitment to, efforts to mitigate and adapt to climate change' (GCF, 2017). Today it is invoked as a general principle, an investment criterion, a process and an outcome (GCF, 2019a), muddling understanding and contributing to an analytical bluntness. The Fund's Independent Evaluation Unit (IEU) was mandated to conduct a study of the principle. The Report published in 2019 (ibid.) highlighted issues and re-stated the necessity for an expansive and flexible interpretation. This paper is partly a response to that call.

Referring to more than the partnership between donor and recipient, country ownership calls for intra-national reflection and highlights how the nation state can be afforded a misleading privilege (Winkler & Dubash, 2016) while missing the heterogenous and often conflicting views and interests within a country (Buiter, 2007). This speaks to a lack of clarity about who 'owns' project development, where the priority for quick disbursement can clash with civil society around expectations for inclusion (Kalinowski, 2020: 2). The GCF Board has also sought to maximize engagement with private sectors (GCF, 2014) which introduces more actors still with a stake in project development and raises concerns about co-option and financialization (Bertilsson & Thörn, 2021). Zamarioli et al. (2020) have shown that there is an adequate infrastructure for country ownership at the Fund level but that many developing country institutions lack the capacity to realize the principle. These concerns that focus on the beneficiary country identify deficiencies with how specific stakeholders struggle with ownership without critically engaging with what ownership implies, nor what it would look like.

Country ownership is conceptualized as a scalar transfer from the Green Climate Fund down to the country, through accredited entities, and then down to the local level, through programmes and projects, via grants, loans, guarantees and equity (GCF, 2018). This conception is the root-cause of much of the confusion regarding country ownership.

Country ownership was never defined in an operational sense. The IEU recommended that it stays this way, and practitioners utilize a 'normative definition of country ownership that goes beyond national ownership' (GCF, 2019a: xxix). Scholars and policy actors alike are at something of an impasse with country ownership that geographers can re-enliven with the post-structural conceptions of scale. How this interacts with the GCF's own understanding of scale, as referring to growth in quantity, and other related ideas such as replicability and long-term sustainability facilitate a novel examination of country ownership. This ought to go beyond a priori, reified categories of actors which reproduce and entrench misunderstandings.

Unit of Analysis

Part of the challenge in the appraisal of country ownership is the lack of a viable unit of analysis. Much of the literature cited thus far locates deficiencies in specific actors and processes or focuses on the eventual projects. These struggle to qualify who or what amounts to a country or how those things carry out ownership. I elaborate a relational conception of scale in the next section that is based on an assemblage ontology. I deploy the South Africa Climate Finance Assemblage (SACFA) as an analytical object that is an ordering of the desire to access the Green Climate Fund in South Africa. In making this desire the unit of analysis, I expose how people, things and ideas combine to shape and steer project development. Projects must target paradigm shifts, which 'can catalyse impact beyond a one-off investment…should be accompanied by a robust and convincing theory of change for replication and/or scaling up of the project results' (GCF, 2019b: 2). Projects must have the potential to deliver a considerably greater quantity of results than the initial project scope and finance. In this sense, 'scale' and 'scaling-up' refer to larger portfolios and bigger results. The paradigm shift implies that projects need to be scalable to help turn the billions into trillions (African Development Bank et al., 2015). There is a disconnect between this policy scalar language and the human geography literature on the production of scale. The policy equation of scaling with replication and quantitative increase (Haarstad, 2016) is intertwined with the varied academic interpretation (Papanastasiou, 2017). I now elaborate on how I understand and operationalize scale.

The South African Climate Finance Assemblage: Operationalizing Relational Scale

Relational Scale

Geographers can conflate abstract and metaphorical conceptions (Jonas, 1994) where labels—such as global and local become naturalized abstractions that do little analytically (Moore, 2008). Brenner (2001) highlights the analytical blunting that occurs when scale is blended with other concepts, for example when scales are invoked to describe a specific socio-spatial territory. Distinctions between scale as size and level and associated untenable binaries chiefly macro–micro and global–local motivate arguments to do away with hierarchical conceptions of scale. Marston et al. (2005) demonstrate a 'grid epistemology' that simplifies phenomena into the language of scale that reproduces socio-spatial inequalities (Marston et al., 2005). Following Moore (2008), I use scale as a category of practice rather than a category of analysis. Scaling can be a process of discursive translation and purification, where different knowledge agendas cohere and simplify (Caprotti et al., 2020). Energy transitions in South Africa rely on these dynamics to reproduce scale (ibid.). It moves towards a relational conception, with analysis focused on how scales are made, extended and reproduced. The scalar production of energy precarity in South African households is shown to be shared and contested (Phillips & Petrova, 2021), demonstrating the value of complicating North–South framings. I extend this approach to consider the role of external finance in relational scalar constructions. This employs a flat ontology—as advanced by Marston et al. (2005) and other post-structuralists (DeLanda, 2006; Latour, 2005). Relational scale helps analysts to move beyond pre-figured scalar labels. For scale to remain useful conceptually it can draw on ideas such as the negotiation and construction of flows, connections, networks, sites, places and materiality (Bulkeley, 2005; Leitner et al., 2008). Hierarchical and relational conceptions of scale offer different perspectives on the same social context. Several of these differences are now distilled into analytical categories that will furnish the subsequent empirical analysis. These categories are summarized in Table 5.1.

Table 5.1 Analytical categories to operationalize relational scale vis a vis a hierarchical conception

Hierarchical conception of scale	Relational conception of scale	Analytical category
Up, down, sideways link in tangled hierarchies of scales	Flat ontology between people and things	Ontology
Pre-figured size and hierarchy between levels	Connections: More/stronger connections = 'bigger'	Magnitude
Pre-figured categories/forms (town, country, supra-national block)	Immanent and emergent categories/forms	Endurance
Fixed and constitutive	Fluid and multiple	Multiplicity

Ontology
Relational conceptions of scale employ a flat ontology consistent with post-structural thinking (DeLanda, 2006; Latour, 2005). A flat ontology opens analysis to contingency and politics between human and non-human components, where form is always emergent (Deleuze & Guattari, 1988), which is valuable to scholars concerned with divergent and potential futures (Bridge et al., 2013) as much as what results.

Magnitude
Hierarchical conceptions of scale establish and reinforce structures and entities, such as cities and nation states. There is no a priori privilege of anything over anything else in a relational conception of scale, and 'size' is more a product of the number and strength of connections than pre-given (MacKinnon, 2010).

Endurance
Mackinnon (2010) developed Bergson's (2014) notion of duration in a bid to acknowledge the temporal flows that intermingle and contribute to emergent forms. It refers to how different objects and ideas interact in deeply processual ways leading to 'mutually transformative spatial structure and strategies' (Jones, 2009). Endurance captures the evolving nature of the social forms. It acknowledges the histories that shape social forms in an emergent and contingent way, so helps analysts look past pre-figured categories and consider contestation.

Multiplicity
Contingency and possibility can be explored in greater depth with a relational conception of scale in assemblage theory. Emphasizing multiplicity avoids privileging any socio-spatial dimension over another (Leitner et al., 2008) and looks at how scale interacts with other concepts (MacKinnon, 2010). There is also a performativity in the construction of scale and a representational trope (Jones, 1998).

Hierarchical conceptions of scale are useful for highlighting and describing power dynamics, in part because scalar language contributes to reproduce domination and resistance. Marston et al. (2005) claim that scale is unhelpful in this regard, as it reproduces socio-spatial inequalities and chokes the possibility of resistance, yet equally the scalar constructs, labels and levels are formative and generative of power dynamics. Assemblage theory conceives of power as disbursed and diffuse across human and non-humans, or actants. Where power is not held as a resource or wielded, it operates in concert in a relational sense (Allen, 2011; Lawhon, 2012). This is a critical divergence between the relational and hierarchical conception of scale that underlies each of these analytical categories. These in turn elaborate on why things happen the way that they do.

Scale and Assemblage

Assemblage theory is part of the post-structural turn and is centred around the notion of a flat ontology, consistent with a relational conception of scale (Deleuze & Guattari, 1988). Assemblages are characterized by immanence, they are never fixed but always in flux and in a process of becoming (Bennett, 2009; DeLanda, 2006). For example, actor-network theory has many commonalities, but is focused on the stabilization of effects via relations (Fredriksen, 2014), whereas an assemblage is always fluid. What remains constant is the human desire that orders an assemblage, where desire enrols components—people, things, ideas—and gives these their properties (Buchanan, 2020: 56). Assemblages are in flux and components may come and go but the human desire that distils the purpose of an assemblage is consistent.

In this paper I frame the desire to produce GCF projects as an assemblage, the SACFA. When this assemblage territorializes, when its identity solidifies and it becomes more coherent and established (Baker & McGuirk, 2017), it will have the productive effect of making 'bankable' projects (Ellis & Pillay, 2017). Territorialisation is the process whereby components of an assemblage are ordered to produce an effect (Smith & Protevi, 2008), equally de-territorialisation occurs when these weaken. This ebb and flow demonstrates the complexity and contingency of assemblages. This process of territorialisation occurs with reference to the components of the assemblage: the civil servants and activists, the solar panels and ecosystems, as well as ideas like justice and value for money. Bouzarovski demonstrates similar dynamics in urban low-carbon transformations, where territorialisation is shown to be imminently constituted of politicization, enrolments and the hybridization of human and material agencies (Bouzarovski & Haarstad, 2019). Territorialisation offers an analogy for country ownership in this way. Territorialisation and country ownership both describe how projects take shape in, reflect and reproduce, and are contested and accepted in a national setting. They both describe how a pipeline of projects narrows to become a small number of bankable and implementable activities. Given the diffused and disbursed agency, these components all participate in the powerful ownership of project development. This is a good fit for GCF project development which is a fluid and messy process (Law, 2004), with lots of contingency and possibility. Using assemblage theory makes analysis attentive to the scope of what might happen, rather than just to what does.

The Added Value of the Assemblage

Using the assemblage to explore scalar politics eschews reified generalities. It offers a picture of concrete assemblages instead. These are abstract concepts (generalities) that are made to exist through classification along essential characteristics (reified) (DeLanda, 2006). This is useful in policy analysis as ideal types and hierarchical labels lack explanatory value. Material and relational lenses make visible the *tangible stuff* of policies (Savage, 2018: 310; emphasis in original). This overcomes a critical deficiency in the current scholarship about country ownership: the notion of a 'country'. Relational scale does not jettison such labels, it problematizes them. In the case of the nation state, it makes visible how 'territory cannot be reduced to national or state territory' (Sassen & Ong, 2014: 22). This facilitates analysis to 'expand the category of a territory to a measure of conceptual autonomy from the nation-state' (ibid.). This means that rather than trying to formulate the 'country' we can question how such a pre-existing category came to exist, how it is sustained and what it might achieve (Savage, 2020). Conceptualizing how people and things combine in a flat ontology, how they connect and the quality and quantity of these connections and how these endure will allow me to scrutinize who and what shapes and steers project development.

Problematizing country ownership includes a range of factors and features including, but not limited to those outlined here, in project development. It broadens the set of actors and actants that constitute the country while placing a far greater emphasis on how these combine relationally to contest and shape project development. Ultimately, it arrives at an acceptable project that reflects the history, culture, politics, economics, ideas and prevailing power dynamics in and surrounding the country. Acceptable in this sense refers to the project aligning with and advancing national development plans and receiving a letter of no-objection—the formal GCF requirements. But country ownership is more than policy and letters of no-objection, projects must also fit the resource and infrastructure context of the country, as well as the specific geographical factors and cultural norms including religion and colonial legacy.

Methods

Data Collection

The research draws on fieldwork in South Africa between November 2018 and March 2020. It draws on audio-recorded, semi-structured interviews with actors involved in the GCF project development. This is complemented by ethnographic fieldnotes and observations. The case-study research design (Ridder, 2012) involved joining multiple, inter-related communities with a vested interest in GCF programming in South Africa. Initial field construction was built out from the organizations formally involved in GCF project development in South Africa. A case-study methodology is employed, informed by the critical ethnographic approach to cases as created dialogically through the researcher (Lund, 2014). I employed a purposive approach to sampling that began by producing a stakeholder set through desk-based research and then building my research field with a snow-ball approach through interviews and events.

Case and Approach: South African Climate Finance

This research deploys an assemblage that is an ordering of the desire to programme the GCF in South Africa, where the unit of analysis is the direct access to the Fund. This is organized around the national designated authority (NDA) and two direct access entities (DAEs). These are the formal links to the Fund, around which various other stakeholders cohere. These organizations oversee country ownership and are viewed as a hierarchical scalar conception of the term. The two DAEs lead the project development process and are the primary focus of this paper, from which the dataset was built out. Memorandums of understanding were signed with each which facilitated insider access to staff, events and written materials. Multiple, often repeat, interviews were carried out with various staff and participation in forums that were either arranged or attended by staff furnished further insight into GCF project development. Country ownership is greater, in a processual sense, where beneficiary countries seek direct access to the GCF (2019a). South Africa is unusual in having two DAEs, each accredited in 2016: the Development Bank of Southern Africa (DBSA) and the South Africa National Biodiversity Institute (SANBI). The differences between these are summarized in Table 5.2. The DBSA is a regional development finance institution that is accredited to programme loans and grants for adaptation and mitigation projects, up to USD250m in size. SANBI is a national quasi-governmental conservation organization. It is accredited to programme grants for adaptation up to USD50m in size.

Table 5.2 Accredited entity comparison[3]

	DBSA	SANBI
Entity type	Direct (regional)	Direct (national)
Size	Large (total projected costs exceed USD250m)	Small (total projected costs between USD10 and 50m)
Fiduciary standards	Basic, project management, grant award, on-lending/blending, loans, equity, guarantees	Basic, project management, grant award
Thematic focus	Adaptation and mitigation	Adaptation
Sector	Public and private	Public
Environmental and social risk category	A—significant adverse risk that may be irreversible	B—mild adverse risk that would likely be reversible

[3] https://www.greenclimate.fund/how-we-work/tools/entity-directory.

These two DAEs combined with a high-capacity public sector, an active and engaged civil society and large domestic private and financial sectors, make South Africa an attractive option to explore this research question. I joined many communities focused on climate and energy issues. There is a climate adaptation network, climate change community with a specific focus on electricity issues, a climate justice-oriented community and an academic activist scene. Additionally, ethnographic fieldwork was conducted in and around mining affected communities, especially with communities suffering from the pollution of the coal economy and local activists opposing it. Living and working in South Africa in this time was an opportunity to experience the electricity crisis—regular and lengthy load shedding (blackouts)—first-hand and to learn how it impacts everyone from local communities to suburban families. The material components of climate finance include the coal infrastructure, the urban context that still echoes apartheid planning, the geography and climate. The legacies of colonialism and apartheid still shape the country, while poverty, inequality and unemployment are acute (National Planning Commission, 2013) especially in rural areas and in some of the largest metropolitan centres. Corruption is endemic, with the Presidency of Jacob Zuma (2009–2018) amounting to what has been labelled a 'state capture' crisis (Ashman, 2019). Public resources were drained from services and infrastructure including from the country's state-owned electricity utility, Eskom. South Africa also has a strong constitution and legal system, legislated participatory processes of consultation and a large and active civil society. It is against this backdrop that the GCF is seeking to reproduce its mandate and result areas by extending finance to address climate change.

Analytical Approach

Interview transcripts and ethnographic fieldnotes were coded and analysed thematically (Braun & Clarke, 2006). This is an iterative process that explored how participants understand country ownership with recourse to both hierarchical labels and also the relationships and connections that they consider important. Data collection was attentive to participants' experience and desire around GCF project development and related concerns. For example, actors engaged in the energy transition might speak to their concerns about environmental justice that shape their orientation in the policy space. The analytical categories that are outlined in the previous section formed broad, initial codes from which analysis proceeded. Further coding sought to identify different ways that participants socially construct and make sense of the assembly of GCF projects, within these four scalar categories. This approach develops a partial interpretation that reflects my own bias and interests and will have missed important factors and actors which shape project development.

A Relational Conception of Country Ownership

Flat Ontology

The flat ontological conception of scale emphasizes the range of potential connections. Project development has a clear and concise purpose and actors in this space navigate these connections and seek to make some of them productive to help territorialize projects. Certain organizations and people can help unlock this finance, including those with prior experience of the GCF. The DBSA collaborated with several organizations to distil the Climate Finance Facility (CFF)[4] into a bankable project. This drew on relationships with *'experts in these application processes who know exactly what's going to be passed'* as a consultant I interviewed explained *'so they have experience, or potentially one of the members has actually been part of the GCF appraisals team, but they know the steps very clearly and very well'*.

I label such actors 'green go-betweens'. These are people, usually with technical backgrounds that are adept at forging productive connections and moving the projects forward. Part of their job is to enrol and reflect material components and networks of human-material hybrid agency. One such consultant from a South African energy think tank explained that their efficacy in this regard owed to a close network and rapid access to information.

> *I could walk to three desks away, and ask them what is the biogas price per megawatt? and they pick up a phone, phone a friend in the centre, or the head of biogas industry association.*
> Consultant

---

[4] https://www.greenclimate.fund/project/fp098.

This is an example of a way that material is represented in and shapes project development. Equally, how the technical inputs relating to renewable energy are produced by a diffuse policy community whose membership is characterized by mobility across it. It is very common, for example, for one person to have worked in government, the private sector and the third sector. This consultant was formally a utility developer in South Africa, for example. This forges connections that facilitate quick and effective working and bring order and control.

The role of materiality in country ownership is missed with a hierarchical scalar lens. This hybrid agency complicates notional ownership of the process. Renewable potential and the transmission infrastructure are key determinants in the energy transition and together have prompted solar developers to pursue 'Crazy ideas, like building solar PV in Mpumalanga'. Energy planning in South Africa locates solar development in the Northern Cape where irradiation levels are greatest. The province is sparsely populated and far from load-centres. These material factors combine with the just transition discourse to motivate building solar sub-optimal generation locations.

The CFF seeks to 'crowd in' private sector investment in green activities, changing behaviour over time until 'you no longer need finance to de-risk it. You've de-risked it … it should influence other banks to look at the space differently' (DBSA staff). Risk reduction and credit enhancement are rubrics of connection in this flat ontology, whereby actors combine around shared objectives and mutual benefit. The territorialisation of projects is gradual and will reduce the need or additionality of the project. This means that the scale that is produced by the project is intentionally partial. Crowding in the private sector will catalyze spending on renewable energy and other climate objectives. Indeed, staff in the NDA conceive of the GCF as a means to 'buydown risk to scale up action' so that in time the GCF could be used for increasingly challenging sectors and problems, re-focusing on water and adaptation.

Participants deploy scale in various ways when they discuss the possibility of expansion and opportunities associated with project development, including outside of South Africa. Solutions and technologies may form new export products. South Africa has an advanced industrial sector and geographically has 'the biggest untapped market in the world over the border, of close to 600 million people who don't have access to electricity'

(Government policymaker). This is an example of the scalar connection and construction of opportunity. In the adaptation space people are thinking about how to market innovations:

> Maybe relocate wine production. Alternatively, maybe we can generate an asset that could be sold and become intellectual property that becomes valuable in other wine producing countries.
> (NDA staff)

Flat ontology collapses categories and distances and makes visible the productive connections between people, things and ideas. Disbursed power and agency can be harnessed to territorialise projects.

Magnitude

The pre-figured idea of a country is misleading to scholars and policymakers alike while the national government is a poor proxy for one. The notion that a country 'owns' development cooperation is metaphorical and serves to shut-down a more flexible understanding of the term. Thinking differently about the 'country' in country ownership can be productive. There is relatively little national oversight in South Africa.

> the NDA has never come to any GCF events. They never come. They never accept invitations, they never engage on issues. From the Fund's perspective they are disengaged.
> (GCF Advisor)

The NDA has created a context where the DAEs lead on project development. This might be a deliberate diffusion of agency to orchestrate the assemblage at arm's length from the ruling African National Congress (ANC) party. Project development is shaped by the ANC which is all-pervasive in institutions and consciousness, but has no formal role. Rather, actors navigate and avoid the ANC:

> There is a block, and it is the government in the middle, blocking... I think it is more like a maze. Things might get through, but it will take a long time and things will get watered down.
> (Climate Justice Activist)

While the national government and the abiding notion of a country is misleading, it remains important to a relational analysis. How actors work with, evade and reflect these pervasive categories is central to project advancement. The ANC conforms neatly with a hierarchical categorization with provincial, municipal and community level structure. Yet this fails to account for the influence and agency of the apparently weakened Party. Informal links of corruption better account for the magnitude of the ANC, where the civil service has, according to a solar developer, been reduced to 'extract economic rent out of the system. It is helpful to avoid the trope of corruption—which closes discussion—and instead highlight how the ANC works. The most senior figures in the ANC, including the President and the Minister for Energy fall on alternate sides of a power struggle around energy. This context shapes South Africa and is a barrier to progress:

> *the ANC can't deal with real world issues now because it is still fighting its own battles, who's going to be next in this feeding frenzy? If Cyril wins, will it be a feeding frenzy as because Cyril hasn't won yet. He's the president but he ain't in power yet.*
> (NGO Director)

This is deterministic of energy policy and accounts for the pressures and challenges of project development better than pre-figured, reified notions of a country. Eskom is a related force that shapes South Africa. The just energy transition seeks to transition the energy economy from a centrally planned, vertically integrated monopoly to one that is far more distributed. Eskom is in crisis, in no small part due to ANC corruption and mismanagement. The crumbling coal-fired infrastructure cannot meet demand and Eskom is billions of dollars in debt. Eskom is totally pervasive in energy and climate change discourses, and in day-to-day life thanks to load shedding. This amounts to a 'huge' presence, where it touches everything. Emphasizing its magnitude in this way better accounts for agency and determinism which is missed without a relational lens. Many community members in the Highveld, where most of Eskom's infrastructure is located, refer to individual power stations simply as 'Eskom'. This reflects a framing, employed by the community group I spent time with, as a unitary and coherent whole. This captures its monolithic significance which also reflects the dependence and entitlement to free electricity in the post-apartheid democracy. The constitution is 'very pro poor' an Eskom staff member told me 'we have a lot of human rights, for example, the right for electricity. Where else do you have a right for electricity?'. The connectedness and agency of Eskom augments the conception of South Africa in terms of the challenge and restrictions in climate finance.

Endurance

Project development targets climate action to contribute towards the GCF's aggregate objectives, such as resilience and emissions reduction. Domestic actors must advance national development agendas with ambitious and catalytic projects. Assemblage theory emphasizes the emergent and immanent categories of actors that shape this work and the role of these in the production of scale. Projects must reflect beneficiary country contexts and become symbiotic to advance pre-existing, shared objectives. For example, the private sector has reacted to institutional failings in utility provision by 'becoming more responsive to providing it themselves … business people are sane people. They need energy, if the government cannot provide it, they will provide it' (DBSA staff). This is a motivation for many off-takers of credit-enhanced products via the CFF. Actors are using the CFF loans to secure their access to electricity. Bankers and private sector parties are unified by a motivation that is not primarily environmental. One commercial banker claimed that 'Eskom is an opportunity. If it wasn't for Eskom the cost of renewables would be years behind where it is now. Why is my house predominantly off the grid? Because I have no faith in Eskom' (Commercial banker). This is a widely held belief that the energy transition is less to do with environmental justice and 'came about through maintenance issues of the power stations' (Central Government staff). Eskom, and the desire to hedge against supply issues, shapes an emergent category of actors with a shared goal to bring down the cost of renewable energy. As such, this provides a better explanation of 'ownership' of the GCF programme.

In November 2019 the DBSA hosted a team of consultants employed by the GCF as part of its Learning-Oriented Real-Time Impact Assessment (LORTA). This explored the early stages of the CFF with a view to conducting an impact evaluation. The week-long mission was an opportunity to learn the mechanics of the project and to meet some of the off-takers of finance, including real-estate firms. The sector is important in the move for roof-top solar to counter-act load shedding. During a tour of a supermarket near Johannesburg a property developer extolled the value of the climate-related measures. The reliability and pay-back of solar, let alone on the ability to keep in-store lighting on during load shedding. The store is vast and windowless. I know from experience how sinister a shopping mall is when the lights, music and customers all disappear. Another client invokes Eskom supply as the greatest driver of roof-top solar a PowerPoint introduction. We then had a tour of an aerospace factory where the sound of heavy machinery fills the cavernous warehouse. Jonas is showing us around. He explains the impact of load shedding, how teams must work overnight and weekends, whenever the power comes back on, to keep up with orders. The CFF meets the demand of an emergent category of potential off-takers relating to the Eskom crisis. This group and the CFF have strengthened and territorialized symbiotically, and sub-projects were in the final stages of preparation as the COVID-19 lockdown came into force. The pandemic highlights the immanence of this. Reduced electricity demand during lockdown briefly ended load shedding. It did not address systemic issues, but it temporarily removed supply issues. This highlights the immanent and emergent nature of ownership, where actors cohere around enduring need.

Multiplicity

GCF projects must be catalytic and transformational rather than an end in itself and this way produce partial scalar effects. This chimes with the confusion about whether country ownership is a process or an outcome, a means or an end. The DBSA's engagement with the GCF is part of a much larger scaling exercise to become a major Green Bank in Africa.

> *90% of concessional funding is targeted towards preventing climate change in the developing market, this is an enormous opportunity. I told my boss ... I want to set up a green bank.*
> (Director, DBSA)

The DBSA is looking to expand across the continent and the GCF offers a stepping-stone to build up its green finance credentials and solidify experience. Their relationship with the Fund produces the necessary scale effects in terms of its results but also lays the foundations for both transformations in South Africa and in the bank itself. Emphasizing desire in assemblage makes this multiple purpose visible. Indeed, the multiplicity in targeted results contributes to the lack of clarity around country ownership in general, where the diffuse future benefit and ownership are necessarily un-specified. The intended growth of the DBSA as a green bank is well known and understood, but it goes beyond the formal scope of their GCF partnership.

There is a degree of confusion in South Africa, outside of the official GCF partners, regarding the scope to participate in project development and access to the Fund. This partly reflects the lack of clear national oversight from the NDA, but also that SANBI has raised expectations in civil society. SANBI produced a climate finance strategy that covered the period 2017–2022 which refers to the GCF having 'no country cap, and no limitation on the number of projects a country or Accredited Entity may submit for approval' (SANBI, 2017: 3). This carried forwards into their approach to raising awareness and encouraging a broad and diffuse sense of ownership and participation. There is a long association with the USD100bn figure that the GCF is contributing towards mobilizing. This contributes to confusion and raised opportunities, including in government where 'people get taken in by the 100bn, and the media feed on that, in reality it's very tough and it's very difficult to deal with' (Director, NDA). Expectations around the GCF have been falsely raised. SANBI engaged in a lengthy consultative process that involved a call for proposals which led many actors to believe that they could participate when this was never an option.

> *you wonder how that finance is going to be managed with reference country ownership and I am not sure about the GCF, it was discussed at COP17 in Durban, and as you said…how should civil society groups access such funding?* (Climate Justice Activist)

This generated a broad sense of buy-in from a range of stakeholders. Many CSOs and other organizations collaborated to submit projects, often in partnership with a government agency. Although most of these proposals were unsuccessful this engendered a sense of ownership across civil society that means that even those dissatisfied actors feel included. The Director of this climate finance programme at SANBI did this quite deliberately, as part of a commitment to transformation. This not only reflects an institutional commitment to good practice but is also close to the GCF's stated goals around participation and ownership. Their approach has been lauded at the GCF.

> *If you're going to consult then you must do properly and if you want people to buy into the kind of intervention that they are trying to build. They are taking their time to plan carefully so that when they do actually draw on the funds, they can be very effective.*
> (GCF Advisor)

SANBI acknowledges the trade-off between 'this huge amount of interest. The limited resources we have to do the process and the need to move quickly' when it comes to enacting country ownership. SANBI sought to include a wide range of actors beyond the notional government orientation of a country that a hierarchical conception of scale invokes. Their approach comes at a cost given that it has still, as of the thirtieth Board meeting in October 2021, yet to secure an approved project. Equally, there are frustrated people who were encouraged to participate and saw their proposal rejected. The alternative would have been to centrally orchestrate project development in a target sector, which is a more common approach in other countries.

> *I'm not convinced that just choosing one would have been the right thing to do. I think we would have undermined what we're trying to do here. Direct access can create a whole lot of transformative delivery that I don't think you would achieve in other ways.*
> (Director, SANBI)

Hierarchical conceptions of country ownership suggest that SANBI is unable, or unwilling, to fix the scalar effects of the GCF in South Africa. This is despite clearly 'being ready to secure a project' (NDA staff). It might frame this as a blockage. Relational ontologies instead emphasize the multiplicity in their approach which is expressly designed to target the complex and elusive transformation that GCF policy seeks. There is a risk that project developers will trade-off transformation in favour of speed, reflecting the pressure that all parties are under.

The raised expectation of civil society to be able to participate via SANBI has had an unintended side effect. The CFF provides loans exclusively to private actors so is quite separate to the stakeholders SANBI engaged. The raised expectation in civil society engendered possibility and hope that anyone can apply and participate in GCF programming. This placated criticism of GCF programming in South Africa, and specifically of the DBSA. The CFF is owned by and will benefit the private sector offtakers. It confers a narrow benefit on this group while not advancing the adaptation and developmental agenda. Civil society might be expected to have opposed this and called for a different use of the GCF resources had they not been operating under the expectation that the resources will flow freely via other channels. Misconceptions about the different sources of money[5] also contribute to maintain a sense of possibility for civil society and activists.

Connected to this is the broad and malleable category of the just transition, that resonates and has multiple meanings across the research context. The sense of multiplicity surrounding the just transition also contributes to quell resistance. Central government, labour, the private sector, academia, the community and civil society have all held workshops, published research and sought to define the just transition. The national government convened in a nationwide, nine-province structured dialogue to seek consensus around the term and what it means for South Africa in an environmental context (National Planning Commission, 2019). The conflation of the just transition with a renewable energy transition in South Africa has restricted progress for both (National energy policy-maker). Multiple divergent views can be carried along under the inclusive rubric of a just transition. The CFF will play a part in this by increasing renewable energy capacity in South Africa which is better than nothing for some groups that might be expected to criticize. Without this broad possibility, project development would have faced greater challenges. All this paints a fragmented picture of ownership of the GCF country programme in South Africa.

Discussion

Concrete Assemblage of a Country

Relational conceptions of scale provide concrete assemblages of the component parts of a country and what they do, rather than providing reified generalities (DeLanda, 2006: 35). As a GCF project territorializes, the processes, actors and things that shape it, that it must avoid, that it must satisfy and work with are visible. This offers a sense of the magnitude of a country, its constituent parts, and the way that components interact. Countries are not neat containers nor a level of government. Actors cannot work or think in this space without recourse to reified generalities

---

[5] The South African Green Fund and the Green Climate Fund, for example.

such as 'country', but this contribution provides a critical re-interpretation of this label. I challenge the a priori spatial or institutional notion of South Africa—rejecting 'the fixed coordinates' (Savage, 2020: 327)—and instead train my focus on the relations that are established across this space. This highlights the paucity of explanatory value offered by a fixed notion of territorial scale (Allen & Cochrane, 2010). Any combination of people, ideas and things can shape the assembly of a country, but the inter-related examples of the ANC and Eskom demonstrate the formative and deterministic effects of these complex sets of relations. Each of these shapes projects development by precluding options creating problems and prompting avoidance. This determines what scalar effects the DBSA can produce via its GCF partnership, leading to a private sector focus that meets a specific and feasible demand. This demand is a hybrid effect of human and material interactions (Bouzarovski & Haarstad, 2019) where the electricity grid, solar irradiation levels and a political economy of corruption shape project development to a large extent.

Assemblage theory provides useful analytical tools to support this analysis. The emphasis placed on the coming together of components, or territorialisation around an outcome accounts for a far wider range of human and non-human agency than a hierarchical scalar conception of project development. The GCF's understanding of country ownership is especially shaky where the private sector is concerned. The private sector is poorly accounted for as a level or label in a hierarchical sense. The GCF's internal policy frames the private sector as an important stakeholder. However, it also finds that private sectors are insufficiently integrated and that project pipelines remain limited (GCF, 2019a: 147). The private sector is better conceived of as a dynamic of interconnectedness that spans individuals and multinational corporations and that is highly reflexive to material reality. Actors like 'green go-betweens' play a linking role to help cohere this private sector and forge human-material links.

Diffuse and Emergent Ownership

Power is understood to be diffuse and disbursed across people and things in a relational ontology. Emphasizing the co-constitution of agency in this way enlivens a varied conception of ownership that better explains how GCF project development works. I have shown how shapes understandings of transformation in different human and material combinations in the country. The DAEs are gatekeepers of sorts and manage the direct communications between the GCF and South Africa, but by destabilizing this linear image of a transfer a relational ontology exposes the complex way that actors and actants enrol in service of the desire to secure GCF projects. Even in the case of DBSA which has worked efficiently and quickly to secure two projects, ownership is shown to be an emergent identity that forms as much to hedge against Eskom supply issues as it reflects climate ambition. This enduring category of actors and actants looks to have 'purified' (Caprotti et al., 2020) the knowledge discourse around renewable energy into a financial proposition that is clear and agential. An important contribution of this paper is to show the formation of categories of actors, as an alternative conception of private sector ownership.

Project development is full of contingent possibility. SANBI's approach demonstrates how inclusivity and diffuse ownership conferred potential on the country programming that was never there. The GCF requires a pipeline of projects such that this can be whittled down into strong concepts and then projects for approval, most of which will not be funded. This invokes a liner imagery, narrowing like a funnel producing bankable projects. This is enticing in its simplicity. Assemblage theory usefully complicates this picture. Project development is required to consult with stakeholders, but this conception fails to account for how conflicting perspectives are then accommodated. Multiplicity can help scholars to consider how outcomes are reached without making its achievement inevitable. This is missing in a hierarchical scalar conception of country ownership. Multiplicity highlights how the South African project development accommodates diverse and broad participation in such a way that placates criticism, echoing the 'tyranny of participation' critique (Cooke & Kothari, 2001). The consultative processes surrounding GCF programming and progress towards a just transition provide an example of the enrolment of would-be critics to quell resistance. Confusion about the different funds and a misconception that applications are open to all, specifically via SANBI, have allowed the DBSA's projects to go under the radar. SANBI's approach provides an important insight into the potential of country ownership. It makes clear the trade-off between expedient results and deep transformation. Relational scale makes this plainly visible and facilitates debate around the potential for this to support greater ambition, especially relating to climate justice agendas.

Partial Scale Effect

The GCF has a stated objective to instigate systems-level change and transformation, yet much of the attention resorts to mitigation and adaptation outcomes. The experience of the LORTA mission brings home that it is challenging to qualify and measure these bigger transformational goals. Catalysis and paradigm shift are central concepts for the GCF which require actors at the Fund and also involved in project development to relinquish control of activities. Hierarchical conceptions of country ownership suffer due to an inability to do this, which partly explains why there is often a stubborn notion of ownership ascribed to central government. This analysis has demonstrated the value of thinking about country ownership as a process of assembly. This is less focused on questions of who is doing what and instead recalls Deleuze and Guattari's encouragement to ask what an assemblage is for, or what it can do (Deleuze & Guattari, 1983). By emphasizing multiplicity and endurance, this contribution makes the contingency of project development visible, clarifying how these processes lead to partial scale effects. This orientation explains how human and material forces combine in pursuit of bigger objectives, that include but exceed the GCF. The scale that is produced is intended to be catalytic, as a means rather than an end in itself. Assemblage theory demonstrates this effect as ongoing work by focusing on the objectives, while a hierarchical conception of scale stops short after describing the work of building an enabling environment.

Conclusion

Country ownership is paradoxical. It is totally pervasive in development cooperation policy and best practice (GCF, 2017; OECD, 2005) yet most practitioners are exasperated by this un-implementable and pluralistic concept. This paper was motivated in part to the GCF IEU's assessment of country ownership (GCF, 2019a) which provided perhaps the most detailed interrogation of the concept without offering a clear definition nor clarifying many of the inconsistencies. The writing was on the wall when there was such universality in the call for its inclusion in GCF policy (Zamarioli et al. (2020) from all parties. The IEU report recommended a definition that goes beyond national government. This paper has addressed this conceptual impasse by paying attention to concrete assemblage rather than the reified generality of country ownership (DeLanda, 2006; McGregor & Knox, 2017). This looks at how desire to programme the GCF enrols things, people and ideas that constitute South Africa rather than a territorial notion. I distil four analytical categories: flat ontology, magnitude, endurance and multiplicity which distinguish a scalar conception of scale from a hierarchical one. This captures the co-constituted agency and the material-human hybrid scalar formation. These combine to offer an alternative to hierarchical conception of scale that ought to benefit policy actors while also re-affirming the value of scale in human geography.

The theoretical approach and the analytical dimensions offer a heuristic generalization and can equally be applied in any GCF beneficiary country, across sectors, financial instruments and in the public or private sectors. It is more likely to yield interesting findings in countries that are pursuing direct access to the Fund and have open and consultative processes. The IEU also cites confusion about the term: is it a principle, an investment criterion, an outcome or a process? This confusion stems from the lack of specificity in country ownership. The analytical framework deployed in this paper has focused on country ownership as a process, drawing on assemblage theory to explain how it is operationalized.

The conceptual issue facing an analysis of country ownership is how to account for the diversity of actors, things and ideas. This diversity of agency is better accounted for by drawing on a flat ontology. It is helpful to emphasize the immanent and emergent categories of actors that project development either enrols or creates which stand to benefit from projects. These actors and actants do not 'own' project development. They focus attention on the scalar effects of the GCF and how these territorialise. This approach offers opportunities to critical scholars of human geography and international development to consider the potential of interventions like the GCF. The contingent and emergent nature of this scalar conception makes a wide range of possibility visible. It includes ideas and positions that might not be 'bankable' in a conventional sense but has important implications for social justice agendas in highlighting the scope for transformation. This is a benefit of SANBI's approach to project development which offers a window into the desire for transformation in South Africa in a way that the DBSA's narrower project development does not.

Bibliography

African Development Bank, Asian Development Bank, European Bank for Reconstruction and Development, European Investment Bank, Inter-American Development Bank, International Monetary Fund, & Group, W. B. (2015). From billions to trillions: Transforming development finance. *Washington, DC.* https://doi.org/10.1017/CBO9781107415324.004

Allen, J. (2011). Powerful assemblages? *Area, 43*(2), 154–157. https://doi.org/10.1111/j.1475-4762.2011.01005.x

Allen, J., & Cochrane, A. (2010). Assemblages of state power: Topological shifts in the organization of government and politics. *Antipode, 42*(5), 1071–1089. https://doi.org/10.1111/j.1467-8330.2010.00794.x

Ashman, S. (2019). Financialised accumulation and the political economy of state capture. *New Agenda: South African Journal of Social and Economic Policy, 2019*(75), 6–11. https://hdl.handle.net/10520/EJC-1aa47860fb

Baker, T., & McGuirk, P. (2017). Assemblage thinking as methodology: Commitments and practices for critical policy research. *Territory, Politics, Governance, 5*(4), 425–442. https://doi.org/10.1080/21622671.2016.1231631

Bennett, J. (2009). *Vibrant matter: A political ecology of things.* Duke University Press.

Bergson, H. (2014). Time and free will: An essay on the immediate data of consciousness. *Routledge London.* https://doi.org/10.4324/9781315830254

Bertilsson, J., & Thörn, H. (2021). Discourses on transformational change and paradigm shift in the Green Climate Fund: The divide over financialization and country ownership. *Environmental Politics, 30*(3), 423–441. https://doi.org/10.1080/09644016.2020.1775446

Bouzarovski, S., & Haarstad, H. (2019). Rescaling low-carbon transformations: Towards a relational ontology. *Transactions of the Institute of British Geographers, 44*(2), 256–269. https://doi.org/10.1111/tran.12275

Braun, V., & Clarke, V. (2006). Using thematic analysis in psychology. *Qualitative Research in Psychology, 3*(2), 77–101. https://doi.org/10.1191/1478088706qp063oa

Brenner, N. (2001). The limits to scale? Methodological reflections on scalar structuration. *Progress in Human Geography, 25*(4), 591–614. https://doi.org/10.1191/030913201682688959

Bridge, G., Bouzarovski, S., Bradshaw, M., & Eyre, N. (2013). Geographies of energy transition: Space, place and the low-carbon economy. *Energy Policy, 53*, 331–340.

Buchanan, I. (2020). *Assemblage theory and method: An introduction and guide.* Bloomsbury Academic.

Buiter, W. H. (2007). 'Country ownership': A term whose time has gone. *Development in Practice*, *17*(4–5), 647–652. https://doi.org/10.1080/09614520701469856

Bulkeley, H. (2005). Reconfiguring environmental governance: Towards a politics of scales and networks. *Political Geography*, *24*(8), 875–902. https://doi.org/10.1016/j.polgeo.2005.07.002

Caprotti, F., Essex, S., Phillips, J., de Groot, J., & Baker, L. (2020). Scales of governance: Translating multiscalar transitional pathways in South Africa's energy landscape. *Energy Research & Social Science*, *70*, 101700. https://doi.org/10.1016/j.erss.2020.101700

Cooke, W. N., & Kothari, U. (2001). *Participation: The new tyranny?* Zed Books.

De Renzio, P., Whitfield, L., & Bergamaschi, I. (2008). *Reforming foreign aid practices: What country ownership is and what donors can do to support it*. Department of Politics and International Relations, University College Oxford. http://eprints.lse.ac.uk/id/eprint/24724

DeLanda, M. (2006). *A new philosophy of society: Assemblage theory and social complexity*. A&C Black.

Deleuze, G., & Guattari, F. (1983). *Anti-Oedipus: Capitalism and schizophrenia* (R. Hurley, M. Seem & H. R. Lane, Trans.). Athlone, 1984.

Deleuze, G., & Guattari, F. (1988). *A thousand plateaus: Capitalism and schizophrenia*. Bloomsbury Publishing.

Dornan, M. (2017). How new is the 'new' conditionality? Recipient perspectives on aid, country ownership and policy reform. *Development Policy Review*, *35*, O46–O63. https://doi.org/10.1111/dpr.12245

Ellis, C., & Pillay, K. (2017). *Understanding 'bankability' and unlocking climate finance for climate compatible development*. Climate and Development Knowledge Network (CDKN). https://media.africaportal.org/documents/CDKN_unlocking-climate-finance.pdf

Fredriksen, A. (2014). *Assembling value(s) what a focus on the distributed agency of assemblages can contribute to the study of value* (LCSV Working Paper Series No. 7). Leverhulme Centre for the Study of Value. http://hummedia.manchester.ac.uk/institutes/gdi/publications/workingpapers/archive/lcsv/lcsv-wp7-fredriksen.pdf

GCF. (2014). *Decisions of the board – seventh meeting of the board, 18–21 May 2014*. https://www.greenclimate.fund/sites/default/files/document/gcf-b07-11.pdf

GCF. (2017). *Guidelines for enhanced country ownership and country drivenness*. https://www.greenclimate.fund/documents/20182/751020/GCF_B.17_14_-_Guidelines_for_Enhanced_Country_Ownership_and_Country_Drivenness.pdf/12096654-ec65-4c97-87d7-e38d8894ff5d

GCF. (2018). *GCF handbook: Decisions, policies and frameworks as agreed by the Board of the Green Climate Fund from B.01 TO B.21.* https://www.greenclimate.fund/documents/20182/296788/GCF_Handbook__Decisions__Policies_and_Frameworks__updated_December_2018_.pdf/25fd22ec-4f81-44ee-b5d1-20bceb2c9264

GCF. (2019a). *Independent evaluation of the Green Climate Fund's country ownership approach.* https://www.greenclimate.fund/sites/default/files/document/gcf-b24-13.pdf

GCF. (2019b). *Investment criteria indicators.* https://www.greenclimate.fund/sites/default/files/document/investment-criteria-indicators.pdf

Haarstad, H. (2016). Who is driving the 'smart city' agenda? Assessing smartness as a governance strategy for cities in Europe (pp. 199–218). https://doi.org/10.1057/978-1-137-52710-3_9

Herod, A. (2010). *Scale.* Routledge.

Jonas, A. E. G. (1994). *The scale politics of spaliality.* SAGE Publications Sage UK. https://doi.org/10.1068/d120257

Jones, K. T. (1998). Scale as epistemology. *Political Geography, 17*(1), 25–28. https://doi.org/10.1016/S0962-6298(97)00049-8

Jones, M. (2009). Phase space: geography, relational thinking, and beyond. *Progress in Human Geography, 33*(4), 487–506. https://doi.org/10.1177/0309132508101599

Kalinowski, T. (2020). Institutional innovations and their challenges in the Green Climate Fund: Country ownership, civil society participation and private sector engagement. *Sustainability, 12*(21), 8827. https://doi.org/10.3390/su12218827

Latour, B. (2005). Reassembling the social an introduction to actor-network-theory. In MyiLibrary & A. C. of L. Societies (Eds.), *Introduction to actor-network-theory.* Oxford University Press.

Law, J. (2004). *After method : Mess in social science research.* Routledge.

Lawhon, M. (2012). Relational power in the governance of a South African e-waste transition. *Environment and Planning a: Economy and Space, 44*(4), 954–971. https://doi.org/10.1068/a44354

Leitner, H., Sheppard, E., & Sziarto, K. M. (2008). The spatialities of contentious politics. *Transactions of the Institute of British Geographers, 33*(2), 157–172.

Lund, C. (2014). Of what is this a case?: Analytical movements in qualitative social science research. *Human Organization, 73*(3), 224–234. https://doi.org/10.17730/humo.73.3.e35q482014x033l4

MacKinnon, D. (2010). Reconstructing scale: Towards a new scalar politics. *Progress in Human Geography, 35*(1), 21–36. https://doi.org/10.1177/0309132510367841

Marston, S. A., Jones, J. P., & Woodward, K. (2005). Human geography without scale. *Transactions of the Institute of British Geographers, 30*(4), 416–432. https://doi.org/10.1111/j.1475-5661.2005.00180.x

McGregor, C., & Knox, J. (2017). Activism and the academy: Assembling knowledge for social justice. *Ephemera: Theory & Politics in Organization, 17*(3), 509–532.

Moore, A. (2008). Rethinking scale as a geographical category: From analysis to practice. *Progress in Human Geography, 32*, 203–225. https://doi.org/10.1177/0309132507087647

National Planning Commission. (2013). *National development plan vision 2030.*

National Planning Commission. (2019). *Pathways for a Just Transition Concluding Conference.*

OECD. (2005). *Paris declaration on aid effectiveness.* OECD Publishing.

OECD. (2011). *Policy Brief No. 4: Country ownership of development: Political correctness or a practical key to better aid?.*

Omukuti, J. (2020). Challenging the obsession with local level institutions in country ownership of climate change adaptation. *Land Use Policy, 94*, 104525.

Papanastasiou, N. (2017). How does scale mean? A critical approach to scale in the study of policy. *Critical Policy Studies, 11*(1), 39–56.

Phillips, J., & Petrova, S. (2021). The materiality of precarity: Gender, race and energy infrastructure in urban South Africa. *Environment and Planning a: Economy and Space, 53*(5), 1031–1050. https://doi.org/10.1177/0308518X20986807

Ridder, H. -G. (2012). Yin, Robert K.: Case study research. Design and methods. *Zeitschrift Für Personalforschung, 26*, 93–96.

SANBI. (2017). *SANBI GCF Funding Framework for the period 2017–2022 in support of SANBI's GCF programme of work.* https://www.sanbi.org/wp-content/uploads/2018/04/sanbi-gcf-funding-frameworkoctober-2017.pdf

Sassen, S., & Ong, A. (2014). The carpenter and the bricoleur. In *Reassembling International Theory* (pp. 17–24). Springer.

Savage, G. C. (2018). Policy assemblages and human devices: A reflection on 'assembling policy.' *Discourse: Studies in the Cultural Politics of Education, 39*(2), 309–321. https://doi.org/10.1080/01596306.2017.1389431

Savage, G. C. (2020). What is policy assemblage? *Territory, Politics, Governance, 8*(3), 319–335.

Savedoff, W. D. (2019). *What is "country ownership"? A formal exploration of the aid relationship.* Center for Global Development.

Smith, D., & Protevi, J. (2008). *Gilles Deleuze.*

Winkler, H., & Dubash, N. K. (2016). Who determines transformational change in development and climate finance? *Climate Policy, 16*(6), 783–791. https://doi.org/10.1080/14693062.2015.1033674

Zamarioli, L. H., Pauw, P., & Gruning, C. (2020). Country ownership as the means for paradigm shift: The case of the Green Climate Fund. *Sustainability, 12*(5714), 1–18.

CHAPTER 6

Towards Accountability in Climate Finance: Lessons from Nepal and Indonesia

Cathy Shutt and Brendan Halloran

INTRODUCTION

Vast amounts of finance must be mobilized to address the climate crisis. There is much debate on who has responsibility for contributing and managing climate finance at the global level (e.g. Khan, Robinson et al., 2020; Lundsgaarde et al., 2018) as well as concern about the fragmented nature of the international system (e.g. Pickering et al., 2017). Despite these complexities, there is considerable agreement among civil society actors that the poor and marginalized people who are worst affected by climate change must have their say in determining how this money is spent (e.g. see Colenbrander et al., 2018; Crick et al., 2019; Krishnan, 2020; Patel et al., 2020; Rahman et al., 2020; Sarker et al., 2022).

C. Shutt
University of Sussex, Brighton, UK

B. Halloran (✉)
International Budget Partnership, Washington, DC, USA
e-mail: info@internationalbudget.org

© The Author(s), under exclusive license to Springer Nature Switzerland AG 2022
C. Cash and L. A. Swatuk (eds.), *The Political Economy of Climate Finance: Lessons from International Development*, International Political Economy Series, https://doi.org/10.1007/978-3-031-12619-2_6

A nascent theoretical and empirical literature outlines measures on how to support such aims and make climate finance more responsive to the needs of vulnerable communities. Authors identify familiar obstacles to realizing these objectives. Citizens and community-based organizations are often unable to access relevant information (Crick et al., 2019), and politics and power relations exclude the voices of women and other marginalized groups from decision-making processes in many contexts (Crick et al., 2019; Price, 2021). In addition, subnational tiers of government tend to be disempowered, having relatively little influence over national climate adaptation policies and plans (Colenbrader et al., 2018).

Such contributions usefully enhance our understanding of the potential roles of civil society organisations (CSOs) in seeking to make actors responsible for managing climate finance and adaptation more responsive and accountable and the difficulties they face in achieving this. Krishnan (2020) emphasizes the need to take approaches informed by political economy analysis to overcome these challenges, including in the context of donor-funded climate adaptation and mitigation programmes. Yet generally the literature on climate change and climate finance has a gap with respect to front line experiences of civil society actors who try to navigate the complicated power dynamics and fragmented systems that characterize public finance and development planning needed to ensure that resources meet the 'last mile' climate adaptation needs of vulnerable communities.

This chapter aims to make an original contribution to this relatively unexplored area. We recount lessons from a two-year (2020–2021) pilot project supported by the Swedish Postcode Foundation implemented in Nepal and Indonesia by Forest Resource Studies and Action Team (ForestAction) Nepal, the Indonesian Traditional Union of Fisherfolk (KNTI) and the National Center for Indonesia Leadership (INISIATIF) with support from the International Budget Partnership (IBP). The pilot tested approaches for ensuring that public resources meet the needs of excluded groups to address challenges associated with climate change. It set out to explore the functioning of the ecosystem of public finance actors and processes involved in delivering resources for local climate adaptation projects in each location and the strategies that could be employed by various actors, especially CSOs, to promote responsiveness and accountability. Research led by one of the authors was undertaken to understand and document the efforts of CSOs supported through this pilot project. The project was completed between August and December

2021; employed a desk review, interviews, and focus groups as data collection methods. The research team reviewed project documents and notes from reflection sessions that IBP hosted with the implementing CSOs during the project. In addition, the team held interviews with IBP and the main implementing CSOs in English. In Indonesia, these interviews and discussions were complemented by local language interviews and focus groups with the staff of implementing CSOs and other community-level actors who acted as local facilitators during the project. In Nepal, ForestAction contributed to the research by undertaking an additional community-level investigation to deepen understanding of how local actors involved in the project viewed their efforts and accomplishments. ForestAction, INISIATIF and KNTI all reviewed and helped to shape a report on which the empirical contributions to this chapter are based.

We begin this chapter with a brief discussion of the experience and evidence related to civic actors seeking to advance responsiveness and accountability for public resources and development outcomes. This includes a turn to more holistic thinking about navigating the 'accountability ecosystem' of actors and spaces at various levels of fiscal governance. We then describe ForestAction and INISIATIF/KNTI's approaches to navigating public finance accountability systems and make them more responsive to those most vulnerable to climate change impacts. We conclude that politically informed engagement that employs citizen evidence, leverages local incentives and builds capacity of local government to respond to climate adaptation priorities can enable collaboration and generate positive responses from government actors. However, longer-term support for broad coalitions will likely be necessary to translate these into more durable changes in behaviours, norms and processes indicative of meaningful government responsiveness and accountability to the adaptation needs of marginalized individuals and groups adversely affected by climate change.

NAVIGATING THE ACCOUNTABILITY ECOSYSTEM—THE THEORY

Public accountability can be broadly defined as the obligation of those in power to take responsibility for their actions. Accountability is a relational process through which individuals and institutions interact, often seeking to ensure response and responsiveness to priorities and claims raised by diverse constituencies. Accountability often depends on formal institutions that seek to ensure representatives are responsive to those that elected them or provide checks and balances on power holders. Less formal, but often equally important, accountability relationships and processes lie outside the state, as citizens make more direct demands for responsiveness from those in positions of authority and media plays an important watchdog role. Private sector actors play diverse roles in engaging and shaping responsiveness and accountability in ways that may or may not align with those of citizens or some government actors.

Accountability and responsiveness are realized, or not, through diverse pathways and forces embedded in a system. This "accountability ecosystem" can be understood as the interlinked and dynamic landscape of state and social actors, institutions, spaces, mechanisms and influences, both formal and informal, related to the process of realizing answerability and responsiveness of government action in a defined context. Power shapes and is shaped by relationships throughout the accountability ecosystem, both in the workings (and failings) of formal accountability institutions and mechanisms, and through the efforts of citizens to demand that authorities be accountable for their actions.

There is a growing body of evidence about the limitations of many governance reform efforts supported by international actors, especially those seeking to strengthen government responsiveness and accountability. Authors draw attention to simplistic assumptions about the nature of change leading to isolated 'solutions' that fail to address the causes of weak accountability (e.g. Carothers & De Gramont, 2013; de Gramont, 2014; Gaventa & McGee, 2013). Many early approaches were highly focused on transparency and information disclosure, based on the idea that 'sunlight is the best disinfectant', not fully appreciating the limits of transparency and information to generate government responsiveness or enable citizen action (for example, Lieberman et al., 2013). In other words, these 'first generation' efforts paid inadequate attention to the power relations, capacities and incentives required for meaningful openness that enables citizens to leverage such disclosures to advance their accountability claims. It follows that more attention must be paid to causal pathways by which transparency might activate accountability (Tsai et al., 2019), understanding that these must be through political engagement to contribute to government accountability (Peixoto, 2012).

Similarly, evidence from a citizen or community-led monitoring efforts, often referred to as social accountability, has pointed to the need to go beyond narrow and tool-based approaches, to more explicitly engage with the political and social context, connecting to broader networks or movements, or to support government to respond to citizen demands (Fox, 2015; Hickey & King, 2016). Although civic actors often play important roles in navigating and strengthening accountability ecosystems, citizen mobilization is no silver bullet (Waddington et al., 2019). Many protests or other collective civic efforts have failed to generate meaningful and sustainable change, and citizens or media 'naming and shaming' powerful actors can elicit considerable blowbacks that make advancing accountability agendas both difficult and dangerous (Jones et al., 2019; Larsen, 2015).

This has led to a search for new collaborative approaches and synergies among citizen groups, professional CSOs and media, and government reformers and oversight actors (Larsen, 2016). It also suggests more complex intermediation (including translating information in ways that are relevant and actionable by specific stakeholders) roles are required to connect these actors and spaces (Brock & McGee, 2017). Recent evidence suggests that CSO intermediaries skilled in participatory approaches can make progress on the thorny issue of ensuring the voices of poor and marginalized people are heard and taken seriously. These organizations work iteratively to build confidence and contextual understanding of the causes of inequality in informal spaces. Learning from such experiences can then be applied to building more inclusive and accountable relationships between marginalized citizens and duty bearers in different spaces and levels of accountability ecosystems (Howard et al., 2018).

These various insights from research and practice have fueled interest in testing and supporting more strategic and system-wide approaches to accountability, grounded in an appreciation of the power dynamics involved in these relationships. An accountability ecosystem perspective emphasizes the need to connect the dots between levels of governance and pro-accountability efforts (Fox, 2015), while being sure to 'work both sides of the citizen-state equation' (Benequista & Gaventa, 2011), including understanding why and how government reformers respond positively to citizen engagement (Joshi & McCluskey, 2018).

The idea that accountability seeking strategies should differ depending on the broader accountability ecosystem has important implications for reform tactics and the interpretation of responses from other ecosystem actors. Those navigating and strengthening public finance accountability ecosystems need to learn to distinguish between *discretionary one-off responses* by politicians and civil servants that might be due to pressure from specific actions or contextual events (e.g. corruption scandal) versus more institutionalized and inclusive *responsiveness* underpinned by stronger accountability dynamics. One-off responses to specific asks or priorities may be read as a government listening to citizens. However, they are not necessarily indications of the kinds of meaningful shifts in incentives, processes or relationships that are required to achieve accountable responsiveness, particularly to the poorest and most marginalized members of society.

There are still considerable questions about what it takes to advance responsiveness and accountability, and what role civic actors can play. The broad message from evidence and practices suggests that citizen-led accountability is most successful when it is undertaken through "relatively complex, strategic, multi-stranded, politically-savvy long-term processes" (McGee & Edwards, 2016). Given the challenges and fragmentation in the governance of public finance and local development implicated in meeting the climate change adaptation needs of vulnerable groups, it's important to better understand what roles and approaches are most effective in the climate finance accountability ecosystem. This chapter examines how ForestAction in Nepal and KNTI and INISTIATIF in Indonesia explored accountability dynamics around the climate adaptation needs of vulnerable groups in each context. It describes how they deepened their understanding of power dynamics that shape the responsiveness of public finance and local development decisions, and tested out engagement strategies to best navigate and shift these.

CLIMATE FINANCE IN INDONESIA AND NEPAL

Research supported by IBP prior to and during the implementation of the projects found that formal national CFA ecosystems in Indonesia and Nepal share some similarities. Both countries are extremely vulnerable to climate change hazards that have enormous impacts on poor and vulnerable populations.

In 2019, the Climate Risk Index ranked Nepal and Indonesia as the 12th and 14th most climate-impacted countries in the world, respectively (Eckstein et al., 2021). Both are seen as global leaders in climate change adaptation and mitigation given that they have made addressing climate change a national policy priority, supported by concrete plans to address it. National budget commitments have been significant in each case, averaging Indonesian Rupiah (IDR) 89.6 trillion (US$6.3 billion) per year between 2016 and 2018 in Indonesia,[1] and 372 billion Nepalese Rupee (US$3 billion) per year for the financial years 2017/2018 and 2018/2019 in Nepal.[2]

Such significant climate finance budget commitments have been associated with new financial frameworks and systems. Climate Change Fiscal Frameworks that were established in 2012 in Nepal and 2014 in Indonesia, map out legal and institutional approaches for planning, execution and reporting of climate finance at the federal level. There have also been efforts to extend these to the subnational level. In the case of Nepal, the Environment Friendly Local Governance (EFLG) Framework introduced in 2013 aimed to integrate climate change issues into local level planning and budgeting to ensure that climate finance is effectively managed at the local level. Additionally, the 2011 Climate Change Policy commits at least 80% of the climate responsive budget to be spent on local-level climate change priorities.

Fiscal frameworks adopted in each setting set out roles and responsibilities for different ministries in budget processes. They also designated formal roles for parliamentary committees and auditing authorities in oversight of climate finance as well as provisions for citizens to participate in planning, monitoring and oversight of climate finance budgets during the budgeting, implementation and auditing cycles.

Such reforms have been accompanied by measures to track and monitor climate finance commitments. In Indonesia the government has set up a Climate Change Trust Fund for the implementation of climate change plans. In addition, both countries have, with support from UNDP, adopted computerized budget tagging systems that make it easier to report on budgetary provisions for climate change. The Government of Nepal introduced a climate change budget code (CCBC) in 2012 in its fiscal planning and budgeting processes to help track climate change

---

[1] See IBP, IIED and PEFA (2021) Climate Budgeting and Participation, IBP, IIED and PEFA, p. 38.

[2] Freedom Forum (2019). *Nepal's Citizen Climate Budget: Where Is Nepal's Money Being Spent? 2018-2019.* https://reliefweb.int/report/nepal/nepals-citizen-climate-budget-where-nepal-s-money-being-spent-2018-2019-enne.

programmes and related finance. The Indonesian government implemented a comparable system in 2016. In theory, the use of special budget codes in each country's Financial Management Information System (FMIS) should have enabled them to implement climate tracking from national to local levels. However, in 2019 the new budgeting code that was used by provincial governments in Nepal had not yet been implemented at the local government level. Research in Indonesia around the same time reported comparable findings.

Delays in implementing technical systems may undermine accompanying policy for oversight by parliamentary committees and audit authorities; however, these bodies face their own constraints in advancing accountability. As in many other countries, even where effective audits are undertaken in Nepal and Indonesia, the findings and recommendations of these are often not acted upon by relevant government entities (International Budget Partnership, 2020). Oversight at the subnational level is likely weaker still. Generally, progress in increasing citizen participation in planning, monitoring and audit has also been slow. In Indonesia, spaces for citizens to participate in pre-budget consultations, as well as fairly nominal climate budget tracking and monitoring, have been limited at all three tiers of government. The same can be said in Nepal.

In Nepal, civil society actors have sought to address some of these issues and strengthen participation in different phases of climate finance planning and budget cycles. Furthermore, cases of NGOs successfully using public hearings to enable citizens to demand accountability on climate finance have been documented at the subnational level. Functioning informal mechanisms for public engagement also exist. Though potentially powerful, institutionalization has been difficult and many of these mechanisms are reported to be dominated by men from higher castes.

In both countries, there have been efforts to build media engagement on climate change. However, until recently, few of these have directly focused on domestic climate finance and accountability systems, except in relation to accessing international climate finance in Nepal. Such reportage frequently refers to the Global North's responsibility for causing climate change, making it responsible for financing adaptation and mitigation in the Global South. The argument made by CSOs covered in the media in Nepal is that local systems needed strengthening if the country is to avail of international climate finance. Yet, this has not led to independent, and systemic investigative work on climate change financing, with the notable exception in Nepal of a programme by Transparency International that uses media to press for the implementation of climate policy decisions.

In summary, the governments in Indonesia and Nepal have made some progress in advancing formal and technical elements of their climate finance systems. However, there remains a significant need to improve the functioning of these systems to enable meaningful accountability. The pilot project that generated insights described in this chapter aimed to enable learning on how this might be done, particularly from the experience of frontline CSOs in Nepal and Indonesia.

NAVIGATING THE ACCOUNTABILITY ECOSYSTEM—THE PRACTICE

Nepal

ForestAction's Aims and Approach
ForestAction Nepal is a learning-oriented CSO that focuses on research and policy dialogue for productive, equitable and sustainable forest and natural resource management. Since its establishment in 2000, the organization has blended expert knowledge with citizen organizing and deliberative engagement with the government to advance more inclusive and sustainable policies. Despite extensive experience supporting communities and local organizations to reflect on governance and impacts of climate and environmental policy at the local level, ForestAction had no prior experience working on climate finance. Participating in the pilot provided the organization an opportunity to experiment with integrating climate finance into their work on resource governance issues including principles of equity, transparency and accountability.

ForestAction intended to use participatory action research (PAR) that engaged women and other vulnerable constituencies such as Dalits (low caste groups), along with civil society and government, to increase information on how funds to address climate change are managed at the local level. By enabling communities to assess local finance and generate community evidence on the impact of climate change budgets, ForestAction aimed to strengthen relationships between government, civil society, media and other stakeholders and increase their capacity to engage in the management and oversight of climate-financing processes. ForestAction aspired to use evidence generated by these local engagements to advocate the national government to strengthen oversight and accountability for climate financial resources.

The pilot effort set out to build on the formally stated government agenda of reaching climate-vulnerable groups and was in line with local government policy objectives and discourse to strengthen systems to access international climate finance. ForestAction was initially elected to work in two municipalities in Karnali District. However, after positive engagements, COVID-19 restrictions and the monsoon season made the locations inaccessible, forcing ForestAction to shift to more accessible locations, the municipality of Kalia in Rauwa and the municipality of Devchuli in Nawalparasi. These areas are also populated by poor and marginalized groups facing impacts of climate change with whom ForestAction had existing relationships.

To explore the functioning of the public finance governance systems around climate adaptation, ForestAction used politically informed, adaptive and participatory approaches to understand formal and informal actors, institutions and underlying power dynamics. Their initial analysis indicated that top-down policymaking favoured high caste elites and overlooked demands from poor and marginalized communities to have a say in how budgets were spent. Provincial and federal development projects are particularly prone to manipulation in areas where communities and local leaders have low levels of education, giving national and provincial governments more scope to impose their own priorities or to regulate local projects. In comparison, in areas with educated elites, the imposition of national priorities was more difficult as local leaders were more able to scrutinize federal projects. ForestAction identified several government stakeholders for engagement, including subnational government officials and various national ministries with responsibilities related to climate adaptation. Associations of marginalized groups, local CSOs, cooperatives and local media were proposed as potential strategic partners.

Early discussions with multi-stakeholder groups increased local understanding of climate change issues and generated insights on climate change impacts. In addition, these discussions surfaced additional information on the complicated power dynamics that shape participation and accountability. Local government and citizen participation mechanisms were often undermined by provincial and federal political power struggles, as well as slow bureaucratic systems.

Government climate adaptation funding and responsibilities were fragmented and complex. A new national level FMIS had not been fully implemented, and climate-specific funds were mixed with other funds at different levels, making it nearly impossible to trace resources from national to local level. As a result, actual climate adaptation budgets and spending were often higher than was obvious from national and local budget documents. As these additional amounts were invisible to local actors, they were impossible to influence or audit. Furthermore, federal ministries mandated to address climate change impacts did not have a presence at the subnational level and therefore could not be engaged by communities and local government.

Thus, local government bureaucrats, as well as citizens, were relatively disempowered actors in the fiscal governance system. They had little information and opportunity to influence climate adaptation funding based on local priorities, and even struggled to implement what funding they did receive. According to one local government official, "It's really hard to bring in funds at the local level. We have to appease so many people, and finally it comes, but gets frozen. The funds come late, right around the end of fiscal year, and we cannot spend them. They get frozen and we can't spend it."

Local politicians, such as municipal mayors, did have an interest in accessing and shaping climate finance as means to strengthen their political support. However, the politicization of funds that bypassed local government units undermined the ability of local bureaucrats to respond to the needs of women and oppressed groups, such as Dalits (lower caste groups). This was reinforced by social norms and hierarchies, as well as opaque local planning processes in which higher caste groups and those with more direct relationships to local government had significant influence. While official quotas have led to greater political representation of women, a lack of inclusive planning practices limited their influence, along with other marginalized groups such as Dalits.

Navigating Local Power Dynamics
Given the complex governance and power dynamics around climate finance, ForestAction expected that a more formal audit process would be neither acceptable nor successful. Instead, the organization used existing trusting relationships with officials to access financial information for engagement. In addition, the CSO framed its engagements more positively around generating shared knowledge and dialogue on climate change adaptation. Initial discussions with a diversity of local civic and government actors surfaced interest in understanding and improving weak

governance systems to bring tangible improvements to communities and residents, including marginalized groups like women and Dalits. This was partly because local authorities perceived that such measures would enhance their ability to avail themselves of budgets legally earmarked for local climate change adaptation, which could bypass blockages at the provincial level.

Taking advantage of this interest, ForestAction supported other activities that were carefully designed to build the capacity of local communities to understand governance issues around public finance for climate adaptation. The organization helped to establish inclusive local climate justice action groups—comprising local government, citizen committee representatives, women, students and Dalits—with a mandate to engage with citizens and government actors in dialogue around public finance and climate adaptation governance. ForestAction played an intermediary and facilitative role in creating safe and informal spaces, such as the climate action groups, for women and members of Dalit communities to develop the confidence required to engage in more formal spaces. These climate justice action groups had an initial focus on a particular climate adaptation project that they investigated and presented findings to the community at a public hearing.

ForestAction chose to hold a public hearing despite knowing that these are often ritualized spaces that don't enable meaningful engagement. Thus, as the organization worked with the new climate justice action groups, they carefully oriented the logistics, design and facilitation to ensure inclusive and engaged dialogue. The hearing would be held in an accessible and central location, and be widely publicized well in advance by local authorities and citizen leaders.

The public hearing in October 2021 in Rasuwa focusing on a water project in a drought-prone area is illustrative of the process and outcomes ForestAction was able to achieve. Forty people attended the meeting which began with an introduction on the role of the public hearing mechanism followed by a presentation on the drinking water project and examples from ForestAction of its experience encouraging good governance of projects in other areas. Following these presentations, the CSO facilitated an open discussion on the weaknesses of local participatory mechanisms that impacted the effectiveness of the project. It included contributions from an indigenous woman who later reflected on having surprised herself by deviating from cultural norms and daring to ask questions of a local official. In addition, ForestAction was able to bring in analysis of the financing of a particular project to raise broader questions about the functioning of fiscal governance for climate adaptation while channelling these towards potential solutions. Those present remarked that a larger budget would have been required to reach the entire community and that regular local government budgets were inadequate to support the recurring costs associated with long-term maintenance of the infrastructure.

Community-level discussions surfaced various power dynamics that excluded residents from public discussions about such service delivery projects. Upon learning about the legal and institutional requirements for public hearings, residents raised questions on why such meetings had not been conducted before. Ordinary residents claimed they were seldom involved in municipal planning. Existing citizen committees, often dominated by local elites, are not always incentivized to engage broadly with residents. These groups tended to collect signatures from their members to approve projects rather than hold public meetings to deliberate on the pros and cons of plans and budgets for development projects. Employees of the municipality raised concerns that political leaders only cared about budget flows rather than the quality of local projects and that the spirit of public service and social work was fading.

Other power dynamics that affect the ability of poor and marginalized groups to make meaningful contributions to budget planning and monitoring were discussed. Technical discussions of the projects provided by engineers in English were inaccessible to many. Additionally, projects funded by local governments tended to be executed late in the year when people were too busy in rice fields to bear the opportunity costs associated with playing an active role in monitoring implementation.

At the end of the meeting, those present recognized that institutionalizing regular public hearings was one tactic that could encourage greater participation in the financial governance of climate and other development projects. The local government has responded by committing to holding more public hearings. Local journalists also covered the event and recommended that future public hearings should be publicized in local radio and newspapers.

The positive public hearing experiences in both municipalities suggest that ForestAction was correct in its assumption that facilitating and creating an enabling environment for dialogue and engagement involving politicians, bureaucrats, community leaders, citizens, CSO and media representatives together would be productive. The success of the public hearings which led to actions, such as repairing parts of irrigation canals catering to Dalits living on marginal lands was largely due to preliminary work by ForestAction. They succeeded in generating interest in fiscal governance issues around climate adaptation and establishing the climate justice action groups to take the issues forward after the hearing. The data used for the public hearing could also be useful in empowering local government officials and political leaders in their engagement with higher levels of government, and advocate for more transparent and accountable governance around climate finance and adaptation.

The short-term nature of the project and the significant interruptions mean that it has not been able to shift climate finance accountability systems at the local level in very significant ways. Nor has it yet been possible to 'join the dots' with other levels of government. Nonetheless, the project has contributed to promising outcomes at the local level. Through this project, ForestAction itself enhanced its capacity and confidence to integrate climate finance into its governance programmes at both the local and the national levels. The organization learned that their efforts need to move beyond general advocacy for more climate adaptation funds to responsiveness and accountability of multiple levels of government to ensure inclusive and effective implementation. This includes continued engagement at the local level, which has proved to be an effective entry point for building understanding, incentives and opportunities for collective dialogue and action.

Indonesia

KNTI and Inisiatif's Aims and Approach

INISIATIF, a strategic advocacy organization with strong capacity in budget analysis, and KNTI, a nationwide fisherfolk organization with more than 300,000 members and substantial experience working on social accountability initiatives and engaging media and government, sought to strengthen the responsiveness of government to coastal fishing communities and the climate change impacts they faced. However, the roles and responsibilities of various levels of subnational government were unclear, thus the two organizations needed to explore and learn which actors to engage and how to influence them. The initial analysis by INISIATIF and KNTI suggested that provincial policy on climate change adaptation was weak, but that national ministries, including Fisheries, Environment and Forestry, and the planning agency, Bappeda, all had roles to play as well.

The two organizations assumed that KNTI's significant membership base would give it a degree of political clout, particularly since the governor of the Central Java province where the organizations were focused was known to have national political ambitions. KNTI also assumed that strategic relationships with journalists would be helpful, as media actors are coming to view the impacts of climate change on coastal communities as a new and important issue. KNTI had worked closely with the media in the past and saw it as playing an important role in raising public awareness, as well as in holding the government to account. Such experience meant they were easily able to shift from name and fame to name and shame tactics if required.

The two organizations undertook initial mapping activities of coastal communities' climate-related challenges that revealed increasingly severe damage caused by tidal floods. Moreover, fisherfolk and their communities were not properly consulted in efforts to address these issues. This led to ineffective government responses, such as the construction of a sea wall that was too small to mitigate flooding.

Navigating Provincial-Level Power Dynamics
INISIATIF judged that the budget information available did not allow fisherfolk to monitor climate adaptation spending and outcomes or to weigh in on whether funding was being allocated appropriately based on communities' priorities. Based on their previous experience, they assumed it would be difficult to access the relevant planning and budget documents, even though by Indonesian law many of these documents should have been accessible electronically. The organizations were able to easily obtain planning documents for some localities, but freedom of information requests were required to access others. Budget documents proved more difficult to acquire, and KNTI had to rely on INISIATIF's intermediation and access through its informal networks in government. Even once these were obtained, the budget code classifications were on the one hand too restrictive for subnational governments to adapt to local realities and on the other still left ambiguities about the responsibilities of different actors.

KNTI's analysis of subnational budgets and plans found that they were inconsistent and inadequate to address the climate change impacts and solutions for affected coastal communities. There was little money to address the more significant impacts of flooding on household assets, and provincial-level budgets for climate issues facing coastal communities were declining.

KNTI and INISTIAIF aimed to use more formal hearings with provincial agencies to get important climate-related issues on the agenda. Such formal activities were complemented by engaging fisherfolk in informal spaces to discuss their needs and using relations with the governor for more informal lobbying. The two organizations identified other CSOs academics, and journalists as their main strategic partners in demanding greater responsiveness.

Efforts by KNTI and INISIATIF to engage regional and provincial-level governments with findings from their budget analysis and community research deepened their understanding of which actors had responsibilities for addressing community climate change needs. These efforts also revealed much about the resources, technical capacities, incentives and power dynamics that influenced whether and how government institutions could or would take action. Initial analysis and outreach to regional government suggested this level of government lacked the authority and resources to respond to the community's needs; these government actors suggested KNTI and INISTIATIF follow up with provincial government or village-level planning processes.

Opportunities to leverage political incentives meant provincial-level engagements appeared more promising and KNTI and INISIATIF assumed that by combining citizen-generated evidence and budget analysis with their political clout they would be able to make a compelling case for support to coastal communities. They thus convened a multi-stakeholder forum (MSF) at the provincial level, leveraging KNTI's membership base and the existing relationships both CSOs had with relevant actors. They invited civil servants of ministries they had identified as having climate change-related responsibilities, academic allies and a few CSOs. KNTI presented its analysis with clear advocacy requests. One was that the Governor of Central Java should issue a Circular Letter instructing agencies to list coasts and fishermen as targets of climate change adaptation and mitigation in the government's work plan and budget. The other was to increase budget allocations for community-level climate change adaptation and mitigation.

Those present noted that they were impressed with the quality of KNTI's research and arguments, which were endorsed by respected academic allies. As a result, provincial representatives of the most powerful agency present, Bappeda, responded positively and agreed that climate change mitigation and adaptation should form a distinct programme in provincial plans and budgets. In addition, the representative proposed offering grants to district governments that made explicit plans to address climate change impacts on coastal communities. These included offering mayors and district-level authorities grants from discretionary funds under the authority of the Governor. Bappeda suggested making access to grants conditional on district authorities including mitigation and adaptation of the coastal sector among the indicators used to assess the environmental sustainability of three-year development plans in Java, as well as mainstreaming coastal sector issues by including relevant provisions in the annual budget of each district-level agency.

Thus, through analysis and engagement, KNTI and INISIATIF 'joined the dots' and found that provincial authorities were best positioned to respond to the climate adaptation needs of coastal communities. The organizations also learned about the technical and political issues in need of resolution if different levels of government were to respond effectively to KNTI's advocacy—among them, that government was not consulting adequately with communities on their needs, and that the climate change adaptation and mitigation needs of coastal communities were not on the political agenda but that the provincial government had incentives to respond, and that technical issues relating to budget definitions had considerable impact on individual agencies.

KNTI and INISIATIF's diverse and exploratory engagement strategy—mixing KNTI's political clout, INISIATIF's analytical skills and government relationships, and drawing on other allies as needed—proved relatively successful in getting responses to the organizations' concrete demands. One of these was that the provincial governor of Central Java issued a circular letter, instructing agencies to list coasts and fisherfolk as targets of climate change adaptation and mitigation. This action was reinforced by the apparent interest of Bappeda, which also expressed support for the involvement of coastal communities in more regular government consultations on climate adaptation planning. Thus, there are some promising signs that political will within the ecosystem of relevant government actors could lead to responsiveness to the climate change-related issues facing fisherfolk and their coastal communities.

INISIATIF was convinced that a combination of evidence and KNTI's political clout had succeeded in getting the climate change mitigation and adaptation needs of coastal communities firmly on the government's agenda in ways that would lead to ongoing *responsiveness*. KNTI, on the other hand, was not entirely convinced and saw the initial actions and commitments as merely an initial *response*. Moreover, Bappeda acknowledged that the provincial government's power to incentivize other government actors were limited, as the Governor had no power to sanction should the local governments fail to respond to any directives they put in place. Mixed reactions from various agencies meant KNTI felt that the government was not fully supported.

While they differed somewhat in how to interpret initial government commitments and actions, both organizations recognized that for tangible and sustained government actions to take place, there would have to be ongoing coordinated follow-up by the various government and civic actors, none of whom could move this project forward on their own. External resources would be needed for the two organizations to continue their engagements around resources for community climate adaptation needs.

KNTI reported their chapters are better equipped to make accountability demands. As a result of engagement in this project, they have stronger research skills and understanding of climate science. In addition, they now know that government responsibilities around climate finance are not being met. A brief interview with KNTI chapters suggested that local fisherfolk will continue to raise these issues with authorities and to play more effective roles in making collective accountability demands. KNTI is encouraging individual communities to use evidence generated by the project for their own accountability demands.

KNTI has a better understanding of how to navigate the ecosystem and work on blockages to climate finance. KNTI staff learned what documents they need to access in order to influence development plans and budgets and how to access them from government departments. It remains to see whether this will bear fruit, but KNTI is confident that it can replicate the process in other regencies and provinces.

There was no explicit evidence that increased responsiveness of the CFA ecosystem would benefit women and marginalized groups. Women were involved in KNTI activities and stood to benefit from proposals made. But there was less evidence that the project had helped women to overcome barriers to participation.

INISITAIF aims to use its learning on the failure of government budgets to respond to fisherfolk's needs in a strategic advocacy role for the fishing and marine sector. For example, evidence from the project could help make the case to other CSOs about the impacts of climate change on the marine sector. In addition, NISIATIF strengthened its relationship with Bappeda.

Conclusions

ForestAction, KNTI and IINISIATIF used the short-term pilot project to explore and navigate the accountability ecosystem around public finance for local development that addresses climate impacts on badly affected communities. They deepened their understanding of the governance challenges, both technical and political, that limited the possibilities that resources to address climate adaptation could reach these communities. Yet, they also leveraged evidence and collaboration to bring together citizens, bureaucrats, elected officials and other civic actors (media, academics, etc.) in spaces that generated positive initial responses to the needs of communities vulnerable to climate change.

The approaches of the CSOs, while entailing important differences based on context and the nature and positionality of the groups themselves and the communities they engaged with, were broadly similar, reflecting their assumptions about what was most likely to work within local political economies and in the context of short-term efforts. In both Nepal and Indonesia, the groups sought to access government information on public finance and planning for climate adaptation (often relying on existing relationships or Right to Information mechanisms), generate evidence from the experience of marginalized groups themselves, and bring together multiple relevant actors in spaces for collaboration and dialogue framed positively around seeking agreed solutions. In both cases, the CSOs gained important insights about the actors and processes of the accountability ecosystem for climate finance and adaptation at the subnational level. This shaped their approaches and enabled them to inform relevant actors and find some alignment of incentives leading to positive responses by decision-makers. ForestAction was particularly attuned to the realities of achieving meaningful inclusion of marginalized groups in engagement with local elites and decision-makers. KNTI, on the other hand, leveraged its significant membership base to engage and influence government actors more directly. Each organization further strengthened their own capacities in terms of understanding the relevant actors and systems (both formal and informal aspects), and how they can play an effective role in engaging these, and facilitating the engagement of others, particularly from marginalized groups.

This affirms the experience of CSOs in other countries, such as Uganda and Ethiopia (Krishnan, 2020), and illustrates the complexity of public finance accountability ecosystems and the gaps and blockages encountered when trying to ensure that the climate change adaptation and mitigation needs of vulnerable populations are met. It also confirms the value of adaptive, politically informed collaborative approaches to navigating complex climate finance accountability ecosystems. Such approaches can generate positive responses and tangible results in the short term. However, the challenging and fragmented governance systems around public finance and local development that the CSOs encountered suggest that strengthening accountability for more durable responsiveness to the climate adaptation needs of marginalized groups is neither automatic nor straightforward. As the broader evidence and experience around public accountability ecosystems suggests, the kinds of efforts initiated by civic actors in both Nepal and Indonesia would need to be sustained and deepened to achieve more meaningful and lasting shifts (in both formal policies and processes, and informal relationships and norms) that would enable climate adaptation resources, plans and projects to address the needs of vulnerable communities. This would likely entail sustaining accountability coalitions that work across multiple levels of governance to ensure inclusive spaces to engage and monitor decisions and funding flows, while also continuing efforts to create an enabling environment that incentivizes responsiveness and accountability, through continued civic mobilization, media coverage and effective state oversight.

Thus, the broader lessons from the experience of civic actors in Nepal and Indonesia for the climate change community are about the importance of paying attention to and working to strengthen the accountability ecosystem for enabling climate adaptation, particularly for the most vulnerable communities. These efforts must be informed by an understanding of the political and power dynamics that shape the possibilities of inclusive, responsive and accountable climate adaptation governance. Commitments of resources by donor and recipient countries must be matched by efforts to support the efforts of civic actors, local governments and others to strengthen the systems that would enable those funds to be used in an inclusive and effective manner. The experience of CSOs in Nepal and Indonesia suggests that more consideration and support should be given to these actors to understand and navigate national and subnational systems and spaces, and explore contextually relevant approaches to strengthening inclusiveness and accountability of public resources and development activities around climate adaptation.

Acknowledgements The authors thank the staff at ForestAction, Action Aid Bangladesh, KNTI, Inisiatif and IBP for their important contributions to this article, but note that any errors are their own. IBP is grateful to Delaine Mccullough, former head of IBP's Climate Finance Program, whose strategic vision and management of this project made this collaboration possible. We would also like to thank the funder of this work, the Swedish Postcode Foundation.

Bibliography

Benequista, N., & Gaventa, J. (2011). *Blurring the boundaries: Citizen action across states and societies.* Citizenship DRC, 11.
Brock, K., & McGee, R. (2017). *More accountable and responsive governance: How do technologies help make it happen?* Making All Voices Count Event Report.
Carothers, T., & De Gramont, D. (2013). *Development aid confronts politics: The almost revolution.* Brookings Institution Press.
Colenbrander, S., Dodman, D., & Mitlin, D. (2018). Using climate finance to advance climate justice: The politics and practice of channelling resources to the local level. *Climate Policy, 18*(7), 902–915.
Crick, F., Hesse, C., Orindi, V., Bonaya, M., & Kiiru, J. (2019). *Delivering climate finance at local level to support adaptation: Experiences of county climate change funds in Kenya.* Ada Consortium.
de Gramont, D. (2014). *Beyond magic bullets in governance reform.* Carnegie.
Eckstein, D., Künzel, V., & Schäfer, L. (2021). *Global climate risk index 2021.* Germanwatch e.V. https://reliefweb.int/sites/reliefweb.int/files/resources/Global%20Climate%20Risk%20Index%202021_1_0.pdf
Flores, W. (2018). *How can evidence bolster citizen action?* (p. 2). Learning and adapting for accountable public health in Guatemala.
Fox, J. A. (2015). Social accountability: What does the evidence really say? *World Development, 72*(2015), 346–361.
Gaventa, J., & McGee, R. (2013). The impact of transparency and accountability initiatives. *Development Policy Review, 31,* s3–s28.
Hickey, S., & King, S. (2016). Understanding social accountability: Politics, power and building new social contracts. *The Journal of Development Studies, 52*(8), 1225–1240.

Howard, J., López Franco, E., & Shaw, J. (2018). *Navigating the pathways from exclusion to accountability: From understanding intersecting inequalities to building accountable relationships*. Institute of Development Studies.

IBP, IIED and PEFA. (2021). *Climate budgeting and participation*.

Jones, E., Amidu, I.-T., & Sefa-Nyarko, C. (2019). *Formative evaluation of the 'I Am Aware' social accountability project in Ghana*. Oxford Policy Management (OPM).

Joshi, A., & McCluskey, R. (2018). *The art of 'bureaucraft': Why and how bureaucrats respond to citizen voice*. Institute of Development Studies.

Khan, M., Robinson, S. A., Weikmans, R., Ciplet, D., & Roberts, J. T. (2020). Twenty-five years of adaptation finance through a climate justice lens. *Climatic Change, 161*(2), 251–269.

Khan, M., Watkins, M., Aminuzzaman, S., Khair, S., & Khan, M. Z. H. (2020). *Climate change investments in Bangladesh: Leveraging dual-use characteristics as an anti-corruption tool*.

Krishnan, N. (2020, September). *Following the money isn't enough: How civil society organizations provide accountability for climate adaptation finance*. World Resources Institute.

Larsen, J. (2015). *Uganda: Winning human resources for health: Case study*. International Budget Partnership.

Larsen, G. (2016). *You cannot go it alone: Learning from cooperative relationships in civil society budget campaigns*. International Budget Partnership.

Lieberman, E. S., Posner, D. N., & Tsai, L. L. (2013). *Does information lead to more active citizenship. Evidence from an Education Intervention in Rural Kenya* (Massachusetts Institute of Technology Political Science Department Working Paper [2013-2]).

Lundsgaarde, E., Dupuy, K., & Persson, Å. (2018). *Coordination challenges in climate finance* (No. 2018: 3) (DIIS Working Paper).

McGee, R., & Edwards, D. (2016). Introduction: Opening governance—Change, continuity and conceptual ambiguity. *IDS Bulletin, 41*(1), 1–21.

Patel, S., Soanes, M., Rahman, F., Smith, B., & Steinbach, D. (2020). *Good climate finance guide: Lessons for strengthening devolved climate finance* (IIED Working Paper). IIED. http://pubs.iied.org/10207IIED

Peixoto, T. (2012). The uncertain relationship between open data and accountability: A response to Yu and Robinson's the new ambiguity of open government. *UCLA Law Review and Discourse, 60*, 200.

Pickering, J., Betzold, C., & Skovgaard, J. (2017). Managing fragmentation and complexity in the emerging system of international climate finance. *International Environmental Agreements: Politics, Law and Economics, 17*(1), 1–16.

Price, R. (2021). *Access to climate finance by women and marginalised groups in the Global South*. Institute of Development Studies.

Rahaman, M. A., & Rahman, M. M. (2020). Climate justice and food security: Experience from climate finance in Bangladesh. In *Environmental policy: An economic perspective* (pp. 249–268). Wiley.

Rahman, S. H., Islam, M. N., & Mukta, Z. H. (2020). Exploration of issues in local-level climate finance transparency and accountability in Southwest Bangladesh. *Bangladesh Journal of Environmental Research, 11*, 12–21.

Sarker, M., Islam, N., Peng, Y., Khatun, M., Alam, G. M., Shouse, R. C., & Amin, M. (2022). Climate finance governance in hazard prone riverine islands in Bangladesh: Pathway for promoting climate resilience. *Natural Hazards, 110*(2), 1115–1132.

Tsai, L., Morse, B., Toral, G., & Lipovsek, V. (2019). *Information and accountability: Evidence synthesis of within government and citizen-government accountability pathways*. MIT Governance Lab.

Waddington, H., Sonnenfeld, A., Finetti, J., Gaarder, M., John, D., & Stevenson, J. (2019). Citizen engagement in public services in low- and middle-income countries: A mixed methods systematic review of participation, inclusion, transparency and accountability (PITA) initiatives. *Campbell Systematic Reviews, 15*, e1025.

CHAPTER 7

Delivering Adaptation Finance Through the Market? The Trouble with Using Carbon Offsets to Finance Climate Adaptation in the Global South

Kate Ervine

Introduction

Concentrations of carbon dioxide (CO_2) in the atmosphere, measured at 418 parts per million at the time of writing, have not been this high for at least 3.6 million years (NOAA, 2021). Global emissions of heat trapping gases, of which CO_2 is the most abundant, have rebounded dramatically from the slump experienced during the first wave of the global pandemic, with the International Energy Agency (IEA) projecting that energy-related CO_2 emissions in 2021 will increase by 1.5 billion

---

K. Ervine (✉)
Department of Global Development Studies, Saint Mary's University, Halifax, NS, Canada
e-mail: kate.ervine@smu.ca

© The Author(s), under exclusive license to Springer Nature Switzerland AG 2022
C. Cash and L. A. Swatuk (eds.), *The Political Economy of Climate Finance: Lessons from International Development*, International Political Economy Series, https://doi.org/10.1007/978-3-031-12619-2_7

tonnes, the second highest growth rate ever recorded, driven predominantly by an increase in the use of coal, followed by natural gas and oil (IEA, 2021a). With global heating of 1.2 °C above pre-industrial levels already recorded in 2020, this surge in fossil-fuelled emissions departs dramatically from estimates that global CO_2 emissions must decrease by 7.6% per year through to 2030 in order to limit global heating to 1.5 °C (UNEP, 2019). As the frequency and severity of catastrophic storms, heatwaves, droughts, floods, crop failures and more continue to increase, communities across the globe, and especially those that have contributed the least or not at all to the climate crisis, are confronted with rising insecurity, vulnerability and the loss of livelihoods. Updated emissions reduction pledges made in 2021 by countries to the Paris Agreement, which could lead to an estimated 2.4 °C of warming by the end of the century, thus fail to reflect the urgency and temporal imperatives of climate breakdown. More troubling, actually existing policies put the level of projected warming at an estimated 2.9 °C or more by the end of the century (Climate Action Tracker, 2021).

It is within this context that adaptation to climate breakdown sits as a core theme in global climate negotiations and governance processes, particularly with respect to the contentious politics of climate finance. Dominant understandings of climate adaptation present it as a process through which actions are taken to limit or avoid the negative impacts of climate breakdown, while simultaneously leveraging potential opportunities (UNEP, 2021b). Observers highlight that whether or not adaptation takes place, in turn, depends on the availability and sufficiency of sustainable levels of finance, with the principle of common but differentiated responsibilities and respective capabilities (CBDR-RC) offering a basis from which countries in the Global South can make claims upon those in the Global North to pay their fair share given the North's disproportionate contribution to climate breakdown, in addition to its greater capacity to respond. CBDR-RC has been central to negotiations under the United Nations Framework Convention on Climate Change (UNFCCC), including its Kyoto Protocol and the Paris Agreement, with the Copenhagen Accord of 2009 committing wealthy nations to mobilize US$100 billion in climate finance a year by 2020. Estimates, however, reveal a consistent failure to fulfill climate finance targets, with adaptation finance receiving proportionately less than finance directed to mitigating climate breakdown. Financing for loss and damage is even more critically inadequate. Though likely an underestimate, official figures peg adaptation costs at approximately $70 billion per year presently, growing to an estimated $140–300 billion by 2030 and $280–500 billion by 2050 (UNEP, 2021a: xiv). Much of the scholarly literature and policy work is thus focused on determining how sufficient funds to finance adaptation will be raised and from where they will come. This challenge is perceived as especially acute given the absence of incentives for private sector investment in adaptation projects.

Under the Kyoto Protocol's Clean Development Mechanism (CDM), two per cent of carbon offsets produced in the Global South and sold to emitters in the Global North to comply with their emission reduction commitments under the Protocol, were mandated to go to the UNFCCC's Adaptation Fund to be monetized and sold, with the revenue funding adaptation. This share of proceeds (SOP) model, which has raised over $200 million for the Adaptation Fund, is grounded in a *quid pro quo* dynamic whereby the acquisition of carbon offsets allows the purchaser to continue to emit at the source and to claim legally binding emission reductions under the Kyoto Protocol, in return for financing projects in the Global South through which carbon offsets are produced. The SOP model is thus celebrated for identifying an innovative channel through which private sector investments can be directed towards adaptation ends that otherwise lack opportunities for profitable returns. With plans to replace the CDM with a yet-to-be finalized offsetting mechanism under Article 6.4 of the Paris Agreement, the Adaptation Fund and its SOP model will serve the Agreement, with current negotiations focused on whether or not a share of proceeds should be delivered via a monetary share of offsets sold or an in-kind contribution of a percentage of offsets issued; what percentage the contribution should be set at; and whether or not to extend the SOP to also cover international emissions trading that will take place under Article 6.2 of the Agreement. The negotiations are among the most contentious within the Paris Agreement, divided along somewhat traditional South/North lines.

The purpose of this chapter is to offer a critical intervention in discussions and debates on the related themes of adaptation finance and adaptation to climate breakdown. The former is often linked, conceptually, to themes of ecological debt. Foregrounding the history of carbon- and resource-intensive economic growth and development in the Global North, along with colonial and post-colonial relations of exploitation globally that have facilitated uneven development and overlapping ecological crises on a planetary scale, the concept of ecological debt demands that nations in the Global North take responsibility for this history, paying for, among other things, the costs of adaptation in the Global South. Furthermore, demands that adaptation finance be new, additional and adequate are framed as a matter of climate justice, with adaptation finance offering one vehicle among many to address historical inequities. Nevertheless, while references to justice, ecological debt and CBDR-RC frame much of the discourse globally on adaptation finance, this paper argues that raising adaptation finance through a share of proceeds from international carbon offsetting represents a profound depoliticization of adaptation finance and adaptation to climate breakdown. Representative of the specific post-political moment that frames contemporary global environmental governance, in which the politics of particular problems are replaced with market-driven and techno-managerial policymaking and in which consensual multistakeholderism and rule by elites stand in for democratic deliberation and debate (Gleckman, 2018; Swyngedouw, 2010; Swyngedouw & Wilson, 2014), the use of carbon offsetting to raise adaptation finance functions such that the political economy of power within which carbon offsetting emerged and operates, and one deeply implicated in producing climate breakdown in the first instance, is largely mystified. Abundant and well-documented evidence shows that carbon offsetting under the Kyoto Protocol allowed polluters in the Global North to avoid taking action, shifting the burden of responsibility for lowering emissions to distant nations and communities; that an overwhelming share of offset projects failed to fulfill their emission reduction commitments resulting in an overall increase in global emissions and that carbon offsetting today represents a dangerous obstacle to achieving real and lasting emission reductions consistent with limiting heating to 1.5 °C above pre-industrial levels (Badgley et al., 2021; Cames et al., 2016; Cullenward & Victor, 2020; Ervine, 2018; Kollmuss et al., 2015). Additionally, offsetting under the Paris Agreement risks undermining climate ambition in the Global North as polluters forego emission reductions at the source, while simultaneously threatening the development of ambitious emission reduction targets in the Global South as countries, in an effort to generate new sources of national revenue, exclude some sectors and options from national mitigation plans in order to produce and sell offsets to purchasers in the Global North (Fearnehough et al., 2021: 37). It is thus that carbon offsetting sustains the conditions under which climate breakdown advances, generating an ever-growing need for adaptation in turn.

By shining a light on these interconnections, this chapter offers an intervention into critically oriented research on adaptation to climate breakdown in the Global South. Much of this literature has documented the problems with adaptation interventions—that they fail to problematize how pre-existing inequalities at the community-level shape outcomes and heighten marginalization; that they fail to interrogate multi-scalar sources and structures of vulnerability and oppression, including relations of production and social reproduction, class, gender, race, and more, thereby threatening to reproduce them; that they fail to offer spaces for democratic dialogue, mutual learning and participatory practice in adaptation projects; and that they conceptualize adaptation as a technical fix in response to external climate threats, thereby mystifying the imperative to understand climate breakdown and the need for adaptation as deeply enmeshed in, and constituted through, globalized socio-economic and political structures to which we must respond as part of adaptation interventions (Bassett & Fogelman, 2013; Eriksen et al., 2015, 2021; Nightingale et al., 2020; Taylor, 2015).

Another body of literature focuses critical attention on adaptation finance specifically, utilizing a climate justice lens to emphasize deep inadequacies in finance to the Global South; to highlight the North's responsibility to scale up new, additional, predictable, transparent and democratically managed funding; and to advocate for public over private approaches to securing financial resources (Gifford & Knudson, 2020; Khan et al., 2020; Roberts et al., 2021). Important to this work has been the argument that dominant approaches to adaptation finance are rooted in a neoliberal understanding of justice wherein private property, market-based strategies and the self-interest of actors are prioritized (Khan et al., 2020). While the problems of applying a neoliberal ethos to adaptation finance are clear, there is a need to interrogate and politicize *sources* of funding in a way that reveals the deep entanglements between, and co-constitutive nature of, climate breakdown, the need for adaptation and adaptation finance. This chapter uses the share of proceeds model from carbon offsetting as a case study to respond to the question: "does the deployment of finance undermine other climate justice goals?" (Gifford & Knudson, 2020: 245). It offers an analysis that underscores the need to consider levels of adaptation finance, its sources and subsequent interventions, as an integrated whole, thereby widening our scope such that contradictions, inconsistencies and dangers are more fully perceived. Too much is risked when "finance become[s] a goal in itself" (Michaelowa, 2012: xviii), such that we fail to examine the politics and relations and structures of power that underpin it.

The remainder of the chapter proceeds with an overview of the state of adaptation finance globally; of the share of proceeds model under the Kyoto Protocol's Clean Development Mechanism and of negotiations on Article 6 of the Paris Agreement under which the share of proceeds will be managed. It then turns to a brief review of the relevant literature on adaptation finance in order to frame the subsequent review of the problems with carbon offsetting and the argument that the scale and scope of these problems demand that they are centralized in current negotiations to use offsetting to raise adaptation finance. The chapter ends with concluding remarks on alternatives for raising adaptation finance for the Global South, while simultaneously recognizing the limits of finance—of monetary compensation—to "somehow set things straight" (Hornborg, 2019: 59).

Global Adaptation Finance: An Overview

At the time of writing, the COVID-19 pandemic and its financial fallout has severely impacted the budgets of many low- and middle-income nations, constraining already limited resources that are required to support climate change mitigation, adaptation and loss and damage. While G7 nations failed to provide detailed plans for scaling-up climate finance to the Global South following their June 2020 meeting, data indicated that they would fail to fulfill their 2009 commitment to provide $100 billion per year in climate finance by 2020, shared equally between mitigation and adaptation. Numbers from the OECD show that in 2018, the most recent year for which official figures are available, a total of $79 billion in climate finance to the Global South was mobilized by developed countries. Of that total, bilateral public climate finance accounted for $32.7 billion, multilateral for $29.6 billion, officially supported export credits for $2.1 billion and private climate finance that can be attributed to developed countries for $14.6 billion (OECD, 2020: 6). In turn, 70% of this finance went to mitigation, 21% to adaptation and 9% to cross-cutting agendas (OECD, 2020: 6). These numbers highlight the failure of developed nations to ensure equal funding between adaptation and mitigation in accordance with requirements laid out in the Paris Agreement. Even more troubling, of the $79 billion total, only 20% was delivered as grants and 74% was delivered as loans. The OECD reports that 20% of the loans from developed countries and 76% from multilateral development banks were in fact non-concessional (OECD, 2020), pointing to deeply flawed reporting practices that see developed nations and donor bodies counting non-concessional loans from which they benefit by way of interest accrued and paid, as legitimate climate finance, even when non-concessional loans disqualify them from counting as Official Development Assistance (ODA) according to OECD guidelines. As noted by Oxfam in its *Climate Finance Shadow Report 2020*, "The excessive use of loans and the provision of non-concessional finance in the name of climate assistance is an overlooked scandal" (Oxfam, 2020: 3). The report goes on to highlight that the bulk of public climate finance over the 2017–2018 period was in the forms of loans and non-grant instruments, including that directed to the world's Least Development Countries (LDCs) which received only 20.5% of bilateral climate finance; approximately half of the finance received by Small Island Developing States (SIDS) was delivered as loans as well, who themselves received only 3% of bilateral climate finance (Oxfam, 2020: 3). LDCs and SIDS are among the most climate vulnerable nations globally, while least responsible for climate breakdown, highlighting further the scandal of counting loans as public climate finance, which is then compounded by the acute insufficiency of delivered funds overall. When analysed through the lens of climate justice and CBDR-RC, these numbers reveal the dramatic failure of developed nations to take responsibility for their historical contribution to climate breakdown.

In fact, Oxfam estimates that officially reported public climate finance figures of $59.5 billion per year for 2017–2018 are much lower, with public "climate-specific net assistance" totaling instead between $19 and 22.5 billion (Oxfam, 2020: 2). The is the result of countries counting loans towards their commitments, in addition to inaccuracies in how they calculate the portion of climate-specific finance within broader development funding. With respect to adaptation funding specifically, CARE International's research documents how official figures are "severely overstated and far too high" (CARE International, 2021b: 1). In its analysis of 112 projects in six countries involving 25 donors, including individual nations and multilateral institutions and a mix of grant and loan-based financing, it found that of the $6.2 billion officially reported by donors as adaptation finance, $2.6 billion was over-reported, reducing the total to $3.8 billion or 58% of their officially reported figures (CARE International, 2021b: 2). This occurs for a number of reasons, including the practice of overstating the extent to which a project focuses on adaptation, thereby inflating the portion of its budget classified as adaptation finance. Japan is specifically noted for "grossly inflating" its adaptation finance with just one example including $470 million of its concessional Post-disaster Standby Loan to the Philippines. Project assessments carried out in country found that the loan, officially intended to ensure liquidity in the aftermath of Typhoon Haiyan so that pre-existing commitments could be financed, went largely to repaying ODA loans, including to Japan. Japan counted its full value as adaptation finance, contending that it "indirectly 'freed up' national funds so that the government could respond to the natural disaster" (CARE International, 2021b: 13). Additionally, CARE's analysis found that it is common for donors to report development finance unrelated to adaptation as adaptation finance, while reporting loans, discussed above, as adaptation finance and at face value, including interest payments (CARE International, 2021b: 24–25).

As a whole, public climate finance to the Global South is critically inadequate and within that, adaptation finance remains "severely underfunded" (Care International, 2021a: 1). If we expand our analysis to include all climate finance flows, UNEP's *Adaptation Gap Report 2020* documents total climate finance flows of $579 billion per year for 2017–2018, with $30 billion, or 5.8%, financing adaptation (UNEP, 2021b: 25). While the discussion above requires us to view these figures critically, they nevertheless underscore the immense gaps that remain for adaptation finance and that show no sign of meaningful redress. It is within this context that the share of proceeds model utilized by the Adaptation Fund should be analysed.

The Adaptation Fund and the Share of Proceeds Model

The Adaptation Fund, operational since 2010 following key decisions taken under the UNFCCC's Kyoto Protocol, was established as a grant-based multilateral financial instrument to finance adaptation in vulnerable developing country parties to the Kyoto Protocol. Many observers highlight the Fund's grant-based structure, its emphasis on host country ownership and its accreditation of domestic implementing entities who can directly access funds, as particular strengths relative to other multilateral funding bodies whose space for meaningful host country ownership remains much more limited (Ciplet et al., 2013: 62–63). The review of the Adaptation Fund is limited here to a consideration of the share of proceeds model through which it raises adaptation finance, rather than providing an assessment of the Fund in its entirety.

As of mid-July 2021, the Fund had received just over $1.1 billion in financial contributions, including $894.5 million from donor nations and $208.38 million from a share of proceeds from the sale of Certified Emission Reductions (CERs) (World Bank, 2021). CERs are carbon offsets produced under the Kyoto Protocol's Clean Development Mechanism (CDM) and which, under the Protocol, are sold to emitters in the Global North to meet their legally binding emission reduction commitments in place of reducing emissions at the source. Known as one of Kyoto's flexible mechanisms, the CDM has allowed for the funding of projects in the Global South that could claim to reduce emissions below a business-as-usual (BAU) scenario, with the reductions then quantified as offsets and available for sale within Kyoto's global compliance carbon market. Emissions reductions below the BAU scenario are measured in tonnes of CO_2 equivalent (tCO_2e), with one CER equal to one tCO_2e. Since its inception the CDM has generated over 2.13 billion CERs, with over 1.48 billion issued during the Kyoto Protocol's first commitment period (2008–2012), and over 659 million during the second (2013–2020) (UNFCCC, 2021).[1]

The SOP model is laid out in Article 12.8 of the Kyoto Protocol which stipulates that a share of proceeds from CDM projects will be used to fund adaptation in climate-vulnerable developing countries that are party to the Protocol, with a decision taken at the 7th Conference of the Parties (COP) in Marrakech in 2001 to have 2% of CERs issued, excluding those generated in LDCs, to go to the SOP (Ratajczak-Juszko, 2012: 97). In turn, as the Fund's trustee, the World Bank is charged with monetizing and selling the CERs. The choice to rely on an in-kind contribution of CERs to the Adaptation Fund left it particularly vulnerable to price volatility within the international market. While in 2008 the price of CERs

---

[1] While the Protocol's second commitment period ended in 2020, the CDM Executive Board continues to issue CERs from projects that operated during the second period and continue to produce them.

neared €25 per tCO$_2$e, a combination of factors combined to generate a crisis of oversupply in global carbon markets, precipitating a dramatic decline in prices from which the CDM has never recovered (Hoch et al., 2015: 47). Since 2013 at least, the market price for a CER has remained largely under €1 per tCO$_2$e, with the average price across project types at the time of writing €1.51 (Lithgow, 2021b).[2] While low prices are especially troubling with respect to climate change mitigation—in theory, we are told that carbon pricing is intended to make emitting more expensive, thereby incentivizing the move to low- to zero-carbon alternatives—low CER prices posed a significant challenge as well for the Adaptation Fund by depriving it of a stable and reliable source of income. This vulnerability is revealed when the in-kind model of the Adaptation Fund's SOP is compared to the SOP that was used to fund the administrative work of the CDM. Specifically, the administrative SOP which levied a fixed monetary contribution from all CERs issued ($0.10–0.20 per CER), had by mid-2019 generated over $350 million for the CDM's Executive Board (Michaelowa et al., 2019: 3).

While the Adaptation Fund's SOP has thus experienced a severe contraction in the finances it has been able to raise as a result of collapsing CER prices, its ability to generate much-needed adaptation finance from a novel source helped to ensure its carry-over into the Paris Agreement. Article 6 of the Agreement, yet to be finalized at the time of writing, provides language on the voluntary use of market mechanisms by Parties to achieve their emission reduction commitments. Article 6.2 deals with emissions trading between parties, citing the voluntary use of "cooperative approaches" that result in "internationally transferred mitigation outcomes" (ITMOs), or emissions reduction units, that can be bought and sold to legally comply with emission reduction targets under the Paris Agreement, while Article 6.4 deals with carbon offsetting, with additional language stating that it "shall aim… to deliver an overall mitigation in global emissions" (OMGE) (UNFCCC, 2015). The language on OMGE distinguishes Article 6.4 from offsetting under the CDM since, unlike

---

[2] The value of CERs vary by project type. During mid-July 2021, CERs generated from wind projects and recorded by the Ecosecurities International Carbon Offset Index were valued at $.79 per tCO$_2$e, while CERs generated from cookstove projects were valued at $15 per tCO$_2$e (Lithgow, 2021b). In selling CERs for the Adaptation Fund, the World Bank is thus able to take advantage of price differentials to earn above average prices when possible (Michaelowa et al., 2019: 9).

offsetting during the Kyoto era when parties from the Global South lacked emission reduction commitments and were thus participating in Kyoto's infrastructure with no implications for their own targets, under the Paris Agreement all parties have submitted Nationally Determined Contributions (NDCs) that include national emissions reduction targets. The reference to OMGE anticipates the distinct nature of offsetting in a world where all parties must lower emissions versus that of the CDM's in which countries in the Global South were, in theory, simply cancelling out the emissions of their northern counterparts. Under the Paris Agreement, they too must lower their emissions, with offsetting potentially providing an incentive for weaker targets so that excess emissions are available to be sold under Article 6.4. OMGE is intended to safeguard against this, although Article 6 negotiations have proven especially contentious and show the extent to which it may be impossible to realize.

With respect to the SOP, Article 6.6 states:

> The Conference of the Parties serving as the meeting of the Parties to the Paris Agreement shall ensure that a share of the proceeds from activities under the mechanism referred to in paragraph 4 of this Article is used to cover administrative expenses as well as to assist developing country Parties that are particularly vulnerable to the adverse effects of climate change to meet the costs of adaptation.
> (UNFCCC, 2015)

In other words, the language identifies offsetting under Article 6.4 as the mechanism from which the adaptation SOP will be levied. Nevertheless, finalizing the so-called rulebook on Article 6 remains one of the last outstanding items to be addressed under the Paris Agreement, with the issue of the adaptation SOP proving especially contentious. In particular, most negotiating blocks and parties from the Global South, including a group of 100 nations that recently endorsed a *Five-Point Plan for Solidarity, Fairness and Prosperity* in advance of COP26 scheduled for November 2021 in Glasgow, are negotiating to have the adaptation of SOP extended to emissions trading under Article 6.2, while also advocating for a minimum of 5% of all proceeds from market activities to go into it (PSA et al., 2021). Many parties from the Global North, including Canada, Japan, New Zealand and the EU bloc, along with private sector actors with an interest in advancing market mechanisms, including the International Emissions Trading Association (IETA) which represents many fossil fuel interests, heavy emitters and offset developers, are opposed to extending the SOP to Article 6.2, citing Article 6.6 and the fact that it only refers to Article 6.4 for the collection of the SOP.[3] These same parties are non-committal with respect to increasing the SOP to at least 5%, although IETA explicitly argues to maintain a 2% levy, suggesting that an increase in the levy and/or its extension to Article 6.2 would constitute higher fees, thus disincentivizing investment (IETA, 2021). In practice, IETA's role as one of the most influential and powerful business lobbies on issues of climate change mitigation, and one that has been intimately involved in global climate governance, has been to advocate aggressively for a neoliberal and market-based approach to climate governance through the use of carbon markets—this allows its members, including companies like Shell and other fossil fuel majors, to pursue offsetting alongside the continued expansion of oil and gas exploration, infrastructure and production. While IETA is willing to accept the status quo for the adaptation SOP, it is also opposed to supporting policies that would increase the cost of business for its members.

This approach fits in part within the broader approach taken by the Global North to climate finance in general, including that for adaptation, wherein adequate and fair financing has its limits. Observers frequently point to the innovative nature of the CDM's adaptation SOP, with good reason. By placing a levy and CERs issued under the CDM, it provided an opportunity to generate finance for adaptation while rich nations simultaneously resisted committing adequate public funds for this purpose. Funds generated from the SOP are also considered new and additional, ticking an important box for countries in the Global North with respect to the claim that they are genuinely providing new sources of finance separate from other ODA commitments. Moreover, the adaptation SOP identified a way to tap into private sector finance, thereby circumventing conditions wherein the incentive to invest in adaptation is low given the lack of opportunities for profitable returns. Indeed, as the impacts of climate breakdown continue to intensify, along with the costs, it has been strategically necessary for many climate vulnerable nations, confronted

---

[3] A database of party submissions to the UNFCCC regarding Article 6 negotiations can be found on the UNFCCC website. Those dealing with the SOP are available here: https://unfccc.int/process-and-meetings/the-paris-agreement/cooperative-implementation/submissions-informal-technical-expert-dialogues-on-article-6-of-the-paris-agreement#eq-1.

with deeply inadequate financial support for adaptive efforts, to advocate forcefully for the expansion of the SOP model under Article 6 of the Paris Agreement. Moreover, current NDCs to the Paris Agreement remain deeply inadequate, with Carbon Action Tracker predicting that current pledges and targets will lead to an estimated 2.4 °C of warming above pre-industrial levels by the end of the century, with current policies instead leading to a projected 2.9 °C of warming (Climate Action Tracker, 2021). If we are to apply the lessons learned from the history of global climate governance thus far to this analysis, the failure of states to meet their pledges and targets is all too common. Both carbon trading and carbon offsetting thus provide countries lacking in adequate emission reduction policies to nevertheless meet their Paris Agreement targets. Indeed, this is how countries like Canada, still aggressively investing in tar sands oil and related infrastructure, and exceptionally far from meeting its NDC which is ranked as "insufficient" by Carbon Action Tracker (Climate Action Tracker, 2021), can at the same time envision a strategy for meeting its target. Carbon trading and offsetting make it possible.

As such, while the adaptation SOP provides a critical source of finance to climate vulnerable nations, with funds expected to increase as Article 6 activities are operationalized, the conditions that furnish the possibility of carbon offsetting, namely the failure to reduce emissions at the source, cannot be lost in debates on the SOP and in relation to those that seek to frame international negotiations on climate finance, climate breakdown, adaptation, and more, as matters of justice and historical responsibility. As the authors of UNEP's *Adaptation Gap Report 2020* note, "strong mitigation action would significantly reduce unavoidable damage costs, particularly in Africa and Asia, which will bear the brunt of future adaptation impacts" (UNEP, 2021b: xiv). In other words, moving decisively to lower emissions will reduce the climate damages and risks that make adaptation necessary. And yet, carbon offsetting works precisely to provide emitters with an alternative to this kind of aggressive action.

CORE ISSUES IN THE ADAPTATION FINANCE LITERATURE

As noted in the introduction to this chapter, a core question informing the analysis here and first posed by Gifford and Knudson (Gifford & Knudson, 2020: 245), is whether or not "the deployment of finance undermine[s] other climate justice goals?" While technical analyses, and the critical scholarly and policy literature on global carbon offsetting under various mechanisms, including the CDM, Reducing Emissions from Deforestation and Forest Degradation (REDD+) and the global voluntary market for carbon offsets, is now extensive, these literatures, discussed below, when addressed to the theme of climate finance, focus largely on mitigation (Baird & Green, 2020; Ervine, 2014; Gifford, 2020; Newell, 2012). This is to be expected—carbon offsetting and trading were developed as policy tools to address mitigation with global financial flows to fund offset projects officially counted as mitigation finance. Climate justice research on carbon offsetting, particularly in the Global South, has thus tended to focus on project impacts: the threats to land rights; community displacement and/or dispossession; the impacts of resource commodification and privatization on access to livelihood needs; human rights abuses and themes of carbon colonialism as Northern nations shift the responsibility for mitigation onto Southern nations and peoples (Böhm & Dabhi, 2009; Bond, 2012; Bumpus & Liverman, 2011; Lohmann, 2001; Newell & Bumpus, 2012). The link between adaptation finance and carbon offsetting is a subject that has yet to receive significant scholarly attention, meaning that there is a need to examine how adaptation finance, when raised from carbon offsetting, can indeed undermine other climate justice goals.

Roberts et al. (2021), summarize some of the dominant issues and problems associated with global climate finance, and that, by extension, frame many of the existing analyses of adaptation finance. They include the severe inadequacy of current financial flows, the significant flaws in the procedures for classifying what counts as climate finance and that permit diverging classifications on the part of donors, and the fact that climate finance is channelled through upwards of 100 different bodies, with the space for developing nations to democratically direct decisions severely constrained. The latter has significant implications for other key issues, including who should be responsible for providing adaptation finance, how it should be allocated, and whether or not some countries should be prioritized in the disbursement of funds (Ciplet et al., 2013; Khan et al., 2020). While the adaptation finance literature does not examine the role of carbon offsetting as a source of adaptation finance, Khan and et al.'s (2020) discussion of how "neoliberal justice" currently frames adaptation finance under the UNFCCC process is useful in allowing us to think conceptually and theoretically about using carbon offsetting to raise funds globally. According to the authors, an approach to adaptation finance that is rooted in neoliberal justice entails, among other things, a preference for private sector and market-based approaches to securing finance, with an emphasis on private property, self-interest and mutual advantage (Khan et al., 2020: 65, 253). Neoliberal justice is distinct from other forms of justice, including distributive, procedural and compensatory, and that would entail an analysis of the structural roots of inequities and injustices, requiring those largely responsible for climate breakdown to take responsibility and to pay their fair share (Khan et al., 2020: 253).

Levying a share of proceeds from carbon offsets to raise money for the Adaptation Fund illustrates well the dominance of neoliberal justice in the provisioning of adaptation finance globally. At its most basic level, carbon offsetting is a project wherein carbon dioxide is commodified, with the right to own it and thus own "carbon space" within the global atmosphere, determined by one's ability to pay. Inherent to this project, as such, is a particular bias that favours those entities possessing the economic and financial power required to secure the property rights that ownership entails. In this, market-based approaches that seek to commodify nature and thus shape control over and access to the resource in question, are neither neutral nor fair. While this particular approach thus affords significant power to actors historically endowed with wealth and political clout as a result of much longer historical processes of uneven development and the colonial and post-colonial ordering of the world's nations and peoples, and in this case we see this borne out with nations and entities in the Global North as the dominant owners of the carbon space purchased through offsetting, its particular connection to climate finance is rooted in a *quid pro quo* dynamic whereby the delivery of finance is dependent on the purchaser getting something in return—namely, the right to continue emitting. This has been the dynamic established with respect to mitigation finance wherein offset purchases are, in theory, intended to fund a range of mitigation activities throughout the Global South. By tapping into these funds via a share of proceeds from carbon offsetting, mitigation finance is redirected as adaptation finance. In turn, the world's most carbon-intensive nations and business interests can shift some of the burdens for financing into the market, while ensuring that climate policy poses minimal threat to their economic growth and overall profitability. By shining a light on these issues, we are better positioned to interrogate and politicize *sources* of funding in order to reveal the deep entanglements between, and co-constitutive nature of, climate breakdown, the need for adaptation and adaptation finance.

THE PROBLEMS WITH CARBON OFFSETTING

As the discussion above indicates, one of the most problematic aspects of carbon offsetting has to do with the role it plays with respect to mitigating climate breakdown in a severely carbon-constrained world. In its landmark Special Report on limiting warming to 1.5 °C above pre-industrial levels, the Intergovernmental Panel on Climate Change notes that global emissions need to be halved by 2030 and brought down to net zero by 2050 (IPCC, 2018). As discussed in the introduction to this chapter, the International Energy Agency is projecting that energy-related CO_2 emissions in 2021 will increase by 1.5 billion tonnes, the second highest growth rate ever recorded, driven predominantly by an increase in the use of coal, followed by natural gas and oil (IEA, 2021a). Pertinent to the continued growth in fossil fuel demand are the results of IEA modelling, released in May 2021, that show "there is no need for investment in new fossil fuel supply," with new investment inconsistent with staying below 1.5 °C of warming (IEA, 2021b: 21). The report goes on to note that current commitments are well below what is required to achieve this critical goal. Indeed, in its analysis of NDCs under the Paris Agreement, Climate Action Tracker identifies only two countries with plans that are compatible with 1.5 °C—Morocco and The Gambia. A further six have plans compatible with limiting warming to 2 °C, while the vast majority of parties, including all of the world's advanced industrial nations, have plans that are ranked as insufficient, highly insufficient and critically insufficient, and that are consistent with close to 3 °C to over 4 °C of warming (Climate Action Tracker, 2021). In sum, the emissions reductions required of the world's nations are without historical precedent, the world's remaining carbon space is narrowing rapidly, and our emissions continue to grow, driven especially by the continued expansion of fossil fuel energy. The wildfires, floods, catastrophic storms, droughts, heat waves, and more, that are raging across parts of the world and that are growing in intensity, underscore the need for rapid and deep emission reductions. In a world in which all parties under the Paris Agreement have committed to lowering their emissions, and in which the majority of these commitments are severely inadequate to avoid catastrophic levels of climate breakdown, there can be no room for carbon offsetting as a compliance mechanism for nations to meet their targets.

A key problem with carbon offsetting, particularly within the framework of the Paris Agreement, is that it allows nations and heavy emitters to claim that they have complied with their targets and commitments under the Paris Agreement, not by lowering their emissions, but by engaging in a market transaction in which they purchase the right to claim another entity's action as their own. While many of the projects and programmes that qualify to produce carbon offsets are of critical importance—avoiding deforestation, planting trees, renewable energy, provisioning cookstoves and water filtration systems to communities, enhanced agro-ecological systems, and more—and require significant injections of financial support to ensure their success, they are not, by definition, the emission reductions of heavy emitters. This is creative accounting such that the Paris architecture, along with the architecture of the Kyoto Protocol that came before it, allows emitters to report actions and log reductions that have not in fact occurred. These reductions are then counted under national registries and submitted to the UNFCCC as proof that nations are on track to achieving their Paris targets. By sanctioning carbon offsetting as a compliance mechanism for achieving Paris commitments, transparency, honesty and accountability are lost. Moreover, the deep and aggressive action that is required in line with climate science, while costly, can be delayed, and the burden shifted to some point in the future.

Beyond delayed action, an extensive body of evidence now exists documenting the dangers and failures of carbon offsetting as a mitigation tool. The concept of "additionality" sits at the heart of offsetting, wherein a project must be able to demonstrate that it was additional to what would have happened in the absence of the project, or from a baseline known as the business-as-usual (BAU) scenario. This BAU scenario is thus a prediction of what the future would entail. In this, project developers must demonstrate that emissions would be higher without the project, then quantifying the projected level of emissions reductions. It is the difference between emissions under the BAU scenario versus that of the project that determines the quantity of offsets the project is eligible to generate, in tonnes of CO_2 equivalent. A further aspect of additionality has to do with whether or not projects are likely to occur on their own, or if the carbon finance provided from offsetting is necessary for their implementation and operation. If they are likely to occur on their own, there can be no claim that the project enables climate action beyond the BAU scenario, and thus no basis for awarding offsets to meet compliance obligations. Overall, research has documented the poor environmental integrity of offset projects globally due to the approval of projects that are not additional, due to the incentive to overinflate baselines to earn a higher quantity of offsets, and as a result of market incentives which have facilitated the gaming of the system (Ervine, 2014; Haya et al., 2020).

While offsetting requires the exact quantification of baseline emissions against which projected emissions reductions will be measured, additionality determined and offsets awarded, the process of doing so can be marked by extreme complexity, defying the kind of certainty required to ensure credible emissions reductions have taken place. Complex ecosystems, many of which comprise the *nature-based solutions* that are driving many offset markets globally and which include forests, grasslands, agricultural lands, wetlands and marine environments, are subject to shifting and variable ecosystemic conditions over time as a result of weather patterns, climatic changes, pest infestations, disease and more. Fluctuations in broader structural and systemic forces shape further their use, exploitation and market value over time. These overlapping variables, many of which are becoming more extreme with climate breakdown and are impacting the viability of nature-based projects, severely constrain the possibility for precision in quantifying historical baselines, BAU scenarios into the future and in the absence of the project, and thus projected emissions reductions. Similar complexity affects baseline determinations for projects at the household level—clean cookstoves and water filtration systems for example, both of which displace the exploitation of trees and biomass for cooking and boiling water—since they require determining historical use patterns and ecosystemic variability in order to quantify emissions reductions (Bumpus, 2011; Ervine, 2018: 99–100; Lohmann, 2005).

These complexities are compounded when offset projects require the calculation of equivalencies between different greenhouse gases (GHG) relative to carbon dioxide, the GHG in which offsets are measured. This requires determining the Global Warming Potential (GWP) of different GHGs, including methane, nitrous oxide and hydrofluorocarbons (HFC), dependent on their specific properties and their resident time in the atmosphere (20, 100, or 500 years), and then calculating their heating potential relative to CO_2. For example, if an offsetting project seeks to reduce methane emissions and methane has a GWP of 265 relatives to

CO_2's GWP of one, the project would receive 265 offset credits for each tonne of methane reduced. It is noteworthy that GWP values from the IPCC, published in its seminal Assessment Reports and used in offsetting systems globally, have been consistently revised from one report to the next, meaning that the number of offsets awarded for particular GHGs has changed over time. For example, the GWP of nitrous oxide over a 100-year time horizon was revised downwards, from 310 in the IPCC's Second Assessment Report (1996), to 298 in its Fourth Assessment Report (2007), to 265 in its Fifth Assessment Report (2014). For HFC-23 the IPCC GWP revisions for the same years went from 11,700, to 14,800, to 12,400, respectively. Both nitrous oxide and HFC-23 offsetting projects produced a significant share of offsets under the CDM, with awarded offsets thus inconsistent depending on the year in question (Ervine, 2018: 93–96).

By allowing for significant imprecision in the development of historical baselines and BAU scenarios within a context of financial motivation, the complexity that marks carbon offsetting has necessarily produced an overabundance of projects globally within which baselines are overinflated and/or activities undertaken that would not have happened otherwise. An EU-commissioned report published in 2016 examined the issue of additionality and environmental integrity with respect to the CDM. As the largest historical purchaser of CERs under the Kyoto Protocol, with over 1.4 billion purchased up to 2017 to legally comply with Kyoto emission reduction targets, the EU's experience with offsets provides crucial lessons. Among the most significant findings detailed in the report were figures estimating that 85% of CDM projects reviewed and 73% of the CERs available between 2013 and 2020 had a "low likelihood" of being additional and not over-estimated (Cames et al., 2016: 11). In turn, the report estimated that only two per cent of reviewed projects and seven per cent of available CERs over the same period had a "high likelihood" of providing emission reductions and of not being over-estimated (Cames et al., 2016: 11). The overall conclusion was that the CDM had "fundamental flaws in terms of overall environmental integrity" (Cames et al., 2016: 11). Another report that analysed Joint Implementation, an additional carbon offsetting mechanism under the Kyoto Protocol with projects concentrated largely in countries with economies in transition, drew similar conclusions. It analysed projects under Kyoto's first commitment period, finding that approximately 75% of the offsets produced did not entail additional emission reductions, meaning that global emissions were potentially 600 million metric tons higher than a scenario in which purchasing nations had reduced their emissions at the source (Kollmuss et al., 2015). A 2019 policy brief that examined forestry offsetting which supplied 80% of all offsets in California's Cap-and-Trade Program found that, as a result of lenient accounting methods, 82% of the offset credits analysed were unlikely to represent "true" emissions reductions, leading to the over-crediting of approximately 80 million tons of CO_2 (Haya, 2019). Additional global studies on forestry-related carbon offsetting have drawn similar conclusions in terms of the tendency to overinflate baselines and thus over-credit projects (Scott et al., 2016; West et al., 2020). In each of these cases, a critical problem with carbon offsetting is revealed beyond that of delayed action discussed above. Specifically, even if an offset lacks environmental integrity, if it is counted towards a nation's emissions reduction commitments, an absolute increase in global emissions follows. This is referred to as "hot air"—offsets that do not represent real emissions reductions but make their way into markets to then be counted as actual emissions reductions. Since the offsets are counted and accepted under the UNFCCC or other jurisdictional systems as real emissions reductions, no official record of this will ever exist to suggest otherwise. On the other hand, the increased levels of CO_2 in the atmosphere will continue to heat the planet, requiring in turn ever greater levels of adaptation.

It is projected that in the years to come the market for carbon offsetting globally is set to expand as parties use offsets to comply with their NDCs under the Paris Agreement. Carbon offsetting via nature-based solutions is the focus of growing interest within this context, with many pointing to the critical role of natural ecosystems in sequestering carbon while simultaneously enhancing and protecting global biodiversity. While the protection and enhancement of natural ecosystems are imperative to addressing multiple and overlapping ecological crises, nature-based offsetting poses particular risks that are worth flagging here. It was based on the uncertainty and complexity associated with natural ecosystems, discussed above, that the EU forbid the purchase of forestry-related offsets to be used to meet emission reduction commitments under the Kyoto Protocol, citing the significant risk that the environmental integrity of forestry-related offsets could not be assured. Forestry-related offsetting suffers from a number of problems, each of which holds lessons for nature-based offsetting more broadly. These include the issue of carbon leakage whereby deforestation, rather than declining with the initiation of an offsetting project, simply shifts to other locations or jurisdictions not covered by the project (Haya, 2019). Indeed, in the absence of strategies to structurally address global demand for forestry products, the risk of forestry offsets sanctioning the overall increase in global emissions is especially acute. The impermanence of trees further undermines the reliability of forestry-based offsets, something illustrated dramatically by devastating forest fires around the world, many of which have directly affected offsetting projects (Kahn, 2021; Lithgow, 2021a; Pontecorvo & Osaka, 2020; Song & Moura, 2019). Even more troubling, recent research has confirmed that the Amazon rainforest, famed for its significant biodiversity and carbon-storing capacity, has now become a net source of carbon dioxide. This is in part a result of climate change induced drought and heat which is undermining the ability of trees to sequester CO_2 (Gatti et al., 2021). This problem is not limited to the Amazon, with recent heatwaves and droughts in western North America underscoring how climate breakdown diminishes the carbon-storing capacity of ecosystems (Coffield et al., 2021). As natural ecosystems are themselves being transformed by a changing climate, plans to extensively expand nature-based offsets in place of emissions reductions at the source thus carry with them significant risks and cannot be relied upon to provide reliable climate solutions into the future.

In concluding this discussion, it is important to consider the source of CO_2 and the difference between terrestrial CO_2 and that associated with fossil fuel extraction, production and combustion. Fossil fuel-related CO_2, prior to extraction, remains locked away within the earth's geological system. Because it is locked away, it cannot circulate in our atmosphere unless extraction occurs—precisely what the IEA says is not necessary on the path to net zero. Carbon offsetting, however, licenses the continued extraction of fossil fuels, and thus the addition of *new* stocks of CO_2 to the atmosphere, thus hastening its warming. Furthermore, forestry- and nature-based carbon offsetting assumes a false equivalency between fossil carbon and terrestrial ecosystems, implying that the capacity exists within global ecosystems to absorb ever-increasing levels of new CO_2 as a result of fossil fuel extraction and burning (Dooley, 2014). The scientific research confirms that this is not possible, with climate breakdown further diminishing the capacity of terrestrial ecosystems to function as reliable carbon sinks. It is thus that the imperative to lower emissions at the source and to aggressively shift away from the use of fossil fuels is more pressing than ever. Not only does offsetting delay this shift, but it also provides a green light for continued exploration, extraction and burning. The rush by fossil fuel companies to purchase offsets and to provide "carbon neutral" products wherein customers can buy their oil and gas, for example, with offsets "neutralizing" their impact (Gardner et al., 2021; Reklev, 2021), illustrates well the profound dangers of using carbon offsetting as a mitigation strategy.

Justice in Adaptation Finance

The track record on adaptation finance is one of deep failure wherein those nations and actors historically responsible for climate breakdown have avoided taking responsibility for its consequences. Developing and climate vulnerable nations are experiencing climate emergencies with increased frequency, while possessing insufficient resources to adapt to the magnitude of the problem, let alone the loss and damage associated with severe climate events. As these crises progress, debating the source of adaptation finance appears less pressing than securing funds to meet the immediate and growing needs of populations impacted by climate breakdown. As this chapter has shown; however, there is a deep indignity associated with requiring nations and peoples to accept finance that has been generated from projects and mechanisms designed precisely to allow emitters to avoid making emission reductions at the source. The share of proceeds model is innovative and offers lessons for how finance might be generated, but it must be detached from carbon offsetting.

As catastrophic climate-related events continue to unfold around the globe, the appetite for truly innovative financing mechanisms may be growing. To this end, applying carbon levies on international shipping and international aviation; applying a polluter pays tax on fossil fuel companies; eliminating fossil fuel subsidies and redirecting funds to climate finance and implementing a global financial transaction tax, represent a small sample of where financial resources exist that could be tapped into. Admittedly, these are the types of interventions that strike at existing power relations and that will entail significant political battles, but the space for business as usual is rapidly disappearing. If justice in adaptation finance is to be achieved, it is time to demand that rather than enabling the current system to persist, the share of proceeds model must itself work to bring an end to the era of fossil fuels.

References

Badgley, G., et al. (2021). *Systematic over-crediting in California's forest carbon offsets program.* Cold Spring Harbor Laboratory.

Baird, I. G., & Green, W. N. (2020). The Clean development mechanism and large dam development: Contradictions associated with climate financing in Cambodia. *Climatic Change, 161*(2), 365–383.

Bassett, T. J., & Fogelman, C. (2013). Déjà vu or something new? The adaptation concept in the climate change literature. *Geoforum, 48*, 42–53.

Böhm, S., & Dabhi, S. (Eds.). (2009). *Upsetting the offset: The political economy of carbon markets.* May Fly Books.

Bond, P. (2012). Emissions trading, new enclosures and eco-social contestation. *Antipode, 44*(3), 684–701.

Bumpus, A. (2011). The matter of carbon: Understanding the materiality of tCO2e in carbon offsets. *Antipode, 43*(3), 612–638.

Bumpus, A., & Liverman, D. (2011). Carbon colonialism? Offsets, greenhouse gas reductions, and sustainable development. In R. Peet, P. Robbins & M. J. Watts (Eds.), *Global political ecology,* (pp. 203–224). Routledge.

Cames, M., et al. (2016). *How additional is the clean development mechanism? Analysis of the application of current tools and proposed alternatives.'* Prepared for DG CLIMA.

Care International. (2021a). *Hollow commitments: An analysis of developed countries' climate finance plans.* CARE International.

Care International. (2021b). *Climate adaptation finance: Fact or fiction?* (CARE International).

Ciplet, D., Roberts, J. T., & Khan, M. (2013). The politics of international climate adaptation funding: Justice and divisions in the greenhouse. *Global Environmental Politics, 13*(1), 49–68.

Climate Action Tracker. (2021). *Global Update: Climate Summit Momentum.* https://climateactiontracker.org/publications/global-update-climate-summit-momentum/. Accessed May 13.

Coffield, S. R., et al. (2021). Climate-driven limits to future carbon storage in California's Wildland ecosystems. *AGU Advances, 2*(3).

Cullenward, D., & Victor, D. G. (2020). *Making climate policy work.* Polity.

Dooley, K. (2014). *'Misleading numbers: The case for separating land and fossil based carbon emissions.'* In FERN (Ed.). FERN.

Eriksen, S., et al. (2021). Adaptation interventions and their effect on vulnerability in developing countries: Help, hindrance or irrelevance? *World Development, 141,* 105383.

Eriksen, S. H., Nightingale, A. J., & Eakin, H. (2015). Reframing adaptation: The political nature of climate change adaptation. *Global Environmental Change, 35*, 523–533.

Ervine, K. (2014). Diminishing returns: Carbon market crisis and the future of market-dependent climate change finance. *New Political Economy, 19*(5), 723–747.
Ervine, K. (2018). *Carbon*. Polity.
Fearnehough, H., et al. (2021), *Analysis of options for determining OMGE, SOP and Transition within Article 6: Implications of policy decisions for international crediting under the Paris Agreement.*
Gardner, T., Adomaitis, N., & Nickel, R. (2021). Clean crude? Oil firms use offsets to claim green barrels. *Reuters*. https://www.reuters.com/article/climatechange-fossilfuels-offsets-insigh/clean-crude-oil-firms-use-offsets-to-claim-green-barrels-idINKBN2C31AO
Gatti, L. V., et al. (2021). Amazonia as a carbon source linked to deforestation and climate change. *Nature, 595*(7867), 388–393.
Gifford, L. (2020). You can't value what you can't measure: A critical look at forest carbon accounting. *Climatic Change, 161*(2), 291–306.
Gifford, L., & Knudson, C. (2020). Climate finance justice: International perspectives on climate policy, social justice, and capital. *Climatic Change, 161*(2), 243–249.
Gleckman, H. (2018). *Multistakeholder governance and democracy: A global challenge*. Routledge.
Haya, B. (2019). *The California air resources board's U.S. forest offset protocol underestimates leakage*. University of California.
Haya, B., et al. (2020). Managing uncertainty in carbon offsets: Insights from California's standardized approach. *Climate Policy, 20*(9), 1112–1126.
Hoch, S., et al. (2015). *Methodology for CDM eligibility criteria definition*. Perspectives GmbH.
Hornborg, A. (2019). *Nature, society, and justice in the anthropocene: Unraveling the money-energy-technology complex*. Cambridge University Press.
IEA Global carbon dioxide emissions are set for their second-biggest increase in history—News—IEA. (2021a). https://www.iea.org/news/global-carbon-dioxide-emissions-are-set-for-their-second-biggest-increase-in-history
IEA. (2021b). *Net Zero by 2050: A roadmap for the global energy sector.*
IETA. (2021). *IETA's input on financing for adaptation and the share of proceeds under Article 6 of the Paris agreement.*
IPCC. (2018). *Global warming of 1.5 °C: An IPCC special report on the impacts of global warming of 1.5°C above pre-industrial levels and related global greenhouse gas emission pathways, in the context of strengthening the global response to the threat of climate change, sustainable development, and efforts to eradicate poverty.*

Kahn, D. (2021). Wildfires rage and a tool to combat climate change goes up in smoke. *Politico.* https://www.politico.com/news/2021/07/27/wildfires-rage-carbon-credits-500830?nname=the-long-game&nid=00000171-5b34-d92d-a5ff-db3ee8890000&nrid=00000170-7960-d847-a5f1-f9e047f70000&nlid=2672637&fbclid=IwAR1UYDp5boegq13G_CYOc9T0cJtdh52aujGSaKhshSV5IIMyu5EQ_MNk64U

Khan, M., et al. (2020). Twenty-five years of adaptation finance through a climate justice lens. *Climatic Change, 161*(2), 251–269.

Kollmuss, A., Schneider, L., & Zhezherin, V. (2015). Has joint implementation reduced GHG emissions? Lessons learned for the design of carbon market mechanisms. *SEI Policy Brief*. Stockholm Environment Institute.

Lithgow, M. (2021a). Washington fire torches second-largest California offset project. *Carbon Pulse.* https://carbon-pulse.com/134578/

Lithgow, M. (2021b). VCM Report: VER issuances, retirements blossom in Q2 as prices increase further. *Carbon Pulse.* https://carbon-pulse.com/133518/. Accessed July 16, 2021.

Lohmann, L. (2001). The dyson effect: Carbon "offset" forestry and the privatisation of the atmosphere. *International Journal of Environment and Pollution, 15*(1), 51–78.

Lohmann, L. (2005). Marketing and making carbon dumps: Commodification, calculation and counterfactuals in climate change mitigation. *Science as Culture, 14*(3), 203–235.

Michaelowa, A., et al. (2019). *Operationalizing the share of proceeds for Article 6.* Climate Finance Innovators.

Michaelowa, A. (Ed.). (2012). *Carbon markets or climate finance? Low carbon and adaptation investment choices for the developing world.* Routledge.

Newell, P. (2012). The political economy of carbon markets: The CDM and other stories. *Climate Policy, 12*(1), 135–139.

Newell, P., & Bumpus, A. (2012). The political ecology of the clean development mechanism. *Global Environmental Politics, 12*(4), 49–67.

Nightingale, A. J., et al. (2020). Beyond technical fixes: Climate solutions and the great derangement. *Climate and Development, 12*(4), 343–352.

NOAA. (2021). *Despite pandemic shutdowns, carbon dioxide and methane surged in 2020—Welcome to NOAA Research.* https://research.noaa.gov/article/ArtMID/587/ArticleID/2742/Despite-pandemic-shutdowns-carbon-dioxide-and-methane-surged-in-2020. Accessed May 13.

OECD. (2020). *Climate finance provided and mobilised by developed countries in 2013–2018.* OECD.

Oxfam. (2020). *Climate finance shadow report 2020.* Oxfam.

Pontecorvo, E., & Osaka, S. (2020). This Oregon forest was supposed to store carbon for 100 years. Now it's on fire. *Grist.* https://grist.org/climate/this-oregon-forest-was-supposed-to-store-carbon-for-100-years-now-its-on-fire/

Power Shift Africa (PSA), ACT 2025 consortium & institute for climate and sustainable cities. (2021). *COP 26 delivering the Paris agreement: A five-point plan for solidarity, fairness and prosperity.* Accessed 8 July 2022. https://climatenetwork.org/resource/cop26-five-point-plan-for-solidarity-fairness-and-prosperity/

Ratajczak-Juszko, I. (2012). The adaptation fund: Towards resilient economies in the developing world. In A. Michaelowa (Ed.), *Carbon markets or climate finance: Low carbon and adaptation investment choices for the developing world*, (pp. 92–116). Routledge.

Reklev, S. (2021). Oil and gas majors stoke Australian offset demand, analysts say. *Carbon Pulse.* https://carbon-pulse.com/135048/

Roberts, J. T., et al. (2021). Rebooting a failed promise of climate finance. *Nature Climate Change, 11*(3), 180–182.

Scott, D., et al. (2016). The 'virtual economy' of REDD+ Projects: Does private certification of REDD+ Projects ensure their environmental integrity?. *International Forestry Review, 18,* 231–246.

Song, L., & Moura, P. (2019). If carbon offsets require forests to stay standing, what happens when the Amazon is on fire? *ProPublica.* https://www.propublica.org/article/if-carbon-offsets-require-forests-to-stay-standing-what-happens-when-the-amazon-is-on-fire

Swyngedouw, E. (2010). Apocalypse forever? Post-political populism and the spectre of climate change. *Theory, Culture & Society, 27*(2–3), 213–232.

Swyngedouw, E., & Wilson, J. (Eds.). (2014). *The post-political and its discontents: Spaces of depoliticisation, spectres of radical politics.* Edinburgh University.

Taylor, M. (2015). *The political ecology of climate change adaptation: Livelihoods, agrarian change and the conflicts of development.* Routledge.

UNEP. (2019). *Emissions gap report 2019.* UNEP.

UNEP. (2021a). *Cut global emissions by 7.6 percent every year for next decade to meet 1.5°C Paris target—UN report.* http://www.unep.org/news-and-stories/press-release/cut-global-emissions-76-percent-every-year-next-decade-meet-15degc. Accessed May 13.

UNEP. (2021b). *Adaptation Gap Report 2020.* Nairobi.

UNFCCC. (2015). *Paris agreement to the United Nations framework convention on climate change.* In UNFCCC (Ed.).

UNFCCC. (2021). *Issuance certified emission reductions.* https://cdm.unfccc.int/Issuance/cers_iss.html. Accessed July 16.

West, T. A. P., et al. (2020). Overstated carbon emission reductions from voluntary REDD+ projects in the Brazilian Amazon. *Proceedings of the National Academy of Sciences, 117*(39), 24188–24194.

World Bank. (2021). *Financial intermediary funds—Adaptation Fund.* https://fiftrustee.worldbank.org/en/about/unit/dfi/fiftrustee/fund-detail/adapt#1. Accessed July 16.

CHAPTER 8

Climate Finance and Neo-colonialism: Exposing Hidden Dynamics

Rebecca Navarro

INTRODUCTION

Carbon markets have become an attractive tool for policymakers and businesses to help mitigate climate change despite their shortcomings, which have been extensively unveiled in the last several years (Forest Trends Ecosystem Marketplace, 2021). Within the last ten years, voluntary carbon markets have experienced a shift from renewable energy-dominated to forest and land-use projects, reaching 55% of the market volume (Forest Trends Ecosystem Marketplace, 2019). This shift is due to the buyers' preferences, which opt for projects beyond simple emission reductions, seeking positive social and biodiversity impacts. Forest Trends Ecosystem Marketplace (2019) also reports the remarkable increase in transactions tied to the distribution of clean-burning cookstoves, which reflect the buyers seeking positive social co-benefits from

---

R. Navarro (✉)
Bonn International Centre for Conflict Studies (BICC), Bonn, Germany
e-mail: rebecca.navarro@bicc.de

© The Author(s), under exclusive license to Springer Nature Switzerland AG 2022
C. Cash and L. A. Swatuk (eds.), *The Political Economy of Climate Finance: Lessons from International Development*, International Political Economy Series, https://doi.org/10.1007/978-3-031-12619-2_8

climate change mitigation. As new actors appear, control mechanisms for appropriate quality standards in carbon trading are challenged, which further threatens carbon credits' credibility, and thereby their legitimacy (Kreibich & Hermwille, 2021).

Often presented as a win–win situation, where carbon offsetting in countries of the Global South creates revenues for poor communities while saving the planet, climate finance is not only the ticket for Global North players to keep their business as usual, but a form of imposing neoliberal environmental governance, and hereby perpetuating neocolonial patterns (Peluso & Lund, 2011). These can reach from physical land grabs (Mariki et al., 2015) to subtle forms of instrumentalization and manipulation (Carton, 2020), through the establishment of capitalist structures and the Western commodity culture (Paterson, 2010), and in a broader sense, through the imposition of Eurocentric knowledge (Heleta, 2018).

In this chapter, a historical perspective of carbon markets covering their evolution and adaptation to emerging criticism is presented, which is crucial to understanding the development and establishment of the existing diversity among actors, commodities and colonial legacies. The introduction of different case studies from previous research further aims to provide insight into the manifold forms of manifestation of neocolonial patterns caused by environmental governance. Finally, different solutions, top-down and bottom-up, are discussed based on findings from the current literature.

Monetizing the Environment: A Historical Perspective on Nature Conservation and Its Implications on Legitimizing Climate Action in the Global South

The legitimacy of carbon markets and their actors are constructed through discourses and narratives, ideas, norms and language (Blum & Lövbrand, 2019), which again are shaped by historical processes, which are a starting point to legitimize players in their actions (Holmes, 2014). Reviewing the history of (Western) conservation of the environment reveals how different discourses have changed the value of nature through time. At the turn of the millennium, the focus moved from romanticized conservation originated in the eighteenth century, which separated nature from culture (Plamper, 1998) to protecting ecosystem functions relevant to humans, so-called ecosystem services (Cadotte et al., 2011; Cardinale et al., 2012). This anthropocentric shift gave nature conservancy a quantifiable value, introducing it into the capitalist system (Sullivan, 2010). At the same time, local communities, Indigenous peoples, which so far had been separated from their nature for conservation purposes, dispossessed by violence, started being considered through the concept of community-based conservation (Colchester, 2004).

Almost in parallel, the concept of sustainable development emerged, which for the first time addressed the need for integrating economic development, environmental protection and social justice and inclusion (Whitfield, 2015). Through the intervention of development work, the damage caused by the colonial era was to be repaired on the one hand, and at the same time, progress (in the sense of Western perception) was to be ensured (Osborn et al., 2015). This can be seen as a mechanism that enables a foothold in the target region through conservation and prepares the terrain for later accumulation through expropriation (Adams, 2020). In this way, Western concepts of nature conservation were adopted in the Global South and thereby also increasingly legitimized, through arguments of "ecological modernization", whereby Indigenous peoples are *educated* and prevented from destroying their resources (Fairhead et al., 2012).

These processes, together with the increasingly thematized global climate crisis affecting ubiquitously all ecosystems, helped set the stage to develop carbon emission trading. Carbon market mechanisms were conceptualized through the Kyoto Protocol in 1997 and adopted in 2005 (Lederer, 2012). The main aim was to limit countries' Greenhouse Gases (GHGs) emissions by setting global emission caps, in the first instance on industrialized countries, the main ones responsible for most of the global emissions (Grubb, 2004). However, instead of reducing emissions by mitigation, emissions acquired economic value and became tradable assets, an idea grounded in the Global North's commodity culture.

The Kyoto Protocol enabled different types of mechanisms for carbon trading, among which the Clean Development Mechanism (CDM) consisted in investing in countries without emissions reduction obligations, mostly located in the Global South, which would allow sustainable development while mitigating climate change. While CDM has made different actors invest in thousands of sustainable projects presumably improving the living standards of people in countries hosting climate compensating measures (UNFCCC, 2018), many authors also highlight the aspect of Western hegemony being perpetuated through new dependencies and its capitalistic nature (Bachram, 2004; Mcafee, 2015). Hereby, the logic of carbon offsetting allows rich states and privileged actors to offset their "carbon indulgences" and continue business as usual (Smith et al., 2007). Nonstate actors also played an important role in carbon markets. The voluntary carbon market perceived higher demand as the reputation of the CDM decreased and the financial crisis hit carbon market prices into the ground (Forest Trends Ecosystem Lane & Newell, 2018; Marketplace, 2019; World Bank, 2015).

Nonstate actors such as private companies, NGOs and individuals are embedded in voluntary carbon markets (Hamrick & Gallant, 2017), which are ruled by voluntary standards and have a greater focus on sustainability than CDM projects (Lovell, 2010). They created however a regulatory uncertainty due to the mixture of public and private authorities included in governing climate change (Green, 2013). The diversity of actors makes both impact evaluation and quality assessment of the offsets difficult. Affected by similar legitimacy problems, voluntary carbon standards compete for their clients' acceptance and their usefulness for private actors (Merger & Pistorius, 2011).

Setting emission caps only on Global North countries under the Kyoto Protocol, allowed buying carbon emission reductions (CERs) from countries without emission caps, relying on the project developer's hypothetical assumption of a certain baseline scenario to justify its implementation, and having clear incentives for over-estimating emissions reductions (Badgley et al., 2022; Fowlie, 2019, 2021; Schneider, 2009). This was taken into account when elaborating on the Paris Agreement in 2015. The Paris Agreement requires all countries to reduce emissions by defining their Nationally Determined Contributions (NDCs) (UNFCCC, 2016), whereby, the delayed emission peak of developing countries is reasonably taken into consideration (UNFCCC, 2019). However, there is no legal obligation to achieve the mitigation targets (Oberthür & Bodle, 2016). While at first, under Kyoto, a small share of Parties had to fulfill legally binding mitigation targets, the large share of "uncapped environment" (Kreibich & Hermwille, 2021) was available for unlimited carbon finance projects. Under the Paris Regime, this mandatory top-down format has been substituted by a more facilitative regime, with non-state actors' "collaborative action, voluntary commitments, win–win solutions, and synergies" (Marquardt et al., 2022). While they play a decisive role in advancing state commitments (UNEP, 2019), the "constructive ambiguity" of Article 6 of the Paris Agreement (Müller & Michaelowa, 2019; Schneider & La Hoz Theuer, 2019) has nurtured accountability problems (Streck, 2020) threatening its effectivity (Chan et al., 2016) and thus its legitimation (Blum & Lövbrand, 2019).

Marquardt et al. (2022) highlight the following risks of non-state actors as "co-optation, tokenization, the substitution of state action, and the depoliticization of the climate issue". Belfer et al. (2019) suggest that this multi-actor movement disguises the self-determination of Indigenous peoples, who will not only be disproportionately affected by climate change (Whyte, 2020) but also by unilateral environmental governance itself, as it perpetuates colonial practices (Cavanagh & Benjaminsen, 2014; Leach et al., 2012). Acknowledging these challenges, mechanisms to involve Indigenous voices within the United Nations Framework on Climate Change (UNFCCC) have been developed and gradually adapted seeking constant improvement. However, as Belfer et al. (2019) conclude, "acknowledgment is not enough to advance fuller participation"; there are still material, procedural and recognition-based constraints that need to be addressed.

Ignoring Indigenous knowledge in environmental governance has further materialized in phenomena captured by the term of "green grabbing". First introduced by the Guardian journalist John Vidal (2008), this concept covers conservation-legitimized interventions in the Global South, which lead to disadvantages for the local population (Fairhead et al., 2012). Environmental markets, under the veil of sustainable development and fuelled by neoliberal globalization (Gardner, 2012) expanded to cheaper land in the developing world. Authors such as Zoomers (2010) speaks here of a foreignization (understood here as outsourcing) of space. There are numerous examples of "carbon colonialism" caused by Western-dominated commodification of forests and natural resources, causing violent land grabs and displacements (Kill, 2015; Lyons & Westoby, 2014). But beyond the physical impact of resource expropriation, the carbon emission trading has further perpetuated a Western-centred definition of development as economic growth, imposing Eurocentric forms of knowledge (as in knowing better how to protect nature), spatial conceptions (as in land rights, imposed in cultures where there is no "ownership" of land) and neo-imperial policies by institutionalizing carbon offsetting initiatives of the Global North in the

Global South, based on the Western commodity culture (Eberle et al., 2019).

All in all, supporters of the "market solution" argue that it will help lower the business costs of transitioning to a post-carbon world, allowing developing countries to circumvent fossil fuel dependency by financing renewable energy solutions (ENTTRANS Consortium, 2008). However, markets are flooded with cheap and dubious offsets, which are further affected by the financial volatility of carbon credits. Despite identifying many loopholes in carbon markets, stakeholders keep seeing them as the main tool for climate change mitigation. Paradoxically, the criticism expressed by carbon market opponents has contributed to helping carbon markets improve their effectiveness (Paterson, 2009). The reasons behind this are the need for legitimizing capitalism, a system that does not benefit all and thus needs to justify itself (Paterson, 2010). From a post-colonial perspective, carbon markets impose climate action on the Global South, stopping developing countries from their development to repair the damage caused by the Global North (Eberle et al., 2019).

The Ubiquitous Nature of Neo-colonialism in Environmental and Climate Action: from Land Grabs to Subtle Forms of Instrumentalization

The most evident forms of green grabbing have been addressed in studies where local communities were evicted from previously public land in order to implement conservation projects, financed by foreign investing entities. However, there are other more subtle forms of perpetuating neocolonial patterns, that do not necessarily require a physical land grab. Green grabbing also may involve instrumentalization of Indigenous communities, an intrusion into local socio-ecological practices, that are erased for the sake of environmental purposes. In both cases, Eurocentric values and power structures are imposed. In order to provide insight into the discursive extensions of what green grabs can be, a selection of case studies are presented, where different forms of Western hegemonic relations are perpetuated for implementing neoliberal environmental action.

The first is a clear example of green grabbing as in resource competition, while the second and third are more subtle forms of imposing

Western supremacy through emission markets. All are examples of capitalization of the environment, where the purpose of investors, articulated through their Western mentality, is superimposed on the real needs of the local communities. Furthermore, both exemplify the ubiquitous nature of neo-colonialism in environmental and climate action, which are essential to address if we are to decolonize environmental action and find appropriate solutions.

Case Study 1: Wildlife Paradise Tanzania

The implementation of the ivory ban in 1989 led to an increase in elephant populations across much of the African continent. According to Thouless et al. (2016), Eastern Africa is home to approximately 20% of the continental herd. Elephant and other 'charismatic megafauna' were to be further accommodated by increasing their rangeland through the development of migratory corridors, transfrontier parks and so on. Protected and conserved land comprises 56.4% of Tanzania's total land area. This is equal to more than 362,000 km^2—a land area larger than all of Germany (IUCN, 2020: 132; World Bank, 2021). An increasing number of protected areas in West Kilimanjaro drove large parts of the Indigenous Maasai out of the forests, and their habitats. This was legitimated by the idea of ecological modernization, which aimed at preventing the local population from using up or destroying their own resources. The implementing actors were external to the local communities, including the Wildlife Division and the Tanzania National Parks (TANAPA), wildlife-based tourism investors and international conservation organizations, such as the African Wildlife Foundation (AWF), mostly funded by USAID. Increasing nature conservation was supposed to increase the attractiveness of the location for tourists, and thus create new jobs in the sector, while at the same time further financing nature conservation.

This led, however, to important evictions of other local Indigenous communities, including 'small-scale farmers who are of Wachagga, Wameru, Waarusha, Wasafa and other ethnicities'. These people were neither paid nor got offered new jobs, as previously promised (Mariki et al., 2015). The 30,000 people who were displaced from the forests of West Kilimanjaro in 2007 were concentrated in the only remaining free space between the newly established protected areas. The displaced population fled to the villages located between the protected areas and found themselves in what was later to be declared a wildlife corridor. Thus, the entire habitat of the Indigenous Maasai was converted for conservation purposes and they were neither involved nor compensated.

Additionally, in 2009, one of the most severe droughts in recent decades had affected Tanzania. The elephants, which can consume about 100–300 kg of greens in a day, set out in search of water and food, and promptly entered the agricultural areas of the reclusive people between the protected areas, where they came across vegetable patches and water sources. In total, the elephants devastated 360 ha and destroyed all water pipes. The affected people had to go in search of water and travel several miles. In the process, they were attacked by another herd of elephants, causing people to be injured and even die. These kinds of incidents had occurred more frequently before, so the inhabitants of the attacked villages had already been looking for solutions. After all the measures taken by the population had failed, and no compensation was paid by the government either, the last and only solution came about, which consisted in using torches to chase the elephants into a gorge where six died (Mariki et al., 2015).

The authors characterize the case of wildlife killing as a militant form of implicit everyday resistance to conservancy, organized through informal networks, by those "who suffer the costs of conservation and who do not have the ability to circumvent the system" otherwise. On the other hand, Mariki et al. (2015) identify this resistance as a response to the 'slow violence' (Nixon, 2013) that is caused by establishing areas for environmental protection thereby dispossessing local populations of their habitats.

This multi-year study showcased how local people were not only evicted from their actual habitat in the name of conservancy but also had to compete for resources with the growing number of (protected) elephants. Perceiving conservation measures as unjust and their livelihoods threatened led them to kill elephants. This act of resistance led to the local governments and responsible entities to adopt measures to improve elephant control and postponed the establishment of the planned wildlife corridor.

According to Mariki et al. (2015), the participation and input of the population in the conservation measures was hardly documented at all, and from the study conducted over the years, a feeling of unfair treatment on the part of the residents was perceived. They felt less relevant than the conservation measures, according to the statements from the interviews conducted there. The originally intended win–win situation thus turned out to be a power imbalance in which only those who make the big investments were heard, in this case meaning the tourism companies and conservation organizations financed by foreign sponsors. The study clearly showcases the perpetuation of Western hegemony through the implementation of the capitalistic logic with foreign investments, combined with the propagation of concepts of nature conservation from the Global North, which further neglect local people's needs and traditions. While this case study is a clear example of a physical land grab, it also entails the cultural dimension of preserving Western superiority through the imposition of Western knowledge as more valuable than local and traditional practices.

Case Study 2: Pyrolysis Stoves for Africa—And the Climate Purse

Besides tree planting and increased efforts in biodiversity conservation and environmental protection, carbon trading also has motivated the development of innovative technologies for climate change mitigation. These can furthermore serve as a tool for achieving sustainable development goals (SDGs) and are thus often allocated in regions of the Global South. Agriculture, as one of the biggest contributors to greenhouse gas emissions, but also one of the most vulnerable sectors to the impacts of climate change, particularly in countries from the Global South, has been recently targeted by climate finance initiatives. Models such as climate-smart agriculture (CSA) have emerged, where innovative technologies aim to bring together food security through climate change adaptation, and mitigation, often financed by emission trading (Richards et al., 2016).

However, as seen before, introducing concepts from the Global North to the Global South can become an intrusion in the sense of imposing new values which undermine local communities' traditions and knowledge forms. When introducing technologies, it is further important to evaluate whether new dependencies are created, motivated by profit, but also for the mere sake of climate compensation, disregarding the long-term impacts on Indigenous peoples of the country targeted for such measures.

One recently very popular technology promoted through climate finance is pyrolysis stoves, which can burn biomass under oxygen-deprived conditions, creating biochar. While recycling agricultural waste, biochar can improve the retention and plant availability of nutrients and water (Razzaghi et al., 2020). The introduction of sophisticated pyrolysis stoves into small farming communities thus allows for saving both wood, needed for cooking, and further protects surrounding forests, since it can use agricultural waste material. Also, cooking smoke and indoor air pollution can be reduced, improving women's health while contributing to climate change mitigation and protecting the environment.

There has been an increasing interest in making the production and application of biochar, which is originally from the Amazon basin, known as *terra preta* or anthropogenic dark earths (ADEs), transferable to other locations, in particular to Africa. This traditional form of soil enrichment cannot improve soil fertility but can also store carbon in the ground for thousands of years (Kuzyakov et al., 2009). It thus has been recently included as a promising negative emissions technology (NET) by the Intergovernmental Panel on Climate Change (IPCC) in the Special Report on Global Warming of 1.5 °C (IPCC, 2022), and started to being listed on voluntary carbon marketplaces (Biochar International, 2021). Thus, it is hypothesized that widespread adoption of these technologies can help promote rural development through the creation of new sources of income from carbon credits and local energy production (Lehmann & Joseph, 2021).

However, to make a significant contribution to carbon sequestration (The Royal Society, 2009), large-scale biochar projects would be necessary, involving technologies unaffordable to most farmers. Furthermore, large-scale biochar production can lead to land grabs by establishing plantations destined to grow feedstock, competing for resources and reproducing controversies around "biofuels vs. food" (Borras, 2010). Many biochar advocates recommend small-scale systems since they are "expected to have a greater positive impact on the diversity of farm management practices and on income than a large scale system would" (Müller et al., 2019). However, as Leach et al. (2012) argue, the high number of small-scale initiatives necessary to reach a comparable level of carbon removals requires creating a reductionist concept of biochar. This standardization is needed to allow cost-effectively reproducing technological implementation (Kochanek et al., 2022). The creation of such a marketable commodity aims to compress the complexity of biochar itself to quantify the carbon benefits within a certification system. However, while carbon sequestration potential can vary depending on feedstock, pyrolysis and post-pyrolysis conditions, and application methods (Camps-Arbestain et al., 2015), these can also affect crop yields, both positively and negatively (Crane-Droesch et al., 2013). Additionally, local pre-existing cropping practices may involve important adaptation barriers to the adoption of biochar technologies (Jeffery et al., 2015). Müller et al. (2019) conclude that biochar systems implementation need to consider place-specific characteristics, beyond physical or economic feasibility, such as "social and cultural conditions, characteristics, and dynamics". The authors define essential "livelihood assets" such as organic waste, capital, farm management, labour and trust, but also accessibility to them, that influence the success of introducing such technology. Biochar, sold as the multiple-win solution in sustainable development, can also have negative effects, such as priming of soil organic matter (Cross & Sohi, 2011) or introducing new contaminants into the soil (Chan & Xu, 2009). As Jeffery et al. (2015) claim, the longevity of biochar, may also imply that "negative effects can endure in soil, potentially for thousands of years".

As Leach et al. (2012) found, ADEs have often already been established in rural communities on the African continent for long as part of socio-ecological practices that have shaped the relationships and history of the practicing people for centuries and enriched their soils. They represent both symbolic and economic capital. Bringing a foreign concept of biochar into these existing structures requires disciplining the local population, in effect making them employees of the carbon industry designed by Global North countries. Furthermore, biochar's feasibility and success are investigated through pilot projects, preparing the ground to endorse markets as soon as they emerge. These experiments may cost time and resources, as field trials on biochar's effect have had very varying outcomes, including negative effects on yields (Crane-Droesch et al., 2013). Additionally, science has been shaped by markets, focusing more on carbon's longevity than on relevant agronomic, soil and ecological aspects (Leach et al., 2012).

This new construct of biochar thus has as its primary goal not food security in the Global South, which on the one hand is used as a legitimizing argument, but the compensation of climate crimes that helps perpetuate the consumption behaviour of the Global North. This reveals how it is ultimately a further capitalization of nature, where Indigenous communities become a cheap labour force while others make a profit, using the image of the smallholder farmer receiving humanitarian aid as a marketing tool for perpetuating corporations' growth. Leach et al. (2012) argue that a green commodity is created, and the commodification of soil carbon takes place and is drawn into a financialized market, skewing revenue flows towards the businesses operating the system, not to the farmers implementing it. These are labelled as "green actors" and "market winners" if they modify their farming practices to fit the mold of carbon sequestration measures. However, Leach et al. (2012) find that biochar projects have been "given little attention to how carbon market revenue streams to farmers might be assured".

While there are evident benefits, as listed above, associated with the introduction of highly efficient pyrolytic stoves which create "clean char", adopting such technologies would still require becoming part of a biochar industry where it is questionable whether it favours the farmers. The implementation of biochar systems in small farming communities would, as a first step, bring about a change in already existing long-established habits. The fact that the Western entrepreneur usurps this right of intervention from a historical legitimization also allows this behaviour to be considered a manifestation of neo-colonialism, by imposing a standardized system into the pre-existing socio-ecological structures. In a subtle way, by changing local behaviour, the local population is subordinated to the global neoliberal market of the big players. These are the "commercial community linking scientists, non-governmental organizations (NGOs), companies, consultancy and venture capital that will all benefit from the establishment of that market" (Leach et al., 2012). The "hypothetical models" they develop pursuing their interests are implemented on the ground, where the local repertoires that do not conform to biochar system logic may be targeted as problematic and in need of conversion, imposing the standardization on farming within the social and ecological diversity in small-scale African rural livelihoods.

Case Study 3: Trees for Global Benefits—Instrumentalization Through the Uneven Geographies of Climate Knowledge

Finally, whether it is competing for resources or disciplining the local communities, climate finance has different ways of involving those who did barely contribute to climate change, to apparently combat it. The following is another "subtle" example, where implementing communities are instrumentalized by permitting an erroneous understanding of the project's goals to "help" keep the living standards of "people overseas, with no mention of the disparity in consumption, emissions, or transfer of responsibility" (Fisher et al., 2018).

The case of the Trees for Global Benefits (TFGB), a best practice (SEED, 2013) carbon forestry project in Uganda that sells its offsets on the voluntary carbon market since 2003, has been subject to some studies regarding the perception of justice (Fisher, 2013; Fisher et al., 2018) and "contradictory knowledge translations" (Carton, 2020).

Both studies (Carton, 2020; Fisher, 2013) found that knowledge about climate finance projects involving tree planting in Uganda differed considerably between actors. The local population, in charge of implementing the projects on-site, had a local understanding of climate change, where the connection between foreign emissions and local climate change was too abstract. This understanding was preserved by the organization in charge of instructing and training the people. Carbon offsets were misunderstood as a form to prevent damage from surrounding industries, and in order to ameliorate the micro-climatic conditions by "attracting the rain", a common belief partly true also found in Winnebah and Leach (2015). The payments they received from foreign sources were understood as altruistic development aid, or because the investors did not have suitable lands for tree planting in their own country. The organization in charge did not put any effort into clarifying this or in explaining the real purpose behind carbon markets. Furthermore, based on their knowledge translation, people assumed that not participating in these tree-planting projects implicated an increase in environmental and health risks. Thus, the organization used this misunderstanding as a medium for the facilitation of tree planting, ensuring its own success.

While the consequences for the local communities were not necessarily bad, but indeed may have helped improve the local climate and economy, the logic behind carbon markets was never explained to them, nor the fact that these trees were planted, so someone else could release carbon into the atmosphere.

The author claims that contradictory knowledge translations are the tool for "a neoliberal and hegemonic practice, that actively reproduces knowledge-power configurations" and that climate finance projects operate through these "uneven geographies of climate knowledge". Actors having different capacities and opportunities of accessing knowledge can be considered a tool of governance. Hall et al. (2015) compile a selection of studies where different forms of resistance to land grabbing (and their absence) are analysed. As they point out, "subtle forms of coercion" involve belonging to a certain economic class. Larder (2015) provides a case study which serves as a prime example of how a poor local community craves being included in a project that was recognized as an iconic land grab by the international social movement organizations.

Carton (2020) found that the lack of understanding of the rationale behind carbon sequestration projects affects the notions of justice (Fisher et al., 2018). While the local communities were only given a symbolic "incentive payment", which would not even cover the opportunity costs of tree planting, their work would allow others in the Global North to carry on with disproportionately costly living standards. Only knowing part of the deal, would let them not ask for more, let alone resist.

Resistance and Regulation

While the smallholder farmer gifted with a pyrolysis oven can be put on the logo of an environmentally conscious brand—without getting rich from it—the sales revenues of the implementing company will be all the greater thanks to the increasing environmental and justice consciousness of the mediatized industrial nations. An environmental awareness that triggers feelings of guilt can be remedied by compensation payments, thus enabling consumers to continue with a clear conscience: a win–win situation, for entrepreneurs and consumers.

While both consumers and investors often act with goodwill ignoring the factual consequences of their environmental intervention, those directly affected can in some cases perceive the negative impact and react.

As has been shown through this chapter, the problems caused by climate finance are diverse and manifold, but also very interconnected through the different dimensions of (in)justice they entail. First of all, the efficacy of carbon markets is questionable, due to the many loopholes they entail, which eventually instead of reducing, even increase GHG emissions. The consequences are tragic to most vulnerable nations, who, at the same time, have contributed less to climate change. On the other hand, climate finance, contrary to its claims of sustainable development, has proven to be a form of perpetuating the North–South power imbalances and eventually stopping less developed countries from developing at their own pace and in their own desired direction.

How can consumers still trust labels that describe products as CO_2-neutral, when this could just as well mean that they have transformed other people's habitats into a photosynthesis paradise, from which the local population can derive no direct benefit? One could argue that the safest way to avoid contributing to this form of neo-colonialism is to avoid climate compensation measures at all and to try to reduce one's own carbon footprint locally by renouncing the "Western lifestyle". Top-down approaches, where investors consider the socio-economic impact of their compensation measures are unlikely to occur unless they are forced to. Besides changes in consumers' demand, this can be due to acts of resistance in the implementing communities, or recently the development of binding regulations.

Resistance has been a recurrent tool to shed light on the dark sides of environmental and climate action in foreign investor-led projects in the Global South. Cavanagh and Benjaminsen (2015) found in this regard different types of resistance, including nonviolent, militant, discursive and formal-legal. The form of expressing resistance strongly depends on the "notions of justice" (Fisher et al., 2018), but also on other factors (Hall et al., 2015), such as the fear of political repression (Mamonova, 2015), which may lead to resistance circumventing direct confrontation with local policies through everyday resistance (Scott, 1989, 2008).

As Brockington (2004) points out, marginalization in conservation can lead to hidden acts of resistance. While they can turn out in conservation entities giving up on their activities, the author also notes that powerful conservation actors keep succeeding in their purpose despite local hidden opposition. In Mariki et al. (2015), the killing of the elephants was the only expression of disagreement by the population that caused a reaction by the local government. Feeling marginalized and disempowered made the villagers opt for forms of "slow violence", avoiding direct confrontation with local policies.

However, as Fisher et al. (2018) analysed, the lack of understanding of the rationale behind carbon offset projects would influence the notions of fairness among participants, limiting the project participants in their claims for justice. As Hall et al. (2015) bring up, accumulation does not necessarily involve dispossession, as "peasants activelsy seek incorporation into new corporate value chains". It is in such cases of misinformation and skewed perception of fairness where resistance is less likely, and especially subtle forms of instrumentalization can take place without any further consequences.

Recent movements of resistance in the Global North have started raising awareness of the climate crisis (Fridays for Future, Extinction Rebellion, etc.), putting policymakers under pressure. This has, however, among other causes, boosted carbon markets, rocketing prices to unforeseen values. The increasing demand has re-opened the dormant carbon markets, but *real* mitigation efforts *in* the Global North, have had less success so far. Raising awareness of the potential consequences and leakages in carbon finance is now necessary to force policymakers and actors to adopt better forms of regulation.

The emergence of non-state actors in climate action has recently led to an increasing depoliticization of pre-existing mechanisms. The ambiguity created through the Paris Agreement has not only made carbon offsets become more questionable in terms of their real mitigation capacity, but further hampered control structures for impact assessment from a socio-ecological perspective on local communities. As Fowlie (2021) argues, rigorous empirical analysis should be implemented *before* carbon offsets are awarded, as a precondition for carbon offset crediting. But not only the offsets, but also social justice issues within them need to be properly addressed through binding policies, in order to decolonize climate finance. These should enforce a priori socio-ecological research (as in Müller et al., 2019) but furthermore ensure truthful knowledge translations in all spheres of decision-making, reaching from the implementing local communities, to the Indigenous delegates in international frameworks. While environmental justice for the Global South will not be achieved through the current climate agenda (Whyte, 2020), it is of utmost importance, despite the narrow time schedule for climate action, to adopt binding regulations which involve a priori research, protecting Indigenous communities from ongoing failures in recognitional and procedural justice.

Conclusion

The emergence of environmental markets offers a unique opportunity for perpetuating the Western consumer society through the implementation of compensation measures, concealed by the shades of altruism and responsibility, encouraging the ongoing 'growthmania' (Weston, 2021) instead of reducing their ecological footprint at the root of emissions. Where once states and governments established themselves in the Global South by conquering resources, it is now entrepreneurs, often also NGOs, hidden in the tailwind of emerging environmental markets in a neoliberal globalized world, who set up businesses where the Global North's indulgences for climate crimes are cheapest to procure.

The history of environmental governance outsourced to the Global South under the veil of sustainable development, prepared the ground for the deployment of carbon markets. These have evolved from allowing unlimited carbon transactions with an 'uncapped' environment to global commitments with no legal binding. Moreover, non-state actors have taken the lead, depoliticizing climate action, hampering quality assessments that safeguard Indigenous peoples' livelihoods, but also their dignity. Climate finance has been widely acknowledged as perpetuating colonial power structures and imposing Western forms of knowledge. While many studies have been addressing overt forms of violent resource expropriation, neo-colonialism also materializes by establishing Eurocentric forms of knowledge, and capitalist structures. The case studies presented in this chapter offer an insight into the broad spectrum of neo-colonialism, by juxtaposing one physical with two subtler forms of green grabbing. The first example reflected a classical land grab, where not only Indigenous communities were evicted, but also resource competition with protected wildlife threatened their livelihoods. The second example showed how foreign technocratic knowledge was superimposed on pre-existing Indigenous knowledge, and in the third example, contradictory knowledge translations were used to implement carbon sequestration projects. While the consequences of the three cases differently affect, positively or negatively, local communities, in all of the cases, local people's dignity was overstepped by providing neither procedural nor recognitional justice through appropriate involvement. However, as discussed above, changing the status quo strongly relies on different forms of resistance, which are more probable to occur in overt than subtle conflicts. In the second and third examples, local communities were not aware of the injustices inflicted upon them, so they would not rise up for a fairer treatment. Top-down regulations that also acknowledge and deal with these subtler forms of exploitation are thus required to ensure real integrity in climate finance.

References

Adams, W. M. (2020). *Green development: Environment and sustainability in a developing world* (4th ed.). Routledge.

Bachram, H. (2004). Climate fraud and carbon colonialism: The new trade in greenhouse gases. *Capitalism Nature Socialism, 15*(4), 5–20. https://doi.org/10.1080/1045575042000287299

Badgley, G., Freeman, J., Hamman, J. J., Haya, B., Trugman, A. T., Anderegg, W. R. L., & Cullenward, D. (2022). Systematic over-crediting in California's forest carbon offsets program. *Global Change Biology, 28*(4), 1433–1445. https://doi.org/10.1111/gcb.15943

Belfer, E., Ford, J. D., Maillet, M., Araos, M., & Flynn, M. (2019). Pursuing an indigenous platform: Exploring opportunities and constraints for indigenous participation in the UNFCCC. *Global Environmental Politics, 19*(1), 12–33. https://doi.org/10.1162/glep_a_00489

Biochar International. (2021). *Biochar in carbon trading markets*. Available online at https://biochar-international.org/protocol/, updated on 2021, checked on 6/21/2022.

Blum, M., & Lövbrand, E. (2019). The return of carbon offsetting? The discursive legitimation of new market arrangements in the Paris climate regime. *Earth System Governance, 2*, 100028. https://doi.org/10.1016/j.esg.2019.100028

Borras, S. M. (2010). The politics of biofuels, land and agrarian change: Editors' introduction. *Journal of Peasant Studies, 37*(4), 575–592. https://doi.org/10.1080/03066150.2010.512448

Brockington, D. (2004). Community conservation, inequality and injustice: Myths of power in protected area management. *Conservation and Society, 2*(2), 411–432. Available online at http://www.jstor.org/stable/26396635, checked on 6/29/2022.

Cadotte, M. W., Carscadden, K., & Mirotchnick, N. (2011). Beyond species: Functional diversity and the maintenance of ecological processes and services. *Journal of Applied Ecology, 48*(5), 1079–1087. https://doi.org/10.1111/j.1365-2664.2011.02048.x

Camps-Arbestain, M., Amonette, J. E., Singh, B., Wang, T., & Schmidt, H.-P. (2015). *A biochar classification system and associated test methods*. Available online at https://www.osti.gov/biblio/1179510,journal=

Cardinale, B. J., Duffy, J. E., Gonzalez, A., Hooper, D. U., Perrings, C., Venail, P., Narwani, A., Mace, G. M., Tilman, D., Wardle, D. A., Kinzig, A. P., Daily, G. C., Loreau, M., Grace, J. B., Larigauderie, A., Srivastava, D. S., & Naeem, S. (2012). Biodiversity loss and its impact on humanity. *Nature, 486*(7401), 59–67. https://doi.org/10.1038/nature11148

Carton, W. (2020). Rendering local: The politics of differential knowledge in Carbon Offset Governance. *Annals of the American Association of Geographers, 110*(5), 1353–1368. https://doi.org/10.1080/24694452.2019.1707642

Cavanagh, C., & Benjaminsen, T. A. (2014). Virtual nature, violent accumulation: The 'spectacular failure' of carbon offsetting at a Ugandan National Park. *Geoforum, 56*, 55–65. https://doi.org/10.1016/j.geoforum.2014.06.013

Cavanagh, C. J., & Benjaminsen, T. A. (2015). Guerrilla agriculture? A biopolitical guide to illicit cultivation within an IUCN Category II protected area. *Journal of Peasant Studies, 42*(3–4), 725–745. https://doi.org/10.1080/03066150.2014.993623

Chan, K. Y., & Xu, Z. H. (2009). Biochar: Nutrient properties and their enhancement. In J. Lehmann & S. Joseph (Eds.), *Biochar for environmental management* (5th ed., pp. 67–84). Earthscan.

Chan, S., Brandi, C., & Bauer, S. (2016). Aligning transnational climate action with international climate governance: The road from Paris. *RECIEL, 25*(2), 238–247. https://doi.org/10.1111/reel.12168

Colchester, M. (2004). Conservation policy and indigenous peoples. *Environmental Science & Policy, 7*(3), 145–153. https://doi.org/10.1016/j.envsci.2004.02.004

Crane-Droesch, A., Abiven, S., Jeffery, S., & Torn, M. S. (2013). Heterogeneous global crop yield response to biochar: A meta-regression analysis. *Environmental Research Letters, 8*(4), 44049. https://doi.org/10.1088/1748-9326/8/4/044049

Cross, A., & Sohi, S. P. (2011). The priming potential of biochar products in relation to labile carbon contents and soil organic matter status. *Soil Biology and Biochemistry, 43*(10), 2127–2134. https://doi.org/10.1016/j.soilbio.2011.06.016

Eberle, C., Münstermann, N., & Siebeneck, J. (2019). *Carbon Colonialism: A postcolonial assessment of carbon offsetting* (J. Verne, Ed.). University of Bonn/United Nations University—EHS.

ENTTRANS Consortium. (2008). *The potential of transferring and implementing sustainable energy technologies through the Clean Development Mechanism*. European Commission Community Research and Development Information Service.

Fairhead, J., Leach, M., & Scoones, I. (2012). Green grabbing: A new appropriation of nature? *Journal of Peasant Studies, 39*(2), 237–261. https://doi.org/10.1080/03066150.2012.671770

Fisher, J. (2013). Justice implications of conditionality in payments for ecosystem services: A Case study from Uganda. In T. Sikor (Ed.), *The justices and injustices of ecosystem services* (Ch. 2). Earthscan.

Fisher, J. A., Cavanagh, C. J., Sikor, T., & Mwayafu, D. M. (2018). Linking notions of justice and project outcomes in carbon offset forestry projects: Insights from a comparative study in Uganda. *Land Use Policy, 73*, 259–268. https://doi.org/10.1016/j.landusepol.2017.12.055

Forest Trends Ecosystem Marketplace. (2021). *Market in motion: State of the voluntary carbon markets 2021 Installment 1*. Forest Trends Association. Available online at https://www.ecosystemmarketplace.com/publications/state-of-the-voluntary-carbon-markets-2021/.

Forest Trends Ecosystem Marketplace. (2019). *Financing emission reductions for the future: State of voluntary carbon markets 2019*. Forest Trends. Available online at https://www.forest-trends.org/wp-content/uploads/2019/12/SOVCM2019.pdf, checked on 6/29/2022

Fowlie, M. (2019). *Are trees getting too much climate credit…or not enough?* Energy Institute at Haas. Available online at https://energyathaas.wordpress.com/2019/06/10/are-trees-getting-too-much-climate-credit-or-not-enough/, updated on 5/26/2022, checked on 6/29/2022.

Fowlie, M. (2021). *Can Carbon Offset loopholes be fixed with better evaluation and rules?* Available online at https://energypost.eu/can-carbon-offset-loopholes-be-fixed-with-better-evaluation-and-rules/, updated on 12/13/2021, checked on 6/29/2022.

Gardner, B. (2012). Tourism and the politics of the global land grab in Tanzania: Markets, appropriation and recognition. *Journal of Peasant Studies, 39*(2), 377–402. https://doi.org/10.1080/03066150.2012.666973

Green, J. F. (2013). Order out of Chaos: Public and private rules for managing carbon. *Global Environmental Politics, 13*(2), 1–25. https://doi.org/10.1162/GLEP_a_00164

Grubb, M. (2004). Kyoto and the future of international climate change responses: From here to where. *International Review for Environmental Strategies, 5*(1), 15–38.

Hall, R., Edelman, M., Borras, S. M., Scoones, I., White, B., & Wolford, W. (2015). Resistance, acquiescence or incorporation? An introduction to land grabbing and political reactions 'from below.' *Journal of Peasant Studies, 42*(3–4), 467–488. https://doi.org/10.1080/03066150.2015.1036746

Hamrick, K., & Gallant, M. (2017). *Unlocking potential: State of the voluntary carbon markets 2017*. Available online at https://forest-trends.org//wp-content/uploads/2017/07/doc_5591.pdf, checked on 6/29/2022.

Heleta, S. (2018). Decolonizing knowledge in South Africa: Dismantling the 'pedagogy of big lies'. *Ufahamu: A Journal of African Studies, 40*(2). https://doi.org/10.5070/F7402040942

Holmes, G. (2014). What is a land grab? Exploring green grabs, conservation, and private protected areas in southern Chile. *Journal of Peasant Studies, 41*(4), 547–567. https://doi.org/10.1080/03066150.2014.919266

IPCC. (2022). Mitigation pathways compatible with 1.5°C in the context of sustainable development. In *Global Warming of 1.5°C: IPCC Special Report on impacts of global warming of 1.5°C above pre-industrial levels in context of strengthening response to climate change, sustainable development, and efforts to eradicate poverty* (pp. 93–174). Cambridge University Press.

IUCN. (2020). *The state of protected areas in Eastern and Southern Africa*. State of Protected and Conserved Areas Report Series No. 1. IUCN ESARO.

Jeffery, S., Bezemer, T. M., Cornelissen, G., Kuyper, T. W., Lehmann, J., Mommer, L., Sohi, S. P., van de Voorde, T. F. J., Wardle, D., & van Groenigen, J. W. (2015). The way forward in biochar research: Targeting trade-offs between the potential wins. *Gcb Bioenergy, 7*(1), 1–13. https://doi.org/10.1111/gcbb.12132

Kill, J. (2015). *REDD: A collection of conflicts, contradictions and lies.* World Rainforest Movement International Secretariat. Montevideo. Available online at https://www.atmosfair.de/wp-content/uploads/redd-a-collection-of-conflict_contradictions_lies_expanded.pdf, checked on 6/28/2022

Kochanek, J., Soo, R. M., Martinez, C., Dakuidreketi, A., & Mudge, A. M. (2022). Biochar for intensification of plant-related industries to meet productivity, sustainability and economic goals: A review. *Resources, Conservation and Recycling, 179*, 106109. https://doi.org/10.1016/j.resconrec.2021.106109

Kreibich, N., & Hermwille, L. (2021). Caught in between: Credibility and feasibility of the voluntary carbon market post-2020. *Climate Policy, 21*(7), 939–957. https://doi.org/10.1080/14693062.2021.1948384

Kuzyakov, Y., Subbotina, I., Chen, H., Bogomolova, I., & Xu, X. (2009). Black carbon decomposition and incorporation into soil microbial biomass estimated by 14C labeling. *Soil Biology and Biochemistry, 41*(2), 210–219. https://doi.org/10.1016/j.soilbio.2008.10.016

Lane, R., & Newell, P. (2018). The political economy of carbon markets. In T. de van Graaf, A. Ghosh, B. K. Sovacool, M. T. Klare, & F. Kern (Eds.), *Palgrave handbook of the international political economy of energy* (Enhanced Credo edition, pp. 247–267). Palgrave Macmillan; Credo Reference (Palgrave Handbooks in IPE).

Larder, N. (2015). Space for pluralism? Examining the Malibya land grab. *Journal of Peasant Studies, 42*(3–4), 839–858. https://doi.org/10.1080/03066150.2015.1029461

Leach, M., Fairhead, J., & Fraser, J. (2012). Green grabs and biochar: Revaluing African soils and farming in the new carbon economy. *Journal of Peasant Studies, 39*(2), 285–307. https://doi.org/10.1080/03066150.2012.658042

Lederer, M. (2012). The practice of carbon markets. *Environmental Politics, 21*(4), 640–656. https://doi.org/10.1080/09644016.2012.688358

Lehmann, J., & Joseph, S. (Eds.). (2021). *Biochar for environmental management: Science, technology and implementation* (2nd ed.). Routledge.

Lovell, H. C. (2010). Governing the carbon offset market. *Wires Climate Change, 1*(3), 353–362. https://doi.org/10.1002/wcc.43

Lyons, K., & Westoby, P. (2014). Carbon colonialism and the new land grab: Plantation forestry in Uganda and its livelihood impacts. *Journal of Rural Studies, 36*, 13–21. https://doi.org/10.1016/j.jrurstud.2014.06.002

Mamonova, N. (2015). Resistance or adaptation? Ukrainian peasants' responses to large-scale land acquisitions. *Journal of Peasant Studies, 42*(3–4), 607–634. https://doi.org/10.1080/03066150.2014.993320

Mariki, S. B., Svarstad, H., & Benjaminsen, T. A. (2015). Elephants over the Cliff: Explaining wildlife killings in Tanzania. *Land Use Policy, 44*, 19–30. https://doi.org/10.1016/j.landusepol.2014.10.018

Marquardt, J., Fast, C., & Grimm, J. (2022). Non- and sub-state climate action after Paris: From a facilitative regime to a contested governance landscape. *Wires Climate Change.* https://doi.org/10.1002/wcc.791

Mcafee, K. (2015). Green economy and carbon markets for conservation and development: A critical view. *International Environmental Agreements: Politics, Law and Economics, 16*, 333–353.

Merger, E., & Pistorius, T. (2011). Effectiveness and legitimacy of forest carbon standards in the OTC voluntary carbon market. *Carbon Balance and Management, 6*(1), 4. https://doi.org/10.1186/1750-0680-6-4

Müller, B., & Michaelowa, A. (2019). How to operationalize accounting under Article 6 market mechanisms of the Paris Agreement. *Climate Policy, 19*(7), 812–819. https://doi.org/10.1080/14693062.2019.1599803

Müller, S., Backhaus, N., Nagabovanalli, P., & Abiven, S. (2019). A social-ecological system evaluation to implement sustainably a biochar system in South India. *Agronomy for Sustainable Development, 39*(4), 1–14. https://doi.org/10.1007/s13593-019-0586-y

Nixon, R. (2013). *Slow violence and the environmentalism of the poor.* Harvard University Press.

Oberthür, S., & Bodle, R. (2016). Legal form and nature of the Paris outcome. *Clim Law, 6*(1–2), 40–57. https://doi.org/10.1163/18786561-00601003

Osborn, D., Cutter, A., & Ullah, F. (2015). Universal sustainable development goals. *Understanding the Transformational Challenge for Developed Countries.* Stakeholder Forum. Available online at https://sustainabledevelopment.un.org/content/documents/1684SF_-_SDG_Universality_Report_-_May_2015.pdf, checked on 6/29/2022.

Paterson, M. (2009). Resistance makes carbon markets. In S. Böhm & S. Dabhi (Eds.), *Upsetting the offset: The political economy of carbon markets* (pp. 244–254). Mayfly Books.

Paterson, M. (2010). Legitimation and accumulation in climate change governance. *New Political Economy, 15*(3), 345–368. https://doi.org/10.1080/13563460903288247

Peluso, N. L., & Lund, C. (2011). New frontiers of land control: Introduction. *Journal of Peasant Studies, 38*(4), 667–681. https://doi.org/10.1080/03066150.2011.607692

Plamper, A. (1998). Von der Kulturlandschaft zur Wunschlandschaft. Die visuelle Konstruktion von Natur in Museen. Zugl.: Berlin, Freie Univ., Diss., 1997. Münster, New York, München, Berlin: Waxmann (Internationale Hochschulschriften, Bd. 271).

Razzaghi, F., Obour, P. B., & Arthur, E. (2020). Does biochar improve soil water retention? A Systematic Review and Meta-Analysis. *Geoderma, 361*, 114055. https://doi.org/10.1016/j.geoderma.2019.114055

Richards, M. B., Bruun, T. B., Campbell, B. M., Gregersen, L. E., Huyer, S., Kuntze, V., Madsen, S. T., Oldvig, M. B., & Vasileiou, I. (2016). *How countries plan to address agricultural adaptation and mitigation: An analysis of Intended Nationally Determined Contributions*. CCAFS dataset. Available online at https://cgspace.cgiar.org/handle/10568/73255

Schneider, L. (2009). Assessing the additionality of CDM projects: Practical experiences and lessons learned. *Climate Policy, 9*(3), 242–254. https://doi.org/10.3763/cpol.2008.0533

Schneider, L., & La Hoz Theuer, S. (2019). Environmental integrity of international carbon market mechanisms under the Paris Agreement. *Climate Policy, 19*(3), 386–400. https://doi.org/10.1080/14693062.2018.1521332

Scott, J. C. (1989). Everyday forms of resistance. *The Copenhagen Journal of Asian Studies 4*, 33. https://doi.org/10.22439/cjas.v4i1.1765

Scott, J. C. (2008). *Weapons of the weak: Everyday forms of peasant resistance*. Yale University Press.

SEED. (2013). *2013 SEED low carbon award winner—Trees for global benefit*. Available online at https://www.seed.uno/enterprise-profiles/trees-for-global-benefit, updated on 6/29/2022, checked on 6/29/2022.

Smith, K., Reyes, O., & Byakola, T. (2007). *The carbon neutral myth. Offset indulgences for your climate sins*. Transnational Institute.

Streck, C. (2020). Filling in for governments? The role of the private actors in the international climate regime. *Journal for European Environmental & Planning Law, 17*(1), 5–28. https://doi.org/10.1163/18760104-01701003

Sullivan, S. (2010). 'Ecosystem service commodities'—A new imperial ecology? Implications for animist immanent ecologies, with Deleuze and Guattari. *New Formations, 69*(69), 111–128. https://doi.org/10.3898/NEWF.69.06.2010

The Royal Society. (2009). *Geoengineering the climate: Science, governance and uncertainty*. The Royal Society (Excellence in science, 10, 2009). Available online at https://royalsociety.org/-/media/Royal_Society_Content/policy/publications/2009/8693.pdf, checked on 6/29/2022.

Thouless, C. R., Dublin, H. T., Blanc, J. J., Skinner, D. P., Daniel, T. E., Taylor, R. D., Maisels, F., Frederick, H. L., & Bouche, P. (2016). *African elephant status report 2016: An update from the African elephant database*. Occasional Paper Series of the IUCN Species Survival Commission, No. 60 IUCN/SSC Africa Elephant Specialist Group. IUCN.

UNEP. (2019). *Bridging the gap: The role of non-state and subnational actors.* United Nations Environment Programme.

UNFCCC. (2016). Conference of the Parties. Report of the Conference of the Parties on its twenty-first session, held in Paris from 30 November to 11 December 2015. Part two: Action taken by the Conference of the Parties at its twenty-first session. Decisions adopted by the Conference of the Parties. Available online at https://unfccc.int/resource/docs/2015/cop21/eng/10a01.pdf, checked on 6/29/2022.

UNFCCC. (2018). *Achievements of the clean development mechanism: Harnessing incentive for climate action.* Available online at https://unfccc.int/sites/default/files/resource/UNFCCC_CDM_report_2018.pdf, checked on 6/29/2022.

UNFCCC. (2019). The Katowice climate package: Making The Paris Agreement Work For All | UNFCCC. Available online at https://unfccc.int/process-and-meetings/the-paris-agreement/katowice-climate-package, updated on 6/29/2022, checked on 6/29/2022.

Vidal, J. (2008). The great green land grab. *The Guardian.* Available online at https://www.theguardian.com/environment/2008/feb/13/conservation, checked on 6/29/2022.

Weston, P. (2021). Top scientists warn of 'ghastly future of mass extinction' and climate disruption. *The Guardian.* Available online at https://www.theguardian.com/environment/2021/jan/13/top-scientists-warn-of-ghastly-future-of-mass-extinction-and-climate-disruption-aoe, checked on 6/29/2022.

Whitfield, K. (2015). *Quick guide to sustainable development: History and concepts.* Brief History of Sustainable Development. Available online at https://senedd.wales/research%20documents/qg15-003%20-%20sustainable%20development%20history%20and%20concepts/qg15-003.pdf, checked on 6/29/2022.

Whyte, K. (2020). Too late for indigenous climate justice: Ecological and relational tipping points. *WIREs Clim Change, 11*(1). https://doi.org/10.1002/wcc.603

Winnebah, T., & Leach, M. (2015). Old reserve, new carbon interests: The case of the Western Area Peninsula forest (WAPFoR), Sierra Leone. In M. Leach & I. Scoones (Eds.), *Carbon conflicts and forest landscapes in Africa* (pp. 200–215). Routledge (Pathways to sustainability). Available online at https://www.taylorfrancis.com/chapters/edit/10.4324/9781315740416-17/old-reserve-new-carbon-interests-case-Western-area-peninsula-forest-wapfor-sierra-leone-thomas-winnebah-melissa-leach

World Bank. (2015). *State and trends of carbon pricing October 2015.* Online-Ausg. The World Bank (World Bank E-Library Archive). Available online at https://www.worldbank.org/content/dam/Worldbank/document/Climate/State-and-Trend-Report-2015.pdf, checked on 6/29/2022.

World Bank. (2021). *Land area (sq km)—Germany*. Available at: https://data.worldbank.org/indicator/AG.LND.TOTL.K2?locations=DE. Accessed 30 June 2022.

Zoomers, A. (2010). Globalisation and the foreignisation of space: Seven processes driving the current global land grab. *Journal of Peasant Studies, 37*(2), 429–447. https://doi.org/10.1080/03066151003595325

CHAPTER 9

Climate Finance and the Peace Dividend, Articulating the Co-benefits Argument

Catherine Wong

Introduction—Climate Finance and the Elusive Peace Dividend

The role and impacts, of climate finance on peace and security in conflict-affected and fragile contexts—many of which are also vulnerable to climate change rank among the lowest recipients of climate finance—is an area still little investigated by either the climate finance, climate

---

The metadata analysis presented in this chapter was made possible through the generous support of UNDP and the Climate Security Mechanism, the full details of which were first published in 2021 study, "Climate Finance for Sustaining Peace – Making Climate Finance Work Better for Conflict-Affected and Fragile Contexts."

C. Wong (✉)
Climate and Security Risk, United Nations Development Programme, New York, NY, USA
e-mail: catherine.wong@undp.org

© The Author(s), under exclusive license to Springer Nature Switzerland AG 2022
C. Cash and L. A. Swatuk (eds.), *The Political Economy of Climate Finance: Lessons from International Development*, International Political Economy Series, https://doi.org/10.1007/978-3-031-12619-2_9

security or environmental peacebuilding fields. A recent UNDP study (2021) conducted with the Climate Security Mechanism and the Nataij Group argues for the need to better understand peace co-benefits. This chapter attempts to fill this void, highlighting that greater attention is needed to the allocation, access and thus distribution, quality and quantity of finance, and therein, the design of climate finance mechanisms and their inherent impacts on equity in conflict-affected and fragile contexts. It examines, synthetically, but not—exhaustively, the literature and underlying arguments from the emerging fields of climate finance, climate security and environmental peacebuilding and the application of a co-benefits approach to strengthen policy coherence, before considering learnings from nascent practice, including the efforts of the UN system. Gaps for further investigation are identified along with key guiding principles on the measurement of peace and security co-benefits or dividends of climate finance and conclusions are drawn from the new meta-analysis by UNDP (2021) and the importance of transdisciplinary approach highlighted (Lawrence et al., 2022; Rigolot, 2020). As one of the first attempts to systematically consider climate finance in climate vulnerable conflict-affected and fragile contexts, it argues that better metrics accounting for peace co-benefits or dividends, reinventing Theories of Change and establishing intersectoral Communities of Practices and special vehicles/calls for proposals could strengthen access and outcomes.

COMPARING AND CONTRASTING GAPS IN THE CLIMATE FINANCE LITERATURE

Climate finance is defined by the UNFCCC as "local, national, or transnational financing—drawn from public, private, and alternative sources of financing—that seeks to support mitigation and adaptation actions that will address climate change" (UNFCCC, n.d.). Established by the 16th COP, the Standing Committee on Finance was established "to assist the COP in exercising its functions in relation to the financial mechanism of the Convention."[1] The foundational and long-established principle

---

[1] For more information see the UNFCCC's Standing Committee on Finance (SCF). https://unfccc.int/SCF.

of "common but differentiated responsibilities and respective capabilities" was enshrined in the Rio Convention in 1992 and serves to reflect that Southern countries bear the overwhelming brunt of climate impacts, whereas Northern countries are responsible for the majority of cumulative greenhouse gas (GHG) emissions. Equitable access to climate finance and addressing those obstacles or gaps may be considered a topic salient to climate security and environmental peacebuilding.

Thus far, climate finance has been essentially blind to conflict and fragility. The literature tackles questions related to commitments under the international negotiations on climate change (in particular, on adaptation vis-à-vis mitigation), allocation and access to climate finance, the needs of Least Developed Countries (LDCs) and Small Island Developing States (SIDS), more recently loss and damage, but largely ignores the specific case of fragile and conflict-affected contexts (UNDP, 2021) and peace and security co-benefits. The research focused on natural resource management, mitigation and adaptation are design and implementation focused, whereas the design and allocation of climate finance, or lack thereof are fundamentally different research questions of concern to the fields of climate finance and climate security/environmental peacebuilding.

Climate finance, as a research theme, is still considered by many, an emerging field. In this vein, Hong et al. (2020) describe a "dearth" of research on climate finance in their 2020 "Review of Financial Studies," a sentiment echoed by others, including Giglio et al. (2020), in their NBER Working Paper, "Climate Finance," Bowen (2011) and in other special volumes/issues of late, endeavouring also fill the gaps, including "The Finance of Climate Change" by the Journal of Corporate Finance (Calvet et al., 2022). The literature broadly encompasses such areas of research as: the effectiveness of climate finance, barriers to access, transparency, environmental and equity impacts of climate finance and the role of private finance (Bhandary et al., 2021; Bowen, 2011; Bowen et al., 2017; Climate Policy Initiative, 2019). There is little specific consideration of access to climate finance by conflict-affected and fragile contexts, if at all.

As a complementary perspective, grey literature on climate finance follows the prevailing logic of the international negotiations closely.[2] Critical insights relate to the gap in adaptation financing and progress towards the US$ 100 billion target, including by the Organisation for Economic Co-operation and Development (OECD, 2021), Oxfam,[3] the World Resources Institute[4] and the Zurich Flood Resilience Alliance.[5] Other studies have examined the impact of COVID-19 on climate finance,[6] and gender and climate finance.[7] Little work specifically investigates countries suffering fragility and conflict. Although a reference point may be found in efforts to highlight the regional gaps in access to climate finance, including by Sub-Saharan African countries, including, inter alia, by Arezki (2020), who notes absorptive capacity, bankability of projects and governance in the energy sector. Recent work by the OECD's International Network on Conflict and Fragility (INCAF) (Poole, 2018) has been the exception, in its focus on fragile states. Mercy Corps also brought attention to the issue with its submission to the UNFCCC Standing Committee on Finance, making a "Call for Evidence: Information and Data for the Preparation of 'The 2020 Biennial Assessment

[2] Developed country Parties to the UNFCCC provide finance to support developing country Parties, under the principle of "common but differentiated responsibility and respective capacities" and a financial mechanism was established to provide these resources. The GEF and the GCF serve as its operating entities of the financial mechanism and the Standing Committee on Finance established to provide guidance to the operating entities. For more information see: https://unfccc.int/topics/climate-finance/the-big-picture/introduction-to-climate-finance.

[3] Carty, T., Kowalzig, J. & Zagema, B. (2020). 'Climate Finance Shadow Report 2020: Assessing Progress towards the $100 Billion Commitment', *Oxfam GB*, p. 32. https://doi.org/10.21201/2020.6621.

[4] Bos. J. & Thwaites, J. (2021). A Breakdown of Developed Countries' Public Climate Finance Contributions towards the $100 Billion Goal. https://files.wri.org/d8/s3fs-public/2021-10/breakdown-developed-countries-public-climate-finance-contributions-towards-100-billion.pdf?VersionId=0luvOD5zVLLxxfRpWad_DyFC3Qh4sjd0.

[5] Alcayna, T. (2020). At What Cost: How Chronic Gaps in Adaptation Finance Expose the World's Poorest People to Climate Chaos. Zurich Flood Resilience Alliance, p. 52. https://www.concernusa.org/wp-content/uploads/2020/07/AT-WHAT-COST.pdf.

[6] Green Climate Fund (2020). Tipping or turning point: Scaling up climate finance in the era of COVID-19. Text. Republic of Korea: Green Climate Fund, p. 44. https://www.greenclimate.fund/document/tipping-or-turning-point-scaling-climate-finance-era-covid-19.

[7] For example, see Australian Aid, Oxfam & PACCCIL (2019, October), Atmadja, S.S. et al. (2020).

and Overview of Climate Finance Flows'" as did a 2021 report by ODI and Supporting Pastoralism and Agriculture in Recurrent and Protracted Crises (SPARC), examining the conflict sensitivity of climate adaptation finance in conflict-affected and fragile contexts in the Horn and the Sahel (Cao et al., 2021).

CLIMATE SECURITY, ENVIRONMENTAL PEACEBUILDING AND THE MISSING FINANCE PIECE

The climate security nexus has been the subject of academic scholarship and ongoing debate, including arguments of causality and contextual pathways through which climate change may affect peace, stability and security (Adger et al., 2014; Burke et al., 2015; Busby, 2018; Dabelko et al., 2013; Hendrix, 2018; Lee, 2022). In this regard, there is not a consensus definition of what constitutes "climate-related security risks." Instead, different security frames of reference are inferred. These include climate change impacts as they relate to the security of the state (Buzan et al., 1998; Oels, 2012); the maintenance of international peace and security under Chapter VII of the United Nations Charter (United Nations, 1945); and the adverse impacts of climate change on human security—the "freedom from fear" and "freedom from want" (UNDP, 1994). In research and policy domains, while acknowledging that many countries suffer the double-burden of climate change and conflict (Moran et al., 2018; Smith & Vivekananda, 2007) the majority accept, as a baseline, that climate change may be a "threat multiplier." This was first observed by the Center for Naval Analyses (CNA) Corporation in its report, "National Security and the Threat of Climate Change" and is widely acknowledged, including in the United Nations Secretary-General's 2009 report, "Climate Change and its Possible Security Implications" (A/64/350). On the subject of causality, opinions diverge greatly, but if the multiplier effect may be considered the common denominator of understanding; based on this, carefully directed climate finance can be part of the solution.

The main corps of the literature on climate security has focused, as abovementioned, on questions of causality, and climate-informed conflict analyses primarily in the country or regional case studies and climate change adaptation and mitigation interventions (e.g. Burke et al. 2009; Hsiang et al., 2011; Lee, 2022; Mach et al., 2019; Miguel et al., 2004).

Challenging earlier thinking on environmental security (De Wilde, 2008; Gleditsch, 1998; Homer-Dixon, 1994; Homer-Dixon & Levy, 1995; Levy, 1995; Mathews, 1989; Schwartz et al., 2000), environmental peacebuilding finds to the contrary, that natural resource and environmental management, and by extension of this, climate change adaptation and mitigation/access to energy can also be entry points to build sustainable peace and social cohesion (Conca & Dabelko, 2002; Ide et al., 2021; Krampe et al., 2021; Swain & Öjendal, 2020).[8] This nascent field has, over the years, tackled inter alia, cooperation over transboundary water resources, the environmental impacts of war and post-conflict situations. In their recent stocktaking, Ide et al. (2021) recall the generational evolution of environmental peacebuilding and describe three overarching dimensions as: security; livelihoods and economy; and politics and social relations and the gaps as including bottom-up approaches, gender, conflict-sensitive programming, use of big data and frontier technology and monitoring and evaluation (Ide et al., 2021; also see Dabelko et al., 2013). Finance is a missing piece in these epistemic fields, neither of which, to date, have meaningfully engaged on the topic thus far.

A Co-benefits Approach to Climate Finance and the Peace Dividend

As a counterpoint and as the subject is finance, the logic of co-benefits and co-costs allows us to bring together these approaches (i.e. climate finance, climate security and environmental peacebuilding) in a way that usefully distinguishes between primary and ancillary benefits and respects the integrity of their different methodological approaches. The Fifth Assessment Report of the IPCC describes co-benefits, as "the positive effects that a policy or measure aimed at one objective may have on other objectives, irrespective of the net effect on overall social welfare' objectives,

---

[8] See Boutros-Ghali, B. (1992) An agenda for peace: Preventive diplomacy, peacemaking and peacekeeping. *International Relations* 11(3): 201–218. https://www.un.org/ruleoflaw/files/A_47_277.pdf; Conca, K. & Dabelko, G.D. (2002). Environmental Peacemaking. Washington, DC: Woodrow Wilson Center Press; and Krampe, F., Hegazi, F. & VanDeveer, S.D. (2021). Sustaining peace through better resource governance: Three potential mechanisms for environmental peacebuilding. *World Development* 144 (2021) 105508. https://doi.org/10.1016/j.worlddev.2021.105508.

irrespective of the net effect on overall social welfare." The IPCC's examination of co-benefits began in its Third Assessment Report (2001) where it was stressed that co-benefits should be considered "at least equally important rationales" as direct climate benefits, while the lexicon of "ancillary benefits" dates back to the Second Assessment Report (1995) and is used interchangeably with co-benefits in this piece. In their synopsis of the scholarship on the concept of co-benefits, Mayrhofer and Gupta (2016) describe the increased predominance of this term, in reconciling climate and environmental objectives with other policy priorities, but highlight the lack of exploration of its definition, pointing out that of the 138 articles shortlisted in their assessment, none tackled taxonomy.

In terms of capturing the co-benefits of climate finance, the field of mitigation is notably further ahead. But overall scholarship, as in the case of climate finance, dates back to the 1990s in relation to GHG emissions (Glomsrød et al., 1992; Pearce, 2000), reflecting the emergence of climate change as a global policy agenda. In their 2020 study of 239 peer-reviewed journal articles, Karlsson et al. (2020) found that co-benefits are often overlooked in policymaking, which can adversely impact policy outcomes. Health and air quality co-benefits of GHG emission reductions are comparatively better examined. Whereas climate adaptation co-benefits and co-costs are little considered (UNECE, 2016), if not underestimated (Karlsson et al., 2020).

Rahman and Mori (2020) concluded that studies on adaptation co-benefits are still limited and poorly communicated and that non-market benefits and equity impacts are particularly underacknowledged (Rahman & Mori, 2020). A study commissioned by the UK's Department of Energy and Climate Change (DECC) investigates mitigation co-benefits for health, economic development and energy security drawing similarly congruent findings. From a desk review of some 400 articles, it concludes (as do others, i.e. Jennings et al., 2020) that potential co-benefits are often local, immediate and important to calibrate for, and greatly exceed adverse effects, which can be minimized through the strong design of risk mitigation strategies (Bhandary et al., 2021; Smith et al., 2016; also see Pearce, 2000), thus arguably from a perspective of climate security and/or environmental peacebuilding, and the optimization of climate finance, a focus on peace co-benefits could help create incentives for more effective allocation, where underinvestment is evident. The DECC-commissioned study finds that research on co-benefits is "extensive but fragmented" (Smith et al., 2016).

In 2010, Tanzler, Maas and Carius highlighted the need for climate finance to "harness the direct co-benefits of adaptation for peacebuilding" on a local, project-based level by designing conflict-sensitive adaptation programmes with transformative outcomes (Tänzler et al., 2010). Similarly, in their 2020 study of all the first-round NDCs, UNDP and the UNFCCC (2020) illustrated that better metrics are needed to quantify and capture peace co-benefits, not only in relation to adaptation finance, but also mitigation and access to energy (UNDP, 2020a, 2020b).

Comparing and contrasting these perspectives, literature originating from the climate security perspective has interrogated questions of maladaptation (Adger et al., 2014) and malmitigation, the "backdraft" (i.e. Dabelko et al., 2013) and building on this, "boomerang" effects (Swatuk & Wirkus, 2018) of climate change adaptation and mitigation, and thus effectively, the "co-costs" of adaptation and mitigation and actually has little guidance to offer on the role and or the co-benefits of climate finance. That recent climate security literature which does address climate finance is limited to conflict risk as it relates to adaptation, *not* mitigation or access to energy (for example, see Sitati et al., 2021), and references the need for conflict sensitivity, the "first, do no harm" principle. "A New Climate for Peace," commissioned under the German G7 presidency, stresses the need for dedicated funding to address climate and fragility risks (Rüttinger et al., 2015).

The UN's Work on Climate Finance and Peace Co-benefits

In the past 15–20 years, these climate change, peace and security interlinkages have received a growing amount of attention not only among researchers, but also within policy circles. While neither the Paris Agreement, nor the Kyoto Protocol, nor the Sendai framework make mention of conflict, fragility, peace or security, (Wong, 2022b), it has been the UN Security Council which has brought attention to this intersection (Conca et al., 2017). A landmark Presidential Statement from 2011 (PRST/2011/15) paved the way for more frequent engagement on the topic and since 2017, a succession of formal outcomes thereon, recognizing the adverse impact of climate change on stability and calling for "adequate risk assessments and risk management strategies by governments and the United Nations."[9]

Within the policy sphere, the UN's recent work, including that of UNDP and the Climate Security Mechanism, established in 2018, to strengthen the analysis of climate-related security risks, has tried to bridge the gap on climate finance and peace. Its 2021 study sought to uncover trends in access to climate finance for countries suffering from conflict and fragility; identify gaps and opportunities to leverage the co-benefits of climate action for peace and security; create strategies for mainstreaming climate-related security risks into climate finance and share recommendations on how to make climate finance work more effectively in contexts affected by conflict and fragility.

Through a metadata analysis of 955 projects (worth US$ 14.4 billion) implemented, under the "vertical funds"[10] in 146 countries, including 56 fragile states (according to OECD 2020 "States of fragility"[11]) over the period 2014–May 2021, conflict and fragility were shown to be salient factors in the access to and implementation of climate finance. It found that:

- Only one of the top 15 fragile state recipients of climate finance was extremely fragile, and just two ranked in the overall top 20, respectively, the Democratic Republic of Congo, at fifteenth, and Haiti, nineteenth.
- On a nominal basis, fragile and extremely fragile countries had a similar number of funded projects, through the vertical funds,

---

[9] S/PRST/2011/15. https://undocs.org/en/S/PRST/2011/15.

[10] The "vertical funds" are development financing mechanisms which allocate resources, derived from different funding sources, to single specific issues or themes. For climate change, there are four main funds: the Adaptation Fund, the Climate Investment Funds (CIFs), the Global Environment Facility (GEF) and the Green Climate Fund (GCF). For more information see: UNFCCC: Introduction to Climate Finance: https://unfccc.int/topics/climate-finance/the-big-picture/introduction-to-climate-finance.

[11] The 2020 OECD fragility framework includes 57 countries and territories. Fragility is characterized as a combination of exposure to risk and insufficient coping capacity of the state, systems and/or communities to manage, absorb or mitigate those risks. In the framework, five different dimensions: economic, environmental, political, security and societal, are each represented by 8–12 indicators. For more information, see: OECD (2020).

though they were far smaller than those in fragile or non-fragile states.
- In fragile states, around half of the approved projects target adaptation as their priority, only 30%, mitigation and the remaining 20%, cross-cutting.
- When measuring funding per capita, extremely fragile and fragile states together averaged just US$ 8.8 per person, in finance from the vertical funds, of which extremely fragile states averaged US$ 2.1 per person compared to US$ 10.8 per person in fragile states and US$ 161.7 per person for non-fragile states (including the SIDS).

This data set comprises only multilateral finance, in part, due to data accessibility and budgetary constraints. Moreover, given that grant-based finance is still the more accessible form of finance in conflict-affected and fragile settings, many of which struggle with high levels of debt distress (which increased during the global pandemic[12]) and thus face barriers to accessing other types of finance, inter alia, due to the cost of capital. Recovery from the COVID-19 pandemic and the war in Ukraine may further impact government revenues, and thus ODA and related financial commitments.

Main Findings

From the study by UNDP (2021), when examined together with perspectives from the literature review and recent experience of both climate change and peacebuilding vertical funds, some key findings emerge that can explain the rationale and delineate the contours of a framework for a co-benefits approach to examining the peace dividend of climate finance.

The Salience of Conflict and Fragility to Climate Vulnerability and Finance

Global climate governance and by extension of this, climate finance largely ignores conflict, effectively disadvantaging conflict and fragility-affected

---

[12] The UN Secretary-General's Independent Expert Group report on climate finance (2020) highlights that 54% of low-income countries already suffer from, or are at risk of debt distress and that increasing levels are also observed in climate vulnerable middle-income countries. For more details, see Averchenkova et al. (2020).

settings, whereas conflict can increase vulnerability to climate change (UNDP, 2021; Wong, 2022b) and by 2030, an estimated half of those living in poverty will reside in countries affected by high levels of violence (UN & World Bank, 2018). Climate finance can better account for contextual conflict and insecurity risk, *firstly*, as conflict impacts climate change vulnerability, so conflict and fragility are not out-of-scope in climate change programming and *secondly*, as an impediment to climate action, so as to do no harm, but also to achieve primary mitigation and adaptation objectives.

In addition to climate change and disaster risk reduction, it is important to consider conflict sensitivity. There are, indeed, very many countries, both in the Southern and Northern hemisphere, which are highly prone to natural—including climate-related—disasters, which will suffer from the increased frequency, intensity and changing distribution of extreme weather events due to climate change. In those countries also suffering from fragility and conflict, climate investments can face quite different challenges from non-fragile settings, including the physical destruction—sometimes intentional—of the very assets required to adapt to and mitigate climate change, the presence and activities of non-state armed groups, changing patterns of migration and forced displacement, etc. (UNDP, 2020a). The geographic overlap in countries that are affected by both climate *and* insecurity, makes a strong case for salience in climate finance, without the need to prove direct causality between climate and conflict, as debated in the climate security literature (Hsiang and Burke, 2013; Lee, 2022; Mach et al., 2019; Miguel et al., 2004).

Having such little access to climate finance and without better addressing vulnerability, including conflict and insecurity risk, climate finance essentially becomes out-of-reach for many countries, and perhaps a vicious cycle as financing often stipulates co-financing requirements. Insufficient climate finance may exacerbate climate-related security risks (UNDP, 2021). Overall, climate finance is still risk averse, access to climate finance in conflict-affected and fragile environments cannot be optimized without consideration of their specific contexts (UNDP, 2021). If a primary climate rationale determines whether an intervention is of value and whether it should be funded, ancillary benefits, particularly for peace, may make a stronger case for funding and may help identify opportunities to de-risk investments.

Beyond a Costs and Co-costs Only Approach

Estimating cost is, of course, essential to calculating benefit. Policymaking shows a natural inherent bias towards cost and co-costs estimation, which Karlsson et al. (2020) argue can lead to "sub-optimal climate policymaking" and "goal failure." As Rohner and Thoenig (2021) stress the scale of conflict-related costs is often underestimated. Operating in fragile and conflict-affected contexts, there are additional but necessary costs which need to be factored in related to the needed security protocol to ensure the safety of staff and local communities. Potential delays in implementation due to violent and/or armed conflict and identifying and deploying expertise in such duty stations means that programming in these environments may take more time and that delays and no-cost extensions are more likely (GEF Independent Evaluation Office, 2020; UNDP, 2021). As a general rule, it is observed that more stable countries with higher absorptive capacity will benefit from greater flows than fragile states, as is the case with development finance (Caldwell & Alayza, 2021).[13] Budgeting experience from humanitarian financing procedures could also an important reference point here. Resources allocated to conflict-affected contexts may also be at risk of elite capture and/or misappropriation and thus impact upon funding commitments (Nett, 2016). It may be the case that finance directed to one geographic area may also result in increased in-migration and change dynamics in natural resource management and inter and intra-communal relations.[14] There is also a need for conflict analysis to inform climate finance.

According to the Sixth Assessment Report of the IPCC, the incidence of maladaptation has increased (IPCC, 2022) and needs to be holistically addressed. A focus only on avoiding maladaptation, as evidenced in

---

[13] WRI's study of 17 developing countries shows decreases in climate budget and delays in implementation. See: Caldwell, M. and Alayza, N. (2021). What COVID-19 tells us about making climate finance resilient to future. Crises. *WRI Insights*, 28 October 2021. https://www.wri.org/insights/making-climate-finance-resilient-future-crises. Also see Mercy Corps (2020). Submission to the UNFCCC Standing Committee on Finance on behalf of Mercy Corps—Call for evidence: Information and data for the preparation of the 2020 biennial assessment and overview of climate finance flows. https://unfccc.int/sites/default/files/resource/SCF%20Submission%20Fragile%20States_Mercy%20Corps.pdf.

[14] Johns, T. (2015). The impacts of international REDD+ finance DRC case study. http://www.climateandlandusealliance.org/wp-content/uploads/2015/08/Impacts_of_International_REDD_Finance_Case_Study_DRC.pdf.

the climate security field, does not encourage the innovation (including large-scale ecosystem regeneration, bankable adaptation initiatives, etc.), new approaches and a xenogenesis in thinking that would be needed to make sure that climate finance contributes to adaptation ambition while aligning with peacebuilding objectives. Concessional climate finance is already highly risk averse and the amounts that reach conflict-affected and fragile contexts are almost nominal, on a per capita basis, as the data set shows, demonstrating socio-economic and peace co-benefits may help change incentives and improve qualitative outcomes.

A peace co-benefit (compared to air quality, health benefits, the costing of a security detail, etc.) may seem abstract or difficult to quantify or qualify. Metrics from conflict prevention and peacebuilding practice and related investments may be informative here. As an example, and as stressed in UN and the World Bank's (2018) "Pathways to Peace – Inclusive Approaches to Preventing Violent Conflict" could save an estimated US$ 5–70 billion a year which, it states, could be reinvested in poverty reduction efforts. Prevention is also, in and of itself, an important lens through which the peace co-benefit of climate finance, in the case of conflict-affected and fragile contexts, could be viewed. As we know, adaptation needs are not static (Chambwera et al., 2014), and neither are the costs, which will invariably increase with time, and without drastic cuts in emissions (UNEP, 2021) and sufficient finance. Early action can present cost savings over longer timeframes and "no" or "low regret" adaptation options and access to renewable energy may yield peace co-benefits, with the effects compounded over time and the avoidance "lock-in" to unsustainable development pathways and the additional costs of retrofitting (UNDP, 2020b). The inverse could also hold true: conflict-affected and fragile contexts face increasing levels of climate change vulnerability due to insufficient access and investments in climate change adaptation and access to energy. Implementation of climate finance at different phases of the conflict cycle is an area which warrants our attention, in addition to conflict-affected and/or peacebuilding contexts.

Peace Co-benefits of Adaptation and Mitigation/Access to Energy

Climate security and environmental peacebuilding often neglect adequate consideration of mitigation, when failure of mitigation, as highlighted, inter alia, by the 2022 Global Risks Report of World Economic Forum, is the greatest threat we face as humankind. Peace co-benefit thinking should not overlook mitigation and access to energy. Globally, 759 million people still lack access to energy, half of whom reside in fragile and conflict-affected settings, and 84% in rural areas, of which an estimated 660 million people will continue to lack access in 2030 (IEA, IRENA, UN, the World Bank and WHO, 2021). According to the World Bank, the percentage of the population which had access to energy in 2020 in South Sudan, was just 7.2% Somalia 49.7%, Central African Republic, 15.5%, Democratic Republic of the Congo, 19.1% and Chad 11.1%.[15] Data compiled by the United Nations High Commissioner for Refugees (UNHCR) from 20 countries over the period 2018–2020 also highlights that in the host communities, access to energy was 33%, whereas that of refugees, was just 18% (IEA, IRENA, UN, the World Bank and WHO, 2021). To achieve SDG 7 will require scaling investments.

Adaptation is underfunded globally, but locally in extremely fragile contexts, the levels of both adaptation and mitigation/access to energy investments are insufficient to meet the need. When adaptation and mitigation investments in extremely fragile countries are *both* so low and underfunded, they should not be presented as an "either/or" scenario as increased investments and likewise understanding of the peace co-benefits of both are important. It is noted that gender is better mainstreamed into adaptation than mitigation financing (OECD, 2016); the same observation could be made in the case of climate-related security risks. In non-conflict settings, given the overall volumes of financing of mitigation and access to energy, more attention is should be given to both potential co-costs and co-benefits. Only focusing on synergies between adaptation and peacebuilding risks missing conflict co-costs and also for missed peace co-benefits. Like the impacts of climate change, co-benefits are multi-temporal and multi-scalar (Mayrhofer & Gupta, 2016), as such, analysis needs to go beyond only local-level direct costs.

The Stimson Center and Energy Peace Partners (2021), in their study of Mali, noted that 50.8% of the population had access to energy overall, but that inequality in access was significant, with the South and centre of

---

[15] The World Bank's Global Electrification Database from "Tracking SDG 7: The Energy Progress Report" is jointly led by the custodian agencies: the International Energy Agency (IEA), the International Renewable Energy Agency (IRENA), the United Nations Statistics Division (UNSD), the World Bank and the World Health Organization (WHO). For further details please see: https://data.worldbank.org/indicator/EG.ELC.ACCS.ZS.

the country at 80% and electrification in North at a mere 2%, which exacerbated underlying inequalities and marginalization. It highlighted that the deployment of renewable energy, including by the United Nations Multidimensional Integrated Stabilization Mission in Mali (MINUSMA) would not only reduce transaction costs, carbon footprint and environmental impact, but also help effectively mitigate security risks related to diesel transportation and the illicit fuel trade, and ultimately help unlock co-benefits in the form of increased access to energy in the North.

Learning by Doing and Intersectoral Partnerships

As there has been little specific analysis of the climate finance "co-benefits" for peace, stability and security in conflict-affected and fragile states, the use of thematic evaluations, dynamic portfolio tracking and convening power of multilateral vertical funds could offer key insights to enhance overall climate finance and programming outcomes. As operational understanding is still in a nascent form and a significant gap. Generating "process knowledge" (Lawrence et al., 2022) is important and a transdisciplinary approach makes sense. Such mechanisms can help forge a dialogue between diverse stakeholders, including peacebuilding actors and create platforms for climate finance, and peace and security.

Worth highlighting, in this regard, is the GEF's work on climate and environmental security, which has been the most extensive to date, of the vertical funds. Beginning with the 2018 report, "Environmental Security: Dimensions and Priorities" produced by its Scientific and Technical Advisory Panel, it examines environmental security considerations throughout the GEF's portfolio and stresses the need to directly address environmental security, conflict risk and the interlinkages between environmental change and vulnerability (Ratner, 2018). The GEF's Global Wildlife Program and the Climate Technology Centre and Network, are examples of the kinds of platforms needed that could support exchange, innovation and mainstreaming priorities in the funds' country-level programmes and set goalposts for project development (UNDP, 2021).

Complementary to understanding the peace co-benefits of climate finance is the need to capture the climate co-benefits of peacebuilding finance. The UN Secretary-General's Peacebuilding Fund (PBF) can also serve as a useful case in point, for its deliberate efforts to outline climate change as a priority, including in their new strategic plan. The 2020–2024 strategy stresses the PBF's increased attention to "provid[ing] more support to managing conflict risks emanating from climate-change related pressures on people and resources," to build and sustain peace. The PBF's stocktaking of its climate security-related portfolio and its thematic review (ongoing at the time this chapter was being written) can offer additional food for thought. The potential for cross-learning, recalibrating metrics and co-financing from climate and peacebuilding vertical funds should also be explored. Aligning climate finance with peacebuilding finance, as the latter is arguably less risk averse, and often includes investments in natural capital, could maximize co-benefits ensuring peacebuilding finance benefits from systematic climate-proofing approaches.

To make climate finance work better for conflict-affected and fragile contexts will require re-envisioning climate governance and policy (UNDP, 2020a, 2020b). NDC finance strategies and financial roadmaps can offer an entry point. In climate adaptation finance, a corollary and similarly important modality for mainstreaming peace co-benefits could be National Adaptation Plans, which are supported in large part by the Green Climate Fund and the GEF (UNDP, 2021). Environmental and social safeguards are critical to "do no harm" approaches. But to contribute positively to peace, the field of climate finance will need to reconstruct its Theories of Change. In the conceptual policy-practice feedback loop, practice is often still underrated, while heuristic approaches are key to solutions.

Co-benefits as a Basis to Define the Peace Dividend of Climate Finance

As we edge closer to the 1.5C line, the risk of triggering irreversible tipping points in sensitive climate systems (Lenton et al., 2020) increases with each fractional degree in increased global warming. All the while the cost of adaptation continues to rise and is estimated to reach US$ 500 billion per year by 2050 in developing countries alone (UNEP, 2021). For comparison, in 2019, multilateral adaptation finance from developed to developing countries was just US$ 20 billion (OECD, 2021). The examination of co-benefits is critically important to the effective allocation of climate finance in times when funding is constrained. As evidenced in the literature (Glomsrød et al., 1992; Nemet et al., 2010; Pearce, 2000), potential cost savings due to air quality and health co-benefits are of similar scale to offset the cost of GHG emissions abatement.

Co-benefits thus provide significant and compelling arguments, particularly when for example, when climate and environment often suffer from de-prioritization in fragile and conflict-affected countries. Climate, environmental and climate actors are typically the weakest actors in their institutional settings and when an emergency sets in and humanitarian response becomes the priority du jour, other types of financing, reflecting in particular, long-term adaptation and mitigation needs may be forsaken, even while these needs do not go away.

To date, however, while literature, research and policy debate on climate finance-related co-benefits in general has progressed (Buchholz & Rübbelke, 2021), treatment of co-benefits for peace, stability and security remains anecdotal at best and formal codification almost non-existent (Wong, 2022a). Taking economic and health co-benefits as a case in point (Rahman & Mori, 2020), with more intersectoral discussion, assessment and awareness raising on peace co-benefits of climate finance, a stronger case could be made for action and investment, in countries which are climate vulnerable and affected by conflict and fragility.

Arguing for the integration of climate change adaptation and mitigation into peacebuilding and peacekeeping, Matthew (2014) describes the "skepticism" and "complacency" by many that more urgent needs should prevail and that climate change adaptation and mitigation should come later. This cycle may become hard to break. Articulating non-climate co-benefits may provide other persuasive arguments to help spur climate action (Bain et al., 2015), in this case, in contexts where climate and environmental considerations alone may not be high on the policy agenda, and simultaneously ensure coherence with primary conflict prevention and peacebuilding objectives.

The climate security debate has recently moved on to begin to tackle climate finance. Having joined the Security Council in January 2022, the United Arab Emirates held an Arria formula meeting entitled "Climate Finance for Sustaining Peace and Security" in March 2022, during which Security Council members debated, for the first time, climate finance and its potential contributions to conflict prevention and peacebuilding strategies. The Government of Kenya, also an elected Security Council member, launched a "Call for Financial Action on the Nexus of Climate and Security" on the sidelines of "Stockholm+50" (the fiftieth anniversary of the 1972 United Nations Conference on the Human Environment) in June 2022. The event's conclusion included: bringing onboard all stakeholders and leaving no one behind; developing climate-fragility frameworks, attracting sufficient financial resources; prioritizing the African continent due to its fragilities and level of development, tailoring approaches to climate adaptation and mitigation, particularly empowering women; attracting adequate resources for the required energy transition towards renewables and moving from commitment to action (IISD Earth Negotiations Bulletin, 2022, June 3).

Conclusions

Climate finance dynamics in countries affected by conflict and fragility are important to climate finance, climate security and environmental peacebuilding fields. Absolute increases in finance are essential, particularly in the case of grant financing for these country contexts, given the low per capita averages. Climate finance is already risk averse and a limited focus on cost and co-costs will not lead to maximally beneficial policy choices. The co-benefits argument pertains not only to access and the quantity of climate finance, but also the quality and effectiveness. Moreover, inherent to finance instruments are incentives or disincentives to fostering desired behaviours and actions; arguments distinct from those in the extant climate security or environmental peacebuilding literature. As the debate continues on the effectiveness of climate finance; metrics and goalposts for climate finance which are conflict-sensitive and capture not only socio-economic, but also peace co-benefits or dividends can incentivize investments that work better for conflict-affected and fragile contexts.

However, without some re-engineering of climate-financing mechanisms, including results management systems and metrics, little may change, as climate finance may continue to remain beyond the reach for some of the most climate vulnerable conflict-affected and fragile contexts (UNDP, 2021). As a result, such countries may become increasingly susceptible to both climate and climate-related development, peace and security risks over time. A balance does need to be struck, and valid concerns addressed related to the "obfuscation" of the climate objectives of climate finance (Buchholz & Rübbelke, 2021; Nemet et al., 2010). Crowding out of peacebuilding finance should not take place, as climate finance should firstly and ultimately fund climate objectives, while calibrating for co-costs and co-benefits; the latter alone not being a sufficient rationale, unless the primary benefits can be established first. A wider lens does not necessarily mean an obscured focus. To the contrary, an overly narrow or technocratic approach that doesn't reflect the nuance of local contextual dynamics is also identified as a contributing factor to maladaptation (Schilling et al., 2017).

Launched in December 2021, 50 Nobel Peace Prize Laureates called on national governments to redirect 2% of their military expenditure each year beginning in 2025, to the Global Peace Dividend Initiative (Smerlak & Rovelli, 2022). This "global peace dividend" of USD 1.3 trillion by 2030, they argued, may be used for pandemics, climate action and extreme poverty (OECD, 2021). The conventional thinking around the "peace dividend" (Aslam, 2007; Chan, 1995)—first emerging from political debate during the Viet Nam War (Melman, 1989), recurring at the end of the Cold War and now during the Ukraine War—supports the belief that reductions in military expenditure in a post-war period will free up resources which can improve a country's economic performance. Nixon, in his acceptance speech in 1972, stressed a concept of not just defined "solely in monetary terms" but instead in the form of "a lasting peace in the world," (Nixon, 1972) thus reflecting a loose conceptual framing that has ubiquitously that also been used by those in the peacebuilding field. This chapter attempted to explain how the logic of co-benefits can be used to determine the peace dividend of investments in climate finance, as an attempt to address a gap in the climate finance, climate security and environmental peacebuilding fields.

Within the constraints of this chapter, multilateral climate finance was the primary focus. However, the same overarching arguments could be applied to private, domestic, etc., climate finance. The subject of the peace co-benefit or dividend in the case of other types of climate finance, humanitarian finance and broader connections to loss and damage, would merit further attention. Issues related to the reporting and transparency of climate finance, etc., are already well-addressed in recent literature and was not the intended scope of this study.

Acknowledgement Sincere thanks are also offered to Dima Reda, Joe Thwaites and Yue Cao for their review and the thoughtful comments kindly provided on the draft text.

REFERENCES

Adger, W. N., et al. (2014). *Human security in: Climate change 2014: Impacts, adaptation, and vulnerability*. Part A: Global and sectoral aspects (pp. 755–791). Contribution of Working Group II to the Fifth Assessment Report of the Intergovernmental Panel on Climate Change (IPCC). Cambridge University Press. https://doi.org/10.1038/s41558-018-0083-3

Alcayna, T. (2020). *At what cost: How chronic gaps in adaptation finance expose the world's poorest people to climate chaos* (p. 52). Zurich Flood Resilience Alliance. https://www.concernusa.org/wp-content/uploads/2020/07/AT-WHAT-COST.pdf

Arezki, R. (2020). Climate finance for Africa requires overcoming bottlenecks in domestic capacity. *Nature Climate Change, 11*, 888–888. https://doi.org/10.1038/s41558-021-01191-7

Aslam, R. (2007). Measuring the peace dividend: Evidence from developing economies. *Defence and Peace Economics, 18*(1), 39–52. https://doi.org/10.1080/10242690600924620

Atmadja, S. S., et al. (2020). *Leveraging climate finance for gender equality and poverty reduction: A comparative study*. Report. CIFOR. https://www.cifor.org/publications/pdf_files/Reports/Climate-UNDP-Report.pdf

Australian Aid, Oxfam & PACCCIL. (2019, October). *Making climate finance work for women: Voices from polynesian and micronesian communities*. https://unfccc.int/sites/default/files/resource/2019Pacific-Climate-Gender%20Report.pdf

Averchenkova, A., et al. (2020). *Delivering on the $100 billion climate finance commitment* (p. 70). The Independent Expert Group on Climate Finance. https://www.convergence.finance/resource/9af77cee-a9f9-4cef-be20-2b0ffdd11606/view

Bain, P., et al. (2015). Co-benefits of addressing climate change can motivate action around the world. *Nature Climate Change, 6*(2), 154–157. https://doi.org/10.1038/nclimate2814

Bhandary, R. R., Gallagher, K. S., & Zhang, F. (2021). Climate finance policy in practice: A review of the evidence. *Climate Policy, 21*(4), 529–545. https://doi.org/10.1080/14693062.2020.1871313

Bowen, A. (2011). Raising climate finance to support developing country action: Some economic considerations. *Climate Policy, 11*(3), 1020–1036. https://doi.org/10.1080/14693062.2011.582388

Bowen, A., Campiglio, E., & Herreras Martinez, S. (2017). An 'equal effort' approach to assessing the north–south climate finance gap. *Climate Policy, 17*(2), 231–245. https://doi.org/10.1080/14693062.2015.1094728

Buchholz, W., & Rübbelke, D. (2021). Overstraining international climate finance: When conflicts of objectives threaten its success. *International*

Journal of Climate Change Strategies and Management, 13(4/5), 547–563. https://doi.org/10.1108/IJCCSM-06-2021-0071

Burke, M., Hsiang S. M., & Miguel, E. (2015). Climate and conflict. *Annual Review of Economics, 7*(1), 577–617 (Volume publication date August 2015). https://doi.org/10.1146/annurev-economics-080614-115430

Busby, J. (2018). Taking stock: The field of climate and security. *Current Climate Change Reports, 4*, 338–346. https://doi.org/10.1007/s40641-018-0116-z

Buzan, B., Wæver, O., & de Wilde, J. (1998). *Security: A new framework for analysis*. Lynne Rienner Publishers. ISBN 978-1-55587-603-6

Caldwell, M., & Alayza, N. (2021, October 28). What COVID-19 tells us about making climate finance resilient to future. Crises. *WRI Insights*. https://www.wri.org/insights/making-climate-finance-resilient-future-crises

Calvet, L., Gianfrate, G., & Uppal, R. (2022). The finance of climate change. *Journal of Corporate Finance, 73*, 102162. ISSN 0929-1199. https://doi.org/10.1016/j.jcorpfin.2022.102162

Cao, Y., Alcayna, T., Quevedo, A., & Jarvie, J. (2021, September). *Exploring the conflict blind spots in climate adaptation finance*. SPARC. https://www.sparc-knowledge.org/sites/default/files/documents/resources/exploring-the-conflict-blind-spots-in-climate-adaptation-finance.pdf

Carty, T., Kowalzig, J., & Zagema, B. (2020). *Climate finance shadow report 2020: Assessing progress towards the $100 billion commitment*. https://doi.org/10.21201/2020.6621

Chambwera, M., et al. (2014). Economics of adaptation. In *Climate change 2014: Impacts, adaptation, & vulnerability. Part A: Global and sectoral aspects. Contribution of Working Group II to the Fifth Assessment Report of the IPCC* (C. B. Field, V. R. Barros, D. J. Dokken, K. J. Mach, M. D. Mastrandrea, T. E. Bilir, M. Chatterjee, K. L. Ebi, Y. O. Estrada, R. C. Genova, B. Girma, E. S. Kissel, A. N. Levy, S. MacCracken, P. R. Mastrandrea, & L. L. White, Eds., pp. 945–977). Cambridge University Press.

Chan, S. (1995). Grasping the peace dividend: Some Propositions on the Conversion of Swords into Plowshares. *Mershon International Studies Review, 39*(1), 53. https://doi.org/10.2307/222692

Climate Change. (1995). *The science of climate change contribution of Working Group I to the second assessment report of the intergovernmental panel on climate change* (J. J. Houghton, L. G. Meiro Filho, IS, A. Callander, N. Harris, A. Kattenberg, & K. Maskell, Eds.) (ISBN 0-521-56433-6 Hardback; 0-521-56436-0 Paperback).

Climate Policy Initiative. (2019). *Global landscape of climate finance 2019*. https://climatepolicyinitiative.org/wp-content/uploads/2019/11/2019-Global-Landscape-of-Climate-Finance.pdf

Conca, K., & Dabelko, G. D. (Eds.). (2002). *Environmental peacemaking*. Johns Hopkins University Press.

Conca, K., Thwaites, J., & Lee, G. (2017). Climate change and the UN Security Council: Bully pulpit or bull in a china shop? *Global Environmental Politics*, *17*(2), 1–20. https://doi.org/10.1162/glep_a_00398

Dabelko, G. D., Herzer, L., Null, S., Parker, M., & Sticklor, R. (Eds.). (2013). *Backdraft: The conflict potential of climate change adaptation and mitigation*. Environmental Change & Security Program report (Vol. 14, Issue 2). Woodrow Wilson international Center for Scholars.

De Wilde, J. (2008). Environmental security deconstructed. In H. G. Brauch (Ed.), *Globalization and environmental challenges: Reconceptualizing security in the 21st century* (pp. 595–602). Springer.

GEF Independent Evaluation Office. (2020). *Evaluation of GEF support in fragile and conflict -affected situations*. GEF/E/C.59/01. https://www.the gef.org/sites/default/files/council-meeting-documents/EN_GEF.E_C59_01_Evaluation_of_GEF_Support_in_Fragile_and_Conflict-Affected_Situations_Nov_2020_0.pdf

Giglio, S., Kelly, B. T. & Stroebel, J. (2020, December). *Climate finance* (NBER Working Paper No. 28226). JEL No. G0.

Gleditsch, N. P. (1998, May). Armed conflict and the environment: A critique of the literature. *Journal of Peace Research*, *35*(3), 381–400.

Glomsrød, S., Vennemo, H., & Johnsen, T. (1992). Stabilization of emissions of CO2: A computable general equilibrium assessment. *The Scandinavian Journal of Economics*, *94*(1), 53. https://doi.org/10.2307/3440468

Hendrix, C. S. (2018). Searching for climate–conflict links. *Nature Climate Change*, *8*(3), 190–191. https://doi.org/10.1038/s41558-018-0083-3

Homer-Dixon, T. F. (1994, Summer). Environmental scarcities and violent conflict: Evidence from cases. *International Security*, *19*(1), 5–40. https://homerdixon.com/evidence-from-cases-full-article/

Homer-Dixon, T. F., & Levy, M. A. (1995). Environment and security. *International Security*, 20(3) (Winter 1995/96), 189–198.

Hong, H., Karolyi, G. A., & Scheinkman, J. A. (2020, March). Climate finance. *The Review of Financial Studies*, *33*(3), 1011–1023. https://doi.org/10.1093/rfs/hhz146

Hsiang, S., & Burke, M. (2013). Quantifying the influence of climate on human conflict. *Science*, *341*, 1235367. https://doi.org/10.1126/science.1235367

Ide, T., Bruch, C., Carius, A., Conca, K., Dabelko, G. D. Matthew, R., & Weinthal, E. (2021, January). The past and future(s) of environmental peacebuilding. *International Affairs*, *97*(1), 1–16. https://doi.org/10.1093/ia/iiaa177

IEA, IRENA, UN, World Bank & WHO. (2021). *Tracking SDG 7: The energy progress report*. World Bank. https://trackingsdg7.esmap.org/data/files/download-documents/2021_tracking_sdg7_report.pdf

IISD Earth Negotiations Bulletin. (2022, June 3). *Global call for financial action towards the nexus between climate and security.* Retrieved June 20, 2022, from https://enb.iisd.org/events/global-call-financial-action-towards-nexus-between-climate-and-security

IPCC. (2001). *Global, regional, and national costs and ancillary benefits of mitigation.* Contribution of Working Group III to the Third Assessment Report of the IPCC.

IPCC. (2022). Summary for policymakers [H.-O. Pörtner, D.C. Roberts, E.S. Poloczanska, K. Mintenbeck, M. Tignor, A. Alegría, M. Craig, S. Langsdorf, S. Löschke, V. Möller, A. Okem (eds.)]. In: *Climate change 2022: Impacts, adaptation and vulnerability.* Contribution of working group II to the sixth assessment report of the intergovernmental panel on climate change [H.-O. Pörtner, D.C. Roberts, M. Tignor, E.S. Poloczanska, K. Mintenbeck, A. Alegría, M. Craig, S. Langsdorf, S. Löschke, V. Möller, A. Okem, B. Rama (eds.)]. Cambridge University Press, 3–33. https://doi.org/10.1017/9781009325844.001

Jennings, N., Fecht, D., & de Matteis, S. (2020). Mapping the co-benefits of climate change action to issues of public concern in the UK: A narrative review. *The Lancet Planetary Health, 4*(9), e424–e433. https://doi.org/10.1016/s2542-5196(20)30167-4

Karlsson, M., Alfredsson, E., & Westling, N. (2020). Climate policy cobenefits: A review. *Climate Policy, 20*(3), 292–316. https://doi.org/10.1080/14693062.2020.1724070

Krampe, F., Hegazi, F., & VanDeveer, S. D. (2021). Sustaining peace through better resource governance: Three potential mechanisms for environmental peacebuilding. *World Development, 144,* 105508. https://doi.org/10.1016/j.worlddev.2021.105508

Lawrence, M. G., Williams, S., Nanz, P., & Renn, O. (2022). Characteristics, potentials, and challenges of transdisciplinary research. *One Earth, 5*(1), 44–61. https://doi.org/10.1016/j.oneear.2021.12.010

Lee, H. F. (2022). Historical climate-war nexus in the eyes of geographers. *Asian Geographer, 39*(1), 93–112. https://doi.org/10.1080/10225706.2020.1768571

Lenton, T. M. et al. (2020/2019). Climate tipping points—Too risky to bet against. *Nature, 575,* 193–197. https://media.nature.com/original/magazine-assets/d41586-019-03595-0/d41586-019-03595-0.pdf

Levy, M. A. (1995, Autumn). Is the environment a national security issue? *International Security, 20*(2), 35–62. The MIT Press. http://www.jstor.org/stable/2539228

Mach, K. J., Kraan, C. M., Adger, W. N., et al. (2019). Climate as a risk factor for armed conflict. *Nature, 571,* 193–197. https://doi.org/10.1038/s41586-019-1300-6

Matthew, R. A. (2014). Integrating climate change into peacebuilding. *Climatic Change, 123*(1), 83–93. https://doi.org/10.1007/s10584-013-0894-1

Mathews, J. T. (1989, Spring). Redefining security. *Foreign Affairs, 68*(2), 162–177; see p. 162. https://doi.org/10.2307/20043906

Mayrhofer, J. P., & Gupta, J. (2016). The science and politics of co-benefits in climate policy. *Environmental Science & Policy, 57*, 22–30. https://doi.org/10.1016/j.envsci.2015.11.005

Melman, S. (1989, December 17). Business forum: The peace dividend; what to do with the Cold War Money. *The New York Times*, p. 3.

Mercy Corps. (2020, June). *Submission to the UNFCCC standing committee on finance on behalf of Mercy Corps—Call for evidence: Information and data for the preparation of the 2020 Biennial Assessment and Overview of Climate Finance Flows*. https://unfccc.int/sites/default/files/resource/SCF%20Submission%20Fragile%20States_Mercy%20Corps.pdf

Miguel, E., Satyanath, S., & Sergenti, E. (2004). Economic shocks and civil conflict: An instrumental variables approach. *Journal of Political Economy, 112*(4), 725–753.

Moran, A., et al. (2018). *The intersection of global fragility and climate risks*. United States Agency for International Development. https://www.straussce nter.org/wp-content/uploads/The-Intersection-of-Global-Fragility-and-Cli mate-Risks-2018.pdf

Nemet, G. F., Holloway, T., & Meier, P. (2010). Implications of incorporating air-quality co-benefits into climate change policymaking. *Environmental Research Letters, 5*(1), 14007.

Nett, K. (2016). *Financing for resilience: 3 lessons to be learned in climate finance*. https://climate-diplomacy.org/magazine/cooperation/financing-res ilience-3-lessons-be-learned-climate-finance-0

Nixon, R. (1972, August 24). Transcript of Nixon's acceptance address and excerpts from Agnew's speech. *The New York Times*. https://www.nytimes. com/1972/08/24/archives/transcript-of-nixons-acceptance-address-and-exc erpts-from-agnews.html

OECD. (2016). *Making climate finance work for women: Overview of bilateral ODA to gender and climate change*. Available at: https://www.oecd.org/development/gender-development/making-climate-finance-work-for-women. htm. Accessed September 25, 2022.

OECD. (2020). *States of fragility 2020*. OECD Publishing (States of Fragility). https://doi.org/10.1787/ba7c22e7-en

OECD. (2021). Climate finance provided and mobilised by developed countries: Aggregate trends updated with 2019 data. *OECD Publishing*. https://doi. org/10.1787/03590fb7-en

Oels, A. (2012). From 'securitization' of climate change to 'climatization' of the security field: Comparing three theoretical perspectives. Hexagon Series on

Human and Environmental Security and Peace (pp. 185–205). https://doi.org/10.1007/978-3-642-28626-1_9

Pearce, D. (2000). *Policy frameworks for the ancillary benefits of climate change policies* (pp 517–560). OECD.

Poole, L. (2018). Financing for stability in the post-2015 era. *OECD*. https://doi.org/10.1787/c4193fef-en

Rahman, S. M., & Mori, A. (2020). Dissemination and perception of adaptation co-benefits: Insights from the coastal area of Bangladesh. *World Development Perspectives, 20*, 100247.

Ratner, B. D. (2018). *Environmental security: dimensions and priorities*. Scientific and Technical Advisory Panel to the Global Environment Facility. https://www.thegef.org/sites/default/files/publications/52103%20STAP%20Report_WEB.pdf

Rigolot, C. (2020). Transdisciplinarity as a discipline and a way of being: Complementarities and creative tensions. *Humanities and Social Sciences Communications, 7*(1), 1–5. https://doi.org/10.1057/s41599-020-00598-5

Rohner, D., & Thoenig, M. (2021). The elusive peace dividend of development policy: From war traps to macro complementarities. *Annual Review of Economics*. Annual Reviews, ISSN 1941-1391, ZDB-ID 2516757-1. Vol. 13.2021, 1, pp. 111–131.

Rüttinger, L., Smith, D., Stang, G., Tänzler, D., & Vivekananda, J. (2015). *A new climate for peace—Taking action on climate and fragility risks*. An independent report commissioned by the G7 members, submitted under the German G7 Presidency. Retrieved from https://climate-diplomacy.org/sites/default/files/2020-11/NewClimateForPeace_FullReport_small_0.pdf

Schilling, J., Nash, S. L., Ide, T., Scheffran, J., Froese, R., & von Prondzinski, P. (2017). Resilience and environmental security: Towards joint application in peace building. *Global Change, Peace & Security, 29*(2), 107–127. https://doi.org/10.1080/14781158.2017.1305347

Schwartz, P., Deligiannis, T., Homer-Dixon, T. R. (2000, Summer). The environment and violent conflict: A response to Gleditsch's critique and some suggestions for future research. *Environmental Change & Security Project Report, 6*(6), 77–94.

Sitati, A., et al. (2021). Climate change adaptation in conflict-affected countries: A systematic assessment of evidence. *Discover Sustainability, 2*, 42. https://doi.org/10.1007/s43621-021-00052-9

Smerlak, M., & Rovelli, C. (2022). Put defence money into planetary emergencies, urge Nobel winners. *Nature, 601*(7893), 318. https://doi.org/10.1038/d41586-022-00096-5

Smith, A., Pridmore, A., Hampshire, K., Ahlgren, C., & Goodwin, J. (2016, June 3). Scoping study on the co-benefits and possible adverse side effects of climate change mitigation: Final report. *Aether*.

Smith, D., & Vivekananda, J. (2007) *A climate of conflict: The links between climate change, peace and war*. International Alert. Retrieved from http://www.international-alert.org/pdf/A_Climate_Of_Conflict.pdf Accessed 8 Mar 2012.

Swain, A., & Öjendal, J. (2020). *Environmental conflict and peacebuilding: An introduction*. Routledge.

Swatuk, L. A., & Wirkus, L. (Eds.). (2018). *Water, climate change and the boomerang effect: Unintentional consequences for resource insecurity*. Earthscan Studies in Water Resource Management Series.

Tänzler, D., Maas, A., & Carius, A. (2010). Climate change adaptation and peace. *Wires Climate Change, 1*(5), 741–750. https://doi.org/10.1002/wcc.66

The Henry L. Stimson Center and Energy Peace Partners. (2021). *From renewable energy to peacebuilding in Mali, MINUSMA's opportunity to bridge the gap*. The Henry L. Stimson Center and Energy Peace Partners. https://www.stimson.org/wp-content/uploads/2021/06/Stimson_FinalRelease_June25.pdf

UNDP. 1994. *Human development report 1994: New dimensions of human security*. UNDP.

UNDP. (2020a). *A typology and analysis of climate-related security risks in the first round Nationally Determined Contributions*. UNDP. https://www.undp.org/publications/typology-and-analysis-climate-related-security-risks-first-round-nationally-determined

UNDP. (2020b). *Re-envisioning climate action to sustain peace and human security*. UNDP. https://www.undp.org/blog/re-envisioning-climate-action-sustain-peace-and-human-security

UNDP. (2021). *Climate finance for sustaining peace: Making climate finance work for conflict-affected and fragile contexts*. UNDP. https://www.undp.org/publications/climate-finance-sustaining-peace-making-climate-finance-work-conflict-affected-and

UNECE. (2016, January). *The co-benefits of climate change mitigation*. Sustainable Development Brief No. 2. https://unece.org/fileadmin/DAM/Sustainable_Development_No._2__Final__Draft_OK_2.pdf

UNEP. (2021). *Adaptation gap report 2020*. UNEP. http://www.unep.org/resources/adaptation-gap-report-2020

UNFCCC. (n.d.). *Introduction to climate finance*. www.unfccc.int. Retrieved June 10, 2022, from https://unfccc.int/topics/climate-finance/the-big-picture/introduction-to-climate-finance

United Nations. (1945). *Charter of the United Nations and the Statute of the International Court of Justice*. https://www.un.org/en/about-us/un-charter/full-text

United Nations & World Bank. (2018). *Pathways for peace: Inclusive approaches to preventing violent conflict*. World Bank. https://doi.org/10.1596/978-1-4648-1162-3.License:CreativeCommonsAttributionCCBY3.0IGO

Wong, C. (2022a, May 18). *Making peace with the Paris Agreement*. Commentary for Royal United Services Institute. https://rusi.org/explore-our-research/publications/commentary/making-peace-paris-agreement

Wong, C. (2022b, March). *Climate finance and the peace dividend: A co-benefits argument*. Green Finance Platform. https://www.greenfinanceplatform.org/blog/climate-finance-and-peace-dividend-co-benefits-argument

World Economic Forum. (2022, January). *The global risks report 2022* (17th ed.). https://www3.weforum.org/docs/WEF_The_Global_Risks_Report_2022.pdf

CHAPTER 10

Toward Just and Effective Climate Action

Larry A. Swatuk and Corrine Cash

INTRODUCTION

In this concluding chapter, we draw together the key points made by contributors to this volume. At the outset of this project we speculated that there were lessons for climate finance to be drawn from the world's long experience with international development. Our goal was twofold: first, avoid the mistakes of the past; second, ensure that the needs and interests of the most vulnerable were placed at the centre of decision-making, planning and action. The logic is quite obvious: as with international development, climate finance proposes a transfer of funds from the rich world (Global North) to the poor(er) world (Global South).

L. A. Swatuk (✉)
Department of Geography and Environment, Mount Allison University, Sackville, NB, Canada
e-mail: lswatuk@uwaterloo.ca

C. Cash
School of Environment, Enterprise and Development, University of Waterloo, Waterloo, ON, Canada
e-mail: ccash@mta.ca

'Rich' and 'poor', like 'developed' and 'developing', 'North' and 'South', are deeply problematic words, suggesting a hierarchy of performance in the socio-political/economic world of states, regions, communities and individuals. In the context of the UNFCCC, this hierarchy is embedded in the lists of Annex 1 (developed) and Annex 2 (developing) countries. Compounding the problems related to hierarchical nomenclatures are measures and metrics which derive from Northern states' belief in best practice. These 'beliefs' are generally portrayed as universal truths grounded in positivist science. As with international development, mainstream approaches to climate action take capitalism (neoliberal and other varieties), private sector involvement, limited state engagement, the rule of law and stakeholder participation as axiomatic. Cross-cutting themes and issues such as poverty, gender, age and ability are to be mainstreamed in planning and action. As several chapters have shown, climate action's increased focus on adaptation draws it ever closer not only to challenges and opportunities for development finance but to a wide range of development projects and programmes as well as to the historically highly divisive development discourse.

LABELS

In principle, the $100 billion/year climate finance threshold is meant to assist Annex 2 countries with limited human, financial and technical resource capacity to mitigate and adapt to climate change. Through the Nationally Determined Contribution (NDC) process, there would appear to be significant scope for creative (public–private–community; public–private; private–community) partnerships to arise in support of renewable energy projects. Developing and implementing sun, wind, water and geothermal projects of a variety of scales should readily absorb at least $100 billion/year. To the contrary, climate finance has become a centrepiece for political grandstanding, finger-pointing, blame-gaming—in other words, it has become riddled with many of the same problems that have long plagued international development.

Part of the problem, it seems to us, is the increasing alignment of climate finance with development finance, in particular Overseas Development Assistance (ODA) and the development of Rio Markers (described by Tomlinson, Chapter 3). Assigning Rio Markers to development projects is akin to slapping a 'climate finance' label on to existing development projects and programmes. This is problematic in several ways.

For one, and as highlighted by Achampong (Chapter 2) and Tomlinson (Chapter 3), the promised $100 billion/year climate finance is meant to be 'new and additional'. While labelling existing programming as climate finance may help a rich state meet its commitment, by double counting, it directly detracts from existing streams of development finance. Second, relabelling as 'climate mitigation' a questionable and/or socially contested development project such as a hydropower dam, increases the likelihood that climate action will result in maladaptation, backdraft or boomerang effects (See Wong, Chapter 9; also Swatuk et al., 2021). A third issue is that by aligning climate finance with development action, all of the 'usual suspects' are drawn into the decision-making circle thus limiting opportunities for innovative, and creative thinking (Ervine, Chapter 7). Lastly, and importantly, given the hierarchical framing of empowered 'haves' (states and companies) assisting disempowered 'have-nots' (states and communities) through Western modes (finance capital) and methods (techno-economic projects), climate finance actions reproduce colonial ways of thinking, being and doing (Navarro, Chapter 8). According to Barnes (Chapter 5), '[t]he conceptual issue facing an analysis of country ownership is how to account for the diversity of actors, things and ideas'.

Pandemic Thinking

While the climate crisis accelerates, its negative effects have been impacted by more than two years of a global pandemic. For Tomlinson (Chapter 3), '[t]he pandemic has revealed the deeply disturbing limits in global solidarity, particularly on the part of the international donor community, in the face of profound vulnerabilities for hundreds of millions of people throughout the Global South.' Highly vulnerable communities have been doubly impacted by these extreme climate and health events. 'Developing and climate-vulnerable nations are experiencing climate emergencies with increased frequency, while possessing insufficient resources to adapt to the magnitude of the problem, let alone the loss and damage associated with severe climate events' (Ervine, Chapter 7). According to Wong (Chapter 9), '[t]he geographic overlap in countries that are affected by both climate *and* insecurity, makes a strong case for salience in climate finance, without the need to prove direct causality between climate and conflict.' Put differently, vulnerable peoples should be at the centre of development and climate policy and planning, not kept at the margins only to be acknowledged during humanitarian crises.

Yet, for Ervine (Chapter 7), '[t]he track record on adaptation finance is one of deep failure wherein those nations and actors historically responsible for climate breakdown have avoided taking responsibility for its consequences'. Moreover, Tomlinson (Chapter 3) argues, '[t]en years on from COP21 in Copenhagen, it is still very difficult to assess even the basics of international climate finance against the 2020 $100 billion target, which is the foundation for trust in moving forward the climate agenda with developing country parties in the UNFCCC.'

Nevertheless, Achampong (Chapter 2) believes that '[i]n the wake of the Covid-19 pandemic, there is an opportunity to ensure that a new norm in climate finance emerges that is structured to ensure that vulnerable communities have access to high-quality financial support, technological assistance and capacity building.'

BUILDING BACK BETTER

In the parlance of Disaster Risk Reduction, it is imperative that communities build back better following a natural disaster. It is well known that the effects on human communities of extreme events such as drought, flood, earthquake, landslide and tsunami are often exacerbated by problems of governance, resource management and land use planning, to name but three obvious contributors to what might be called 'manufactured calamity'. Poorly designed development interventions, sometimes labelled 'white elephants', scatter the physical landscape of the Global South: unfinished buildings, overpasses to nowhere, landscapes scarred by clear-cut agriculture and the proliferation of gated suburban 'communities'. At the same time, resource capture through land and water grabbing pushes already vulnerable communities off the land and into urban slums. Despite well-documented evidence of the impact of fossil fuel-based economic growth on climate change, environmental degradation and social exploitation, much of Africa's 'growth' over the last two decades has centred on resource extraction for export, largely fuelling industry in China. While arguing in support of an energy transition, countries worldwide continue the hunt for hydrocarbons.

This is a socio-ecological terrain that is far from having the sort of resilience or adaptive capacity envisioned by climate or development activists. Moreover, extreme climate events and social conflicts seem to traverse the same sub-tropical/tropical terrain. Conflict-prone societies subject to sustained bouts of organized violence are rarely at the centre of development or climate finance, with development banks being notoriously 'risk averse' (Wong, Chapter 9). This aversion to risk leads to a focus on likely wins.

As climate emergencies overlap with humanitarian crises, international development increasingly finds itself focusing on triage—patching up the 'patient' in hopes that their survival will be assured somewhere down the line. Sound social relationships founded on long-term, mutually beneficial planning and programming are overshadowed by short-term, reactive responses and engagement.

For Wong (Chapter 9), climate finance must address this reality. To 'build back better', she proposes a 'co-benefits approach' to climate action. 'The co-benefits argument pertains not only to access and the quantity of climate finance, but also the quality and effectiveness' (Wong, Chapter 9). Peacebuilding activities must reap climate co-benefits if they are to have long-term positive impacts. At the same time, targeted climate action may serve to support peacebuilding efforts.

In Chapter 2, Achampong puts forward 6 lessons for climate finance from development finance:

(1) Instrumentalizing policies for other interests does not allow for developing country ownership or enable democratic country-driven strategies.
(2) Private sector involvement can be costlier than public service investments and can lead to additional, unplanned costs.
(3) Export-driven approaches to sustainable development have intensified an over-reliance on certain industries to support entire economies.
(4) The economic prowess of certain (richer) economies influences countries' macroeconomic policies.
(5) The involvement of Public Development Banks (PDBs) does not automatically lead to positive development outcomes.
(6) Group dynamics play a significant role in project development and implementation.

These six points constitute the political economic foundation upon which climate finance seeks to build. Put differently, they provide important lessons regarding risk and vulnerability, particularly where large sums of money draw together diverse actors with often non-compatible interests:

behind seemingly altruistic promises lie self-interest; the state is not the singular source of a problem just as the private sector is not a panacea; powerful actors will drive an agenda in their own interest; aid is no substitute for economic diversification; collective action will play out differently depending on a number of variables.

Barnes (Chapter 5) offers a useful methodological way past commonly held assumptions regarding the various actors involved in climate/development finance. Whereas Achampong (Chapter 2) and Tomlinson (Chapter 4) highlight the importance of 'democratic country ownership of climate finance strategies' as a necessity, Barnes asks who exactly are we talking about when we say 'country ownership'? As with international development, the UNFCCC processes are dependent upon a hierarchical, statist ontology: states are the primary actors in development; some are developed or developing; highly indebted or middle-income and so on. This blinds us to the actual terrain of action within and across countries and regions. In his chapter he uses South Africa as a case study to illustrate how different assemblages coalesce around different climate finance projects eliciting completely different results. For Barnes (Chapter 5), 'reified generalities' blind us to the possibilities of climate finance.

Similarly, if we wish to 'build back better', Navarro (Chapter 8) warns against the unreflexive adoption of seemingly non-controversial climate action projects. Drawing on case studies of efficient cook stoves and community-level forest conservation for carbon capture and storage, she argues the "emergence of environmental markets offers a unique opportunity for perpetuating the Western consumer society through the implementation of compensation measures, concealed by the shades of altruism and responsibility, encouraging the ongoing 'growthmania'" (Chapter 8). Ervine (Chapter 7) puts it equally bluntly: '[T]here is a deep indignity associated with requiring nations and peoples to accept finance that has been generated from projects and mechanisms designed precisely to allow emitters to avoid making emission reductions at the source.' While acknowledging that 'the appetite for truly innovative financing mechanisms may be growing', such as the share of proceeds model, 'it must be detached from carbon offsetting' (Ervine, Chapter 7).

Achampong offers useful policy advice regarding the necessities for sustainable, equitable and just climate finance:

- Democratic country ownership of climate finance strategies
- Prioritization of grant-based public climate finance
- Mandatory debt cancellation and debt relief in the aftermath of climate disasters, coupled with direct access to new and additional climate finance
- Support for greater access to finance for women and indigenous communities
- Public Development Banks must embed climate action and biodiversity objectives across all of their operations, investments and macroeconomic frameworks, and apply a 'do no harm' principle to all investments and approved projects
- Creation of a comprehensive monitoring and reporting framework that includes private finance and multilateral finance
- Policy coherence between the Paris Agreement and SDGs
- Country-level institutionalization of engagement and participation processes to ensure that all relevant stakeholders are able to engage in policy and project development and implementation, listening to the views of all marginalized groups within society.

In Chapter 6, Shutt and Halloran focus on the importance of accountability in climate finance. While country ownership is important, being accountable to the citizens particularly those most vulnerable is key to effective and sustainable climate action. Drawing on their experience with pilot programmes in Nepal and Indonesia, they highlight three important points: (i) the need for accountability coalitions; (ii) insight into the political and power dynamics at play and (iii) development of contextually relevant approaches. In their words:

- Building and sustaining accountability coalitions that work across multiple levels of governance to ensure inclusive spaces to engage and monitor decisions and funding flows, while also continuing efforts to create an enabling environment that incentivizes responsiveness and accountability, through continued civic mobilization, media coverage and effective state oversight.
- These efforts must be informed by an understanding of the political and power dynamics that shape the possibilities of inclusive, responsive and accountable climate adaptation governance. Commitments of resources by donor and recipient countries must be matched

by efforts to support civic actors, local governments and others to strengthen the systems that would enable those funds to be used in an inclusive and effective manner.
- Carefully and systematically navigate national and subnational systems and spaces, exploring contextually relevant approaches to strengthening inclusiveness and accountability of public resources and development activities around climate adaptation.

The Future of Climate Finance

As described above, the ways and means for ensuring effective and socially just climate finance are many and varied. Despite the many (self-imposed) barriers, the potential for realizing broad-based socio-ecological benefits is significant. On the mitigation front, the fact that everyone requires energy should help concentrate attention on forms of production that are renewable, sustainable and affordable for all. The fact that the costs of solar energy systems for households and industry have come down considerably while still offering profit-oriented inducement for private companies all along the supply chain show good potential for smart partnerships at a variety of scales. Similarly, micro solar, wind and hydro systems for rural electrification and irrigation for small-scale farmers demonstrate significant benefits (Krampe, 2016). While scale matters, the problems seem to increase in direct proportion to the size of the project: large-scale dams and solar farms displace and marginalize communities at the point of the development intervention. REDD+ and related carbon-sequestration initiatives often do the same, while also dividing communities in terms of winners (direct participants in REDD+ programmes) and losers (those who have lost access to forests for their livelihoods). This reproduces all of the long-standing problems with 'international development' (see Swatuk & Wirkus, 2018 for a series of case studies).

As highlighted by Ervine (Chapter 7) and Navarro (Chapter 8), carbon markets are particularly problematic. While the idea of 'high integrity' voluntary carbon markets (VCMs) was floated by the UK government at COP26 in Glasgow, those that draw Northern sources (of carbon and capital) together with Southern (carbon) sinks raise many ethical issues related to part to country ownership but also to support for business as usual. Saying that the voluntary carbon market must not act as a substitute for, but work in addition to, meaningful emissions reduction provides little hope for the hypothesized outcome. This is particularly the case where there is no means of policing or penalizing polluters who at best will commit to accurate self-monitoring and reporting. Nevertheless, as reported by Ecosystem Marketplace (2021), there is a clear appetite among companies for carbon markets:

> Voluntary Carbon Markets hit a record $1 Billion in 2021 ... Forest and Land Use credits and Renewable Energy credits dominate volume traded. Forestry and Land Use credits account for 61% while Renewable Energy credits account 38% of transactions reported.

Debt for climate swaps—like debt for nature swaps before them—offer up the same sorts of practical difficulties and ethical dilemmas. In the absence of strict regulation, the need for not-for-profit 'carbon watch-dogs' will be more important than ever.

This raises the issue of responsibility. As COP processes are dominated by states and, increasingly, private sector actors, and as the discourse of climate action is infused with the language of national development plans, corporate responsibilities and market forces, this leaves little room—both physical and intellectual—for differently placed and empowered actors, be it within sovereign states as citizens or across states as elements of global civil society. Such a division is consistent with trends in international development. While several chapters in this volume argue in support of (recipient/developing) country ownership of climate strategies, this barely addresses the question of whose interests do these state actors actually represent? Hence the consistent questioning from the margins regarding the voice of women, BIPOC (black, indigenous, people of colour), the poor, ethnic minorities and so on.

Dealing in aggregates (carbon emissions) regarding planetary boundaries and 'tipping points' (Steffen et al., 2015) moves climate decision-making and action even further from the point of impact. Put differently, those most seriously affected by extreme events are often equally negatively impacted by climate action decisions taken in state houses and at global conventions far from their lived realities (Navarro, Chapter 8; Barnes, Chapter 5). How, then, to ensure that climate finance benefits those most likely to suffer in a climate-changed world? In principle, there should be no separating out climate finance from any other sort of finance; all finance should be climate-friendly. Given the extent of the worldwide climate emergency, there is no option for not mainstreaming climate into finance, including pension funds, bank loans, asset-based lending and so on. Granted, we are very far from this ideal condition. But we are even farther from a unified front regarding climate finance alone. The $100 billion/year figure was political from its first utterance. It has since become wrapped up in the divisive question of reparations payments, i.e. 'loss and damages' suffered by the Global South due to more than two Centuries of Global North-devised, carbon-based development. In our perspective, the loss and damages discussion should remain separate from the question of climate finance. At the same time we regret the endless 'bean counting' attached to who has paid how much for what sort of climate action. As we state in Chapter 1, the amount of capital committed to climate finance pales in comparison to the South-to-North flow of debt repayment. Seen this way, debt forgiveness would have a much more significant impact on poor states' capacities to mobilize resources for both mitigation and adaptation, than some minor share of $100 billion. These issues are not mutually exclusive: debt forgiveness can work together with targeted climate finance alongside and in addition to meaningful development aid. In 2022, the German government, as part of its Presidency of the G7 (Group of Seven industrialized countries) emphasized the need for G7 countries to double their climate finance by 2025 and to develop a 'resilience shield' whereby development actions would not add to the burden of Annex 2 countries. This resilience shield would focus on efforts in support of food security, energy security and provision of 'financial and other support for comprehensive poverty-oriented, gender-responsive solutions to manage climate risks and other disasters and to address impacts from rapid-onset events as well as slow-onset processes' (German Watch, 2022). Such an integrated focus provides, in our view, some basis for optimism that climate finance will move in transformational directions.

As highlighted above, the lessons from international development are clear: climate finance is as much political as it is economic; it brings together differently empowered actors in support of diverse interests; the framework of action reflects orthodox meanings and measures of state power (political, economic, military) in the world; it creates space increasingly dominated by private capital and it too often ignores the voices of those most in need. At the same time, and as shown by Barnes in Chapter 5, climate action creates assemblages wherein creative coalitions can emerge in support of mutually beneficial action. Similarly, as shown by Shutt and Halloran (Chapter 6), searching out the ways and means of building these coalitions is essential if business as usual is to be displaced and transformational action supported.

REFERENCES

Ecosystem Marketplace. (2021). *Voluntary carbon markets top $1 billion in 2021 with newly reported trades, a special ecosystem marketplace COP26 bulletin.* Accessed 23 July 2022. https://www.ecosystemmarketplace.com/articles/voluntary-carbon-markets-top-1-billion-in-2021-with-newly-reported-trades-special-ecosystem-marketplace-cop26-bulletin/

German Watch. (2022). *Risk or resilience? G7's 2022 crises response can pave the way.* Accessed 23 July 2022. https://www.germanwatch.org/en/85230

Krampe, F. (2016). Empowering peace: Service provision and state legitimacy in peacebuilding in Nepal. *Conflict, Security and Development, 16*(1), 53–73.

Steffen, W., Richardson, K., Rockstrom, J., Cornell, S. E., Fetzer, I., Bennett, E. M. Biggs, R., Carpenter, S. R., De Vries, W., De Wit, C. A., Folke, C., Gerten, D., Heinke, J., Mace, G. M., Persson, L. M., Ramanathan, V., Reyers, B., & Sorlin, S. (2015). Planetary boundaries: Guiding human development on a changing planet. *Science, 347*(6223), 1259855.

Swatuk, L. A., & Wirkus, L. (2018). *Water, climate change and the Boomerang Effect: Unintentional consequences for resource insecurity.* Earthscan.

Swatuk, L. A., Thomas, B. K., Wirkus, L., & Silva, L. P. (2021). The 'Boomerang Effect': Insights for improved climate action. *Climate and Development, 13*(1), 61–67.

Index

A
accountability, 77, 83, 85, 86, 88–91, 93, 94, 130–134, 136–138, 142, 146, 148
accountability ecosystem, 131–134, 147, 148
accountability power, 239, 240
actor-network theory, 106
adaptation, 206–212, 214, 215, 217, 218, 220–222
adaptation finance, 60–64, 66, 154–158, 160–162, 166–168, 174
Adaptation Fund (AF), 27, 28, 155, 160–162, 167
Adaptation Gap Report, 160, 165
additionality, 169–171
Agreement SDGs, 239
agriculture
 climate-smart, 187
 green actors in, 190
Annex 1(countries), 234
Annex 2(countries), 234

Anthropocene, 4
apartheid, 110
approach Peacebuilding, 237
assemblage theory, 100, 101, 106, 107, 115, 120–123

B
bilateral climate finance, 50, 52–55, 66, 69, 70, 158, 159
biochar, 187–190
 Amazon basin, 188
blended finance, 75, 86–88, 94
budget systems, 15
Busan principles, 77
business-as-usual (BAU) scenario, 161, 169–171

C
Carbon Action Tracker, 165
carbon colonialism, 17, 183
carbon forestry, 191
carbon levies, 174

INDEX

carbon markets, 161, 164, 179–182, 184, 188, 190–195
  non-state actors in, 194, 195
  post-colonial perspectives of, 184
  regulation of, 192
carbon offsetting, 15, 16, 156–158, 162, 165–169, 171–174
carbon trading, 165
Certified Emission Reductions (CERs), 161, 162, 164, 171
China, 8, 23
China co-benefits, 237
citizen engagement, 82
citizen mobilization, 133
civil society, 101, 102, 110, 117–119
Civil Society Organisations (CSOs), 76, 78–80, 83–85, 87, 90, 93, 94, 130, 131, 133, 136–141, 144, 147, 148
Clean Development Mechanism (CDM), 155, 158, 161–164, 166, 171, 181, 182
climate action, 184, 193–195
climate adaptation, 154
climate adaptation spending, 143
climate change, 179, 181–183, 187, 190–192, 205–207, 209–215, 217–219, 221
  adaptation, 187
  and state security, 209, 213
  mitigation, 180, 184, 187, 188
climate crimes, 189, 194
climate disasters, 35
climate finance
  and adaptation, 3, 6, 11, 15, 16, 27
  and co-financing, 215
  and loans, 6, 25
  and mitigation, 3, 6, 15, 27
  and over-reporting, 26, 31
  and the peace dividend, 205, 210, 214, 220

co-benefits of, 210–212, 219, 221, 222
  commitments, 5, 6, 13, 14, 29
  for women and indigenous communities, 35
  gender responsive, 12, 30–32, 36
  grant equivalent, 25–27
  grants for, 6, 25, 35
  impacts of Covid-19 on, 208
  mechanisms, 206, 219, 222
  multilateral, 214, 223
  private sector involvement in, 33
  reporting, 51, 52
  substantial amounts of, 24
  trends, 48, 53, 54, 59, 60
climate impacts on women, 60
climate justice, 156, 157, 159, 165, 166
climate loans, 59, 65, 66
climate negotiations, 154
climate policymaking
  conflict-related costs of, 216
climate security
  backdraft, 212
  boomerang effect, 212
  mechanism, 206, 213
  nexus, 209
climate vulnerable nations, 165
coastal communities, 143–145
collaboration, 131, 147
colonialism, 110
common but differentiated responsibilities and respective capabilities (CBDR-RC), 154, 156, 159
communities, 130, 137–140, 142, 143, 145–148, 180, 181, 184, 185, 187–195, 234
communities Paris, 239
community-based, 37
community-led actors, 133
community-level adaptation, 144

INDEX

community-level mitigation, 144
concessional loans, 52, 65
conflict, 207–209, 212–222
   vulnerability to climate change, 215
conservation, 181, 184–187, 193
   Western, 180
consultants, 111, 112, 115
cook-stoves, 179
cooperation modalities, 75
cooperative approaches, 162
country ownership, 14, 15, 22, 33–35, 78–80, 88, 90, 93, 99–102, 107–111, 113, 116–118, 120–123, 235, 237–241
   materiality in, 112
   unit of analysis of, 103, 123
Covid-19, 7, 8, 10, 13, 21, 22, 24, 25, 35, 37, 158, 214

D

Dalits, 137, 139, 140, 142
damage vulnerable, 242
debt
   cancellation, 35
   crisis, 65
   repayments, 29, 35
   servicing, 6, 29
   trap, 23
debt crisis, 65
Democratic Republic of Congo, 213
development aid budgets, 59
Development Bank of Southern Africa (DBSA), 109, 111, 112, 115–118, 120, 121, 123
development cooperation, 76, 77, 80, 81, 83–90, 93–95
development effectiveness, 75, 76, 78, 87, 88, 94
Development Finance Institutions (DFIs), role of, 86

disaster risk reduction (DRR), 215
drought, 186

E

ecological modernization, 11, 181, 185
ecosystem, 181
   functions, 181
   services, 181
effect maladaptation, 235
elephants, 185, 186, 193
emission reduction policies, 165
emission reductions, 155, 156, 161–163, 168, 169, 171, 172, 174
emissions reduction units, 162
emissions trading, 161
energy, 110–112, 114, 115, 119, 121, 188
   renewable, 179, 184
   solar, 112
   transition, 104, 110, 112, 114, 115, 119
energy affordable, 12, 22
energy transition, 104, 110, 112, 114, 115, 119
environmental governance, 180, 183, 194
environmental peacebuilding, 17, 206, 207, 210, 211, 217, 222, 223
eurocentric knowledge, 180

F

fair financing, 164
financing gap, 27, 37
fisherfolk, 142–146
flat ontology, 100, 104–106, 108, 111–113, 123
food shortages, 7
foreign aid. *See* Official Development Assistance (ODA)

fossil fuel energy, 168
fossil fuel-related CO_2, 173
fragile states, 208, 213, 214, 216, 219
free, informed and prior consent, 87

G
gender, 208, 210, 218
gender equality, 59, 67, 68
gender inequalities, 21, 32
global carbon markets, 162
global environmental governance, 156
globalization, 9, 10
Global North, 180–184, 187, 189, 192–194
Global South, 180, 181, 183, 184, 187, 189, 193, 194
global voluntary market for carbon offsets, 166
global warming, 1, 2, 4
good governance, 36
grant-based resources for adaptation, 60, 63, 65
Green Climate Fund (GCF), 14, 100–103, 106–112, 115–123
green grabbing, 183, 184, 195
greenhouse gas emissions (GHGs), 187
  as tradable assets, 181
greenhouse gases, 59, 181
Growthmania Women, 238
G7 (group of countries), 242
G7 nations, 158

H
Haiti, 213
Holocene, 4

I
Indigenous, 239, 241

Indigenous people, 181, 183, 187, 195
  Maasai, 185, 186
Indigenous Peoples' rights defenders, 83
Indonesia, 130, 131, 134–137, 142, 143, 147, 148
institutions, 2, 8–12, 15, 18, 21, 25, 28, 34, 36
international carbon offsetting, 156
international climate finance, 136, 138
International Emissions Trading Association (IETA), 163, 164
internationally transferred mitigation outcomes (ITMOs), 162
international negotiations on climate finance, 165
IPPC reports, 171

K
Kampala Principles, 87, 88
Kenya, 221
Kyoto Protocol, 16, 154–156, 158, 160, 161, 169, 171, 172, 181, 182

L
land grabs, 180, 183, 184, 187, 188, 191, 192, 195
Least Development Countries (LDCs), 59, 63, 64, 159, 161
livelihoods, 12, 22, 28, 33
local government, 131, 136, 138–142, 146, 148
local government budgeting, 141
local government policy, 138
loss and damage, 4, 6, 14, 16, 26, 27, 71, 207, 223

M
maladaptation, 62, 63, 212, 216, 223

manufactured calamity, 236
marginalized groups, 130, 138–141, 146–148
market-based approaches, 167
market transactions, 169
mitigation, 206, 207, 209–212, 214, 215, 217, 218, 221, 222
mitigation finance, 59, 71
modernization, 18
multilateral climate finance, 51, 53, 57, 158, 160
multilateral institutions, 6, 26, 159
multi-stakeholder forum (MSF), 144
municipal planning, 141

N
National Adaptation Plans (NAPs), 81
Nationally Determined Commitments (NDCs), 65, 89
Nationally Determined Contributions (NDCs), 163, 165, 168, 172, 234
nature-based solutions, 170, 172
nature commidification, 167
neocolonial, 16
neo-colonial(ism), 185, 195
  in climate action, 184, 185
neoliberal justice, 166, 167
Nepal, 130, 131, 134–137, 147, 148
net-zero, 36, 37
non-concessional loans, 52, 53, 55
non-state actors, 81

O
Official Development Assistance (ODA), 3, 6, 29, 32, 59, 65, 69–71, 159, 160, 164

P
pandemic, 7, 8, 10, 13, 21, 22, 35, 37, 158, 214

pandemic loss, 235
Paris Agreement, 13, 22, 26, 31, 36, 37, 46, 48, 49, 51, 55, 57, 58, 60, 63, 65, 69, 71, 154–156, 158, 159, 162, 163, 165, 168, 169, 172
participation, 79, 80, 84, 87, 94
participatory action research (PAR), 137
partnerships, 77, 80, 82–86, 88, 93
peace, 205–207, 209, 210, 212, 213, 215, 219–223
  co-benefits of, 206, 211, 212, 217–223
  sustainable, 210
peacebuilding, 214, 217–222
  environmental, 206, 207, 209–211, 217, 222, 223
peace dividend, 223
  metrics for, 206, 217
planning processes, 139, 144
policy, 14, 16, 17, 22, 24, 25, 28, 30, 32–35, 37
polluter pays, 174
populism, 9
poverty, 15, 18, 22, 24
power, 7, 10, 11, 17, 23, 31, 32, 34, 36, 106, 113, 114, 116, 120
power dynamics, 130, 133, 134, 138, 139, 141, 143, 144, 148
private finance, 157, 158, 167
private sector engagement (PSE), 87, 88
private sector finance, 164, 167
provincial climate policy, 142
public accountability, 131, 134, 136, 148, 149
Public Development Banks (PDBs), 34, 36
public finance, 130, 131, 134, 138, 140, 147, 148
pyrolysis stoves, 187

Q
quid pro quo, 155, 167

R
REDD+ Carbon markets, 240
Reducing Emissions from Deforestation and Forest Degradation (REDD+), 166
repayment forgiveness, 242
resilience shield, 242
resource capture, 236
responsiveness, 130–132, 134, 142, 144–146, 148
Rio Convention, 207
Rio Markers Boomerang, 234
rural development
 technologies for, 188
Russian invasion of, 7, 9

S
scale
 hierarchical, 100, 104–106, 109, 118, 120–122
 in human geography, 100, 123
 in policy, 103
 relational, 100, 103–107, 119, 121
share of proceeds (SOP) model, 155, 157, 158, 160, 161, 165, 174
slow violence, 186, 193
Small Island Developing States (SIDS), 59, 63, 64, 159
Solar energy dams, 240
South Africa, 100, 103, 104, 108–121, 123, 238
South Africa Climate Finance Assemblage (SACFA), 103, 104, 106
South Africa National Biodiversity Institute (SANBI), 109, 117, 118, 121, 123
sovereign state, 2, 7, 10
sovereignty, 11
Sustainable Development Goals (SDGs), 3, 6–9, 13, 22, 24, 31, 37, 81, 83, 87

T
Tanzania, 185, 186
territorialisation, 106, 107, 112, 120
tourism, 187
transformation, 11, 18, 107, 116–118, 120–123
transparency, 51, 52, 56, 57, 59
tree planting, 187, 191, 192
'triple bottom line', 11

U
Uganda, 191
Ukraine, 7, 9, 214, 223
UN Security Council, 212

V
'vicious cycle of poverty', 12
voluntary BIPOC debt, 241
vulnerable communities, 12, 22, 26–28, 30, 35, 37
vulnerable populations, 48, 56, 59, 63, 134, 148

W
West Kilimanjaro, 185
women-led climate change responses, 63
World Bank, 161, 162